Trade and Economic Change on the Gold Coast, 1807–1874

LEGON HISTORY SERIES
General Editor A A Boahen PhD

Trade and Economic Change on the Gold Coast, 1807–1874

Edward Reynolds PhD
Department of History,
University of California, San Diego

Longman   Longman Inc.

Longman Group Ltd
Burnt Mill, Harlow, Essex CM20 2JE

Distributed in the
United States of America
by Longman Inc.
New York

*Associated companies, branches and representatives
throughout the world*

© 1974 Longman Group Ltd

ISBN 0 582 64582 4
Library of Congress Catalog Card No. 74–77603

First published 1974

Made and printed in Great Britain by
William Clowes & Sons, Limited
London, Beccles and Colchester

Contents

Abbreviations   *page* vi

Preface   vii

Introduction   1

CHAPTER ONE
Trade and economic change   5

CHAPTER TWO
Abolition and its aftermath, 1807–1828   37

CHAPTER THREE
The economy in transition, 1828–1850   72

CHAPTER FOUR
The age of African merchants, 1850–1863   103

CHAPTER FIVE
Trade and problems of economic development, 1863–1874   139

CHAPTER SIX
Economic change, conflict and African politics   164

CHAPTER SEVEN
On the threshold of a modern economy   174

Appendices   182

Bibliography   189

Index   201

Abbreviations

A.H.S.	African Historical Studies
B.G.G.A.	Bulletin of Ghana Geographical Association
B.M.A.	Basel Mission Archives, Switzerland
C.O.	Colonial Office, Public Record Office, London
E.B.G.	*Economic Bulletin of Ghana*
E.D.M.	*Elder Dempster Magazine*
E.H.R.	*Economic History Review*
F.C.	Furley Collection, Balme Library, Legon
G.C.R.	*Gold Coast Review*
G.N.A.	Ghana National Archives
G.N.Q.	Ghana Notes and Queries
G.J.	*Guineisk Journaler*, Copenhagen
G.J.S.	*Ghana Journal of Sociology*
G.T.	Geografisk Tidsskrift
Gtk.	Generaltoldkammer og Kommerce – Kollegiets Arkiv, Copenhagen
I.A.S.R.R.	*Institute of African Studies University of Ghana Research Review*
I.F.A.N.	*Bulletin de l'Institut Fondamental de l'Afrique Noire*
I.S.S.J.	*International Social Science Journal*
J.A.H.	*Journal of African History*
J.A.I.	*Journal of the Anthropological Institute*
J.A.S.	*Journal of African Society*
J.E.H.	*Journal of Economic History*
J.S.A.	*Journal of Society of Arts*
M.M.	*Mission Magazine*
M.M.A.	Methodist Missionary Archives, London
P.P.	Parliamentary Papers
T.	Treasury, Public Records Office
T.G.C.T.H.S.	*Transactions of the Gold Coast and Togoland Historical Society*
T.H.S.G.	*Transactions of the Historical Society of Ghana*
T.H.S.N.	*Transactions of the Historical Society of Nigeria*
V.G.R.	Vestindisk-guineisk Rente- og Generaltoldkammer

Preface

It affords me great pleasure to express my sincere gratitude to those who have been of assistance in the writing of this book. My indebtedness to a dedicated scholar, teacher and adviser, Mr Douglas H. Jones, merits a word of deepest appreciation, as this work could not have been written without his expert supervision. I offer him my cordial thanks for suggesting the topic, giving advice and making valuable critical remarks and suggestions that have had a bearing on every part of this work. I am much obliged to Dr Richard Rathbone for friendly advice and perceptive comments which have clarified my views on many points. I owe a debt of gratitude to Mr Ole Justesen of the University of Copenhagen for helping me put into better perspective the activities of the Danes on the Gold Coast. Professor Adu Boahen offered constructive criticisms on an early draft and Dr A. G. Hopkins also read a section of an early draft and helped to resolve some problems on the subject. I am also grateful to Professor John D. Fage for his early comments and suggestions on the work.

I am glad to acknowledge the libraries, archives and persons who have been helpful in gathering material for this work. My thanks are due to the staff of the following libraries and archives: The Public Record Office, The British Museum, The International African Institute, The Royal Commonwealth Society, The Foreign and Commonwealth Library, The Institute of Historical Research, The School of Oriental and African Studies, The Ghana National Archives, The Balme Library at Legon, The Rigsarchiv in Denmark, and the Basel Mission Archives in Switzerland. I am much indebted to the Rev. H. J. Keteku for allowing me to share his first-hand knowledge about the history and activities of the Basel Mission. I am also grateful to the Rev. E. T. Koramoa who has shared with me his unrivalled knowledge and private collection of Basel Mission activities. For allowing me to read drafts of their own work, I am obliged to Kwame Arhin of the University of Ghana and Harvey Feinberg of Southern Connecticut State, U.S.A. My friends Ray Kea and John Miles have also been helpful in sharing the knowledge of their research with me. The encouragement of my friends and colleagues, Mr Kofi Asare Opoku, Professors Ramon Ruiz and Harry Scheiber, is warmly acknowledged.

Nor must I forget to mention the support of my family. The meagre earnings of my mother and grandmother from hawking textiles paid for my early education. The encouragement of my wife Kay has been invaluable for the writing of this book. Her enthusiasm and support for this work make it spiritually hers as well as mine.

This book is based on my revised thesis *Trade and Economic Change on the Gold Coast, 1807–1874* which I presented to the University of London for the Ph.D. degree in January, 1972.

La Jolla, California   EDWARD REYNOLDS
11 June 1973

List of Illustrations

Between pages 22–23

1 Cape Coast Castle
2 The Castle of Elmina
3 Port of Christiansborg, near Accra

Between pages 54–55

4 Ramseyer family and trader captives of the Asante
5 The first day of the Yam custom

Between pages 86–87

6 Governor George Maclean
7 Presentation of the Court of Select audience

Between pages 118–119

8 Basel Mission Factory
9 Basel Mission Carpentry workshop
10 The Palace of Ouso Adoom, the King's nephew

Dedicated to
Kay Bissell Reynolds

Introduction

The complaint that West African economic history is a neglected subject has become banal, but until recently studies dealing with the history of economic development in West Africa were rare except for those by Allan McPhee,[1] W. K. Hancock,[2] and L. C. A. Knowles[3] – to mention some of the better known. Since the middle of the 1960s, however, increasing attention is being paid to the subject.[4] The present work is a contribution to the economic literature of West Africa and more specifically that of the Gold Coast, modern Ghana.

There is no dearth of literature on the economic history limited to the late nineteenth century Gold Coast. H. J. Bevin has surveyed the period just before the era of the onset of the rapid economic development of the country.[5] The period 1874–1905 is examined in R. Dumett's thesis, which is mainly concerned with the official British attitudes towards the economic development on the Gold Coast. This work contains excellent sections on gold mining activities and the rubber trade.[6] Dumett has also covered the rubber trade in a recent article.[7] Robert Szereszewski has studied the period 1891–1922 and provided a good

1 *The Economic Revolution in British West Africa*, London, 1926

2 *Survey of British Commonwealth Affairs*, 2 vols., London, 1942

3 *The Economic Development of the British Overseas Empire*, 2 vols., London, 1928

4 Among the more important works to appear are those of A. G. Hopkins which include: *Economic History of West Africa*, London, 1973; *An Economic History of Lagos, 1880–1914*, unpublished Ph.D. thesis, London University, 1964; 'Economic Imperialism in West Africa, 1880–1892', *E.H.R.* xxi, 1968 and 'Economic Aspects of Political Movements in Nigeria and the Gold Coast, 1918–1939', *J.A.H.* vii, 2, 1966. Other valuable works include Claude Meillassoux, ed., *The Development of African Trade and Markets in West Africa*, London, 1971; Colin W. Newbury, 'Trade and Authority in West Africa from 1850–1880' in L. H. Gann and P. Duigan, *The History of Colonialism in Africa 1870–1914*, Cambridge, 1969; and George E. Brooks, Jr., *Yankee Traders, Old Coasters and African Middlemen, a History of American Legitimate Trade with West Africa in the Nineteenth Century*, Boston, 1970.

5 H. J. Bevin, 'The Gold Coast Economy about 1880', *T.G.C.T.H.S.* ii, pt. 2, 1956, pp. 73–86

6 R. E. Dumett, *British Official Attitudes in Relation to Economic Development in the Gold Coast, 1874–1905*, unpublished Ph.D. thesis, University of London, 1966

7 See R. E. Dumett, 'The Rubber Trade of the Gold Coast and Asante in the Nineteenth Century: African Innovation and Responsiveness', *J.A.H.* xii, 1, 1971, pp. 79–101

theoretical account of the rapid economic change during this period.[1] There are also the two pioneering studies by Polly Hill on cocoa.[2] Her *Gold Coast Cocoa Farmer* deals with the labour systems that are employed in the Ghanaian cocoa industry, while her *Migrant Cocoa Farmers* treats the fascinating process of the movement of Akuapem farmers into Akyem to purchase land for the cultivation of cocoa. The only serious attempts to look at the pre-colonial economy are expressed in recent articles by Stephen Hyman and K. Boaten.[3] There is also Kwame Arhin's useful study dealing with the development of Atebubu and Kintampo as market centres in the late nineteenth century.[4]

The concentration and the attention of economic historians on the period of rapid economic growth in the late nineteenth century is, in the main, just, but the period of transition from the sale of slaves to the sale of natural products on the Gold Coast calls for serious study.[5] The present work on trade and economic change on the Gold Coast from 1807 to 1874 seeks to fulfil such a need.

By the beginning of the nineteenth century the Atlantic slave trade had already made inroads into the traditional subsistence economy of the Gold Coast and elements of a modern economy had begun to emerge; but the interdiction of this trade in 1807 rendered the bulk of the existing commerce illegal. Consequently, other products had to be found by stimulating the export of old staples like gold and ivory and by encouraging the cultivation of agricultural produce in exchange for European goods. This meant a process of commercial and economic change, but wars often interrupted this evolution.

The peace and security the country enjoyed between 1830 and 1850, social and cultural changes effected by Christianity and education, and increased opportunities for entering trade made these decades a key period of economic change. By 1850 this transformation had led to the rise of a class of African merchants who were sensitive to new commercial opportunities and who had the ability and initiative to exploit new avenues of trade. As these African merchants attained more wealth and influence, they began to assume a position and to acquire a power that once had been occupied and held by the traditional rulers, whose social and economic position had been declining since abolition.

Conflicts in the wake of the Asante invasion of the coast in 1863 and wars in

1 R. Szereszewski, *Structural Changes in the Economy of Ghana 1891–1911*, London, 1966

2 Polly Hill, *The Gold Coast Cocoa Farmer: a Preliminary Survey*, London, 1956, and *Migrant Cocoa Farmers of Southern Ghana*, Cambridge, 1963

3 Stephen Hyman, 'Economic Forms in Pre-Colonial Ghana', *J.E.H.* xxx, 1, 1970, pp. 33–50; a useful summary which, despite its title, covers aspects of Asante trade during the eighteenth and nineteenth centuries is K. Boaten's 'Trade among the Asante of Ghana up to the End of the Eighteenth Century', *I.A.S.E.E.* vii, 1, 1970, pp. 33–46.

4 Kwame Arhin, *The Development of Atebubu and Kintampo as Market Centres*, unpublished Ph.D. thesis, University of London, 1969

5 A study that deals with the transitional period from slaves to palm oil trading in another area of West Africa is K. O. Dike's *Trade and Politics in the Niger Delta*, Oxford, 1956. A general study on the transitional period in relation to trade and political power is Patrick Manning's 'Slaves, Palm Oil, and Political Power on the West African Coast', *A.H.S.* ii, 2, 1969, pp. 279–88. See also David A. Ross, 'The Career of Domingo Martinez in the Bight of Benin', *J.A.H.* vi, 1, 1965, pp. 79–90; C. W. Newbury, *The Western Slave Coast and Its Rulers*, Oxford, 1961.

the Volta area affected the country and the trade and commercial operations of the African merchants. This, and the prevailing system of credit, led to a number of bankruptcies and to the ruin of many indigenous traders. The persistent Asante threat, the increasing presence of Britain on the coast, the declining fortunes of African rulers, the decrease in prestige and wealth of chiefs and the talk of British retrenchment from the coast united the people in the formation of a nationalistic organisation for the political and economic development of the country.

Although the economy grew, diversified, and progressed considerably towards a modern economy during the period under study, the formal declaration of the Gold Coast as a Protectorate in 1874 paved the way for a more complete integration of the country's trade into the modern world economy. The era after 1874 marked the decline of African initiative in trading enterprises as well as the emergence of a foreign-dominated oligopolistic regime. This crucial period of trade and economic change between 1807 and 1874 is an important transitional era that links the economy of the Gold Coast based on slaves to that of the modern Ghana based on natural produce.

This study embraces the process of economic growth together with the social, cultural and political changes that were involved. Economic growth is used here not merely to connote the trade and economic process of development that was to lead to 'economic revolution' in the last decade of the nineteenth century, but also to describe a wider process. Implied in the term as used here are the changes in economic roles and relations, institutional organisation, and ideological adjustments of the traditional economy to a new commercial order. Although the term 'Gold Coast' in this work covers most of the present-day southern Ghana, it is used flexibly. On the coast it covers the littoral stretching from Apollonia to Keta which was then occupied by the British, the Dutch and the Danes at the beginning of the nineteenth century. Although, strictly speaking, the term Gold Coast in this period comprises only the states south of the River Pra, Asante has to be taken into account as an inseparable part of all aspects of life on the Gold Coast: militarily and economically Asante dominated her southern neighbours. The Asante hinterland is excluded here, except in so far as it impinges upon this study.

As far as the available trade statistical data permit, the relevant figures have been used. Though incomplete and not wholly reliable, these figures are valuable, and together with dispatches and reports do throw light on Gold Coast economic history during this period. The trade statistics are employed to indicate the trend of developments rather than to show the precise quantification of trade at any particular date. Although some economic historians might take issue with the handling of the statistical data, and rightly so, undue manipulation of the trade figures would probably multiply the errors in already unreliable data. At any rate, the trade statistics often represented only goods on which duty had been paid.

The figures used in the text which represent declared or 'real' value[1] are

1 The best discussion on this subject of 'official' and 'real' values is Albert H. Imlah's *Economic Elements in the Pax Britannica*, Cambridge, Mass., 1958, ch. 2. Until about 1869 British imports and exports were recorded as 'real' or declared and official. Official values, which are not realistic measures of current market values, were started at the end of the seventeenth century when record-keeping of imports and exports in money values began. At the time, tables of prices were prepared with the rates based on current prices. Although

those from the original correspondence, Blue Books, Colonial Statistical Tables 1833–1913 (C.O. 442 Series) and the Parliamentary Papers.

An obvious feature of a growing economy and a vital aspect of the development of a viable modern economy is the increase and movement of population. The movement of the people of Krobo to Akuapem to buy land during the period was the result of an expanding economy and a growing population, and the movement and settlement of Fante traders in Asiakwa Asante,[1] especially in the 1830s, was because of increased trade activities. Although this feature was clearly present on the Gold Coast for the period under study, the paucity of data does not allow a full assessment of the scale of these changes. Another important feature of the economy which is difficult to subject to statistical analysis is the substantial amount of trade and exchange involved in the internal commerce which lay outside the economic sphere of the overseas trade.

The footnotes will reveal the extent to which I have drawn upon economic, anthropological, and sociological studies. These sources have not been used primarily as models, but as tools to help interpret the historical process of trade and economic change on the Gold Coast. These aids, used in conjunction with the relevant trade and economic data in the context of the country's nineteenth-century background, tell the story of Gold Coast economic history from 1807–1874.

---

some adjustments in the initial valuations were made in the early years, for over 150 years the same table was used to calculate official values. It was not until 1854 that this system was overhauled, but even after the new method of valuation was set up, the old system prevailed until 1869. See Imlah, *Economic Elements in the Pax Britannica*, pp. 20–21. Declared values which had begun in 1798 often represented the real value of goods. During the Napoleonic wars when there was the *ad valorem* convoy duty, there existed the possibility of understating value. In 1813, however, a law was passed providing a penalty – a fine of £20 and detention of goods – for fraudulent returns. Admittedly, declared values are not perfect, but they are as close as one can get to the actual value of trade. See Imlah, *Economic Elements in the Pax Britannica*, pp. 23–34.

1 See G. E. Metcalfe, *Maclean of the Gold Coast*, London, 1962 and John Mensah Sarbah, *Fanti National Constitution*, London, 1906

CHAPTER ONE

Trade and economic change

Gold Coast society and its economies at the beginning of the nineteenth century had been subjected to and modified by more than three centuries of European trade and contact which had made a significant impact on the country. Undoubtedly the period of trade with Europeans established patterns of markets, created steady demand for certain European imports and gave rise to vested interests in the overseas trade. It is possible that this trade built on the Gold Coast trading expertise for transfer to legitimate trade after 1807 and that the activities of European traders before abolition contributed to the progress towards a modern economy the country had made by the 1800s.

Early European trade on the Gold Coast

The commercial relationship of the Gold Coast and, to be sure, that of West Africa with the outside world has a long history that predates the inception of Portuguese exploration and trade on the African coast. Since the Middle Ages articles from the West African interior such as gold, pepper, ivory, ebony and slaves had been exported across the Sahara to the North African coast and from there to the outside world.[1] There is no conclusive evidence that the Gold Coast was involved in this trade before the fourteenth century. However, in 1471 when the Portuguese arrived on the Gold Coast there were Mande traders from the western Sudan at Elmina. Seemingly, by the fifteenth century trade connections had developed between the Gold Coast, the western Sudan, North Africa and the outside world with the flow of trade goods in both directions.[2]

The motives behind the arrival of the Portuguese to Africa still remain debatable. It is not known for certain what role the search for gold played in the Portuguese exploration of the West African coast, but it seems that the quest for gold was a prime consideration after 1472.[3] Certainly it was the gold trade that led the Portuguese Crown, Dom João, to make the Guinea trade a royal monopoly in 1474 after Fernão Gomes' contract to explore the coast expired.

Portuguese monopoly and the lucrative trade thereby established on the west

1 C. R. Crone, ed., *The Voyages of Cadamosto and Other Documents*, London Hakluyt Society, 1937, pp. xi–xii

2 Ivor Wilks, 'A Medieval Trade Route from the Niger to the Gulf of Guinea', *J.A.H.* iii, 2, 1962, pp. 337–9

3 C. R. Boxer, *The Portuguese Seaborne Empire: 1415–1825*, New York, 1969, p. 28

coast of Africa did not remain unchallenged, and attempts by other European powers like the French, Dutch and English to gain a share in the trade contributed to serious international rivalry on the Gold Coast.[1]

To promote and to protect their trade, Europeans built factories and castles of which the first European factory was Portuguese – Arguin, constructed in 1445. Probably the best known Portuguese castle built on the Gold Coast was Elmina, which became the centre and headquarters of Portuguese activities on the West African coast. The Portuguese also erected other minor fortresses at Axim, Shama and Accra, but these forts were an ineffective defence against the activities of interlopers.[2]

Europeans who followed the Portuguese to the Gold Coast continued the example of building forts and castles to promote trade – all of which, except for that of Keta, were established with the consent of the local people involved. The normal procedure for erecting these buildings was for the inhabitants of an area to invite a European power to build a fort in their region. The site for the fort was occasionally given as a gift or, as in most cases, leased for an annual rent. The company or country concerned was then given a monopoly of the import and the export trade, in return for which the company undertook to defend the people in case of attack.[3]

From the time of the Portuguese, Europeans sought to maintain an exclusive monopoly on trade. Portugal, for example, instituted severe penalties for interlopers. Illicit traders dealing in Guinea without a licence were liable to be executed and have their goods appropriated by the Portuguese Crown.[4] The Portuguese also forbade Africans in their sphere of influence to trade with other Europeans. There were even instances when the Portuguese ordered the Elminians to destroy a village for trading with interlopers, as when Mouree was burned in 1610.[5] Despite this Portuguese ban upon the Africans' freedom to trade with outsiders, many Africans continued to do so with the result that Portuguese monopoly was never complete.[6]

The Dutch also attempted to engage the Africans in trade with them alone. So did the English, who undertook to secure confirmation from various local people and chiefs that they would trade with no one else.[7] Both the English and the Dutch also attempted to conclude working contracts to prevent the natives from playing one off against the other, but this plan failed. It seems the idea of granting trade monopolies to Europeans was subject to various interpretations.

1 The history of European rivalry on the Gold Coast is well known. Especially see K. Y. Daaku, *Trade and Politics on the Gold Coast 1600–1720*, Oxford, 1970, pp. 7–20; H. A. Wyndham, *The Atlantic and Slavery*, Oxford, 1935 and J. W. Blake, *European Beginnings in West Africa, 1450–1560*, London, 1937.

2 Blake, *European Beginnings in West Africa*, p. 101

3 Wyndham, *Atlantic and Slavery*, p. 26; A. W. Lawrence, *Trade Castles and Forts of West Africa*, London, 1963, p. 66; Daaku, *Trade and Politics*, p. 56

4 Blake, *European Beginnings in West Africa*, p. 76

5 Harvey Michael Feinberg, *Elmina, Ghana: a History of Its Development and Relationship with the Dutch in the Eighteenth Century*, unpublished Ph.D. dissertation, Boston University, 1969, p. 22

6 *Ibid.*   7 *Ibid.*

Africans might have viewed such pacts as simply giving a particular European country a share of the trade. The African custom of showing hospitality to all strangers may also have made the commitments difficult to maintain.[1] Interpretations aside, the agreements were hard to keep when company officials on the coast not infrequently changed loyalties and often engaged in trade on the side.

Local trade

European traders on the Gold Coast seem to have participated in two forms of trade: direct trade between Europe and the Gold Coast, and a local trade between the Gold Coast and the rest of West Africa. It was probably not only the prospects of the gold trade that attracted the Portuguese to the Gold Coast, but also the opportunity to operate as middlemen in the framework of an existing local trade.[2]

The Portuguese established a lucrative trade between the Gold Coast and Benin, building a factory at Gato for this purpose in 1486. Slaves were bought in Benin and sold on the Gold Coast to native merchants who used them as carriers to the interior since they had no beasts of burden. Other items like cotton cloth, panther skins and palm oil were bought in Benin and sold on the Gold Coast for gold.[3] There seems also to have been significant trade in beads between the two coasts.[4]

Local trade did not cease to be noteworthy when the Portuguese were dislodged from the coast. Dutch and English merchants who followed in their tracks continued to carry goods from other parts of West Africa for sale on the Gold Coast. In addition to the Benin trade there was local trade between the Gold Coast, the Dahomean Coast and the Ivory Coast where the famous Quaqua cloth was obtained.[5] Some of the cloth sold in the local trade came from the far interior.

Europeans participated in the local salt trade, too. In 1724, for instance, Europeans were in control of the salt ponds near Accra. So lucrative was this trade to Europeans that they sometimes demanded salt in payment of goods they sold to the people of the Gold Coast. At other times, during the off-season, Africans were given credit to be paid in salt.

Gold and ivory trade

Until at least the beginning of the eighteenth century the mainstay of European–African trade was gold. Europeans came to associate sections of West Africa with the prominent trade items they produced. And, as the name of the Gold

---

1 Daaku, *Trade and Politics*, pp. 59–61

2 Wilks, 'A Medieval Trade Route from the Niger to the Gulf of Guinea', p. 339. Also, J. D. Fage, 'Some Remarks on Beads and Trade in Lower Guinea in the Sixteenth and Seventeenth Centuries', *J.A.H.* iii, 2, 1962, p. 344.

3 Blake, *European Beginnings in West Africa*, p. 93

4 See Fage, 'Some Remarks on Beads and Trade in Lower Guinea in the Sixteenth and Seventeenth Centuries'.

5 Daaku, *Trade and Politics*, pp. 6, 24

Coast implied, the yellow metal abounded which formed the basis of an initial trading with Europeans and attracted the early concentration of European forts on the Gold Coast. It is difficult to obtain an accurate estimate of the total exports of gold from the Gold Coast.[1] It has been suggested that after 1481 Portugal imported approximately 170,000 dobras of gold annually to Portugal. Gold exports began to decline from about 1530, but they did not reach a serious stage until the end of the sixteenth century.[2] Writing at the beginning of the eighteenth century, Bosman calculated that gold exports from the Gold Coast amounted to about 7,000 marks in a good year. This was the equivalent of about £224,000 sterling or £2,000,000 in twentieth-century terms. Of this, Bosman estimated that the Royal African Company received 1,200 marks, then equivalent to about £38,000.[3] On the other hand, between 1682–1692 the Royal African Company exported £250,000,[4] and between 1672 and 1713, 548,327 guineas were coined from gold imported from the Gold Coast. It would seem that Bosman's figures are somewhat exaggerated, but the figures do indicate the scope of the Gold Coast gold trade. By the late eighteenth century, the export of gold began to decline. This led to an increase in the purchasing price of gold and the inhabitants of the Gold Coast began to demand gold as partial payment for their slaves.[5] In 1772 Brew of Anomabo wrote:

> There is no buying slaves now without you give 2 oz. of gold on each to procure which, you must sell your goods 20% under prime cost and may think yourself happy to get it even at that rate. The black traders . . . will not take the primest smoked taffy . . . but will oblige you to give seven ackies of gold in its stead, and they will have gold for any article that is not in ready sale in the market, in short, the nature of the trade is so much altered that a man who was here but two years ago would be at his wits end to make a purchase.[6]

1 N. R. Junner, *Gold on the Gold Coast*, Colchester, 1935, p. 14. According to Junner the annual exports of gold were:

	Annual Average	Total Ounces
1471–1750 (280 years)	40,000	11,200,000
1750–1800 (50 years)	10,000	500,000
1801–1850 (50 years)	40,000	2,000,000
1851–1880 (30 years)	25,000	750,000
	Total	14,450,000

The figures for the first half of the nineteenth century are somewhat higher than those available in official returns for the Gold Coast but those for 1851–1880 compare favourably with available figures. See also Walter Rodney, 'Gold and Slaves on the Gold Coast', *T.H.S.G.* x, 1969, pp. 13–38; Daaku, *Trade and Politics*, p. 23

2 Blake, *European Beginnings in West Africa*, p. 83

3 William Bosman, *A New and Accurate Description of the Coast of Guinea*, London, 1705, p. 89; J. D. Fage, *Ghana, a Historical Interpretation*, Madison, 1961, p. 47 and Daaku, *Trade and Politics*, p. 23

4 K. G. Davies, *The Royal African Company*, London, 1957, p. 225

5 Marion Johnson, 'The Ounce in Eighteenth Century West African Trade', *J.A.H.* vii, 2, 1966, p. 203; Davies, *Royal African Company*, p. 225

6 E. Donnan, ed., *Documents Illustrative of the History of the Slave Trade to America*, 4 vols., Washington, D.C., 1930ff., ii, p. 547

Of course the Asante–Fante dispute in 1765 was among the immediate causes of the hiatus in the gold trade.[1]

The export trade of the Gold Coast was not confined to gold alone as considerable quantities of ivory were involved. Elephants were rather scarce on the Gold Coast and it seems that most of the ivory exported from there originated from Ahafo and Gyaman and other interior markets on the fringe of the forest.[2] That the ivory trade was in the hands of rulers was a common assumption based on the fact that when an elephant was killed on the Gold Coast one of the tusks was given to the chief.

The slave trade

Until the end of the seventeenth century the Gold Coast produced more gold than slaves, but this situation changed in the eighteenth century when the gold trade declined and the slave trade became the main export. It is not unlikely that slaving activities had a disrupting influence on gold mining activities. It was for this reason that the Portuguese and the Dutch attempted to exclude slave trading from the Gold Coast. The Dutch maintained their interest in the gold trade for as long as they could. And it was suggested by an account of 1706 that the local people were said to be accustomed to transporting their slaves to the English and their gold to the Dutch. The Dutch were attracted to the slave trade early in the eighteenth century while still maintaining their interest in the gold trade. Although they considered relinquishing slave trading for a time, paradoxically they encouraged it in order to safeguard their gold markets.[3]

By the beginning of the eighteenth century it was clear the great demand for slaves to work the sugar, tobacco and cotton plantations of the New World had made the slave trade of paramount importance on the Gold Coast. The changing trade situation is reflected in the major English trading objectives. In 1660 the Company of Adventurers of London trading in Africa was founded with the object of searching for gold.[4] However, when the Royal African Company was formed in 1672 the chief aim was to trade in slaves to meet the increasing demands of the English colonies.[5]

By the third decade of the eighteenth century slaves had become the main concern on the Gold Coast and gold a subsidiary one. This, in effect, altered the nature of Afro-European trade. The people of the Gold Coast who up to now had exported both slaves and gold were now exporting captives and demanding payment for them in gold. This derived from the exploitation of Brazilian gold wealth and reached West Africa through resident European merchants at Whydah and Sao Tomé who had gained control of some of the imported metal.[6] In 1729 when this practice of payment for slaves in gold on the Gold Coast

1 Johnson, 'The Ounce in Eighteenth Century West African Trade', p. 204

2 T. E. Bowdich, *Mission from Cape Coast Castle to Ashantee*, London, 1819, p. 332 and Daaku, *Trade and Politics*, pp. 27–28

3 Rodney, 'Gold and Slaves on the Gold Coast', pp. 17–19; Davies, *Royal African Company*, p. 227

4 Davies, *Royal African Company*, p. 41

5 Rodney, 'Gold and Slaves on the Gold Coast', p. 18   6 *Ibid.*

came to their attention the Royal African Company warned their employees that 'It was never intended that gold purchased there [in Whydah and the Island of Sao Tomé] would be brought to the Gold Coast and sunk there; if the natives would not accept English manufactures they should keep their slaves'.[1] By the 1720s, as it was reported, the Gold Coast had indeed become a slave coast.

The Gold Coast was most active in the slave trade during the eighteenth century and Professor Philip Curtin's recent and careful study on the slave trade indicates more accurately the part played by the Gold Coast.[2] The slave exports of the French and the English may be represented by the figures in the table on page 11 which exclude slaves exported by the Danes and the Dutch.

The Danish participation in the African slave trade was about 1% and in most cases they despatched one or two ships to the coast per year.[3] The Dutch participation of the slave trade was also limited. It is likely that most of the Dutch slaves came from the Gold Coast area. According to a recent study based on the available Dutch records, Holland averaged approximately 3,398 slaves a year between 1675 and 1794 and had a 10% share of the total African slave trade. However, the Dutch records are not sufficiently precise in distinguishing between slaves from the Gold Coast and those from other regions of West Africa.[4] But without the Danish and Dutch figures, which will probably not substantially alter the above figures, there is still enough information here to indicate the significant trends of the slave trade on the Gold Coast.

Slave exports from the Gold Coast, as from the rest of West Africa, steadily increased from the 1700s until they reached a plateau in the 1740s. After the middle of the century slave exports fluctuated from decade to decade in response to Anglo-French sea warfare. The number of slaves exported in the Atlantic slave trade fell from 338,100 to 295,000 from the decade of 1741 to 1750 to the decade of 1751 to 1760 whereas the Gold Coast slave trade registered a decline from 67,000 to 41,800 in those same two decades. The only area in Africa with an increase during this period was the Bight of Benin. 1761–1770 showed rises and falls in trade in different areas and during this period the Gold Coast, the Bights of Benin and Biafra and the Windward Coast were the only areas in Africa that experienced an increase in the trade. There was a general decline in 1771–1780, but 1781–1790 manifested increased trade, except for the Windward Coast. The period from 1791 to 1810 reflected the beginning of the downward spiral of the slave trade which coincides with the period of the Napoleonic Wars and the Gold Coast's trade reaction.[5] As the table shows, from the figures available, it seems that the Gold Coast was consistently a leading exporter of slaves during the eighteenth century and invariably responded more than any other area to the supply, demand and fluctuations of the trade.

1 T. 70/54: Royal African Company to Braithwaite, Cruickshank and Peake, 14 August 1729, quoted in Sammy Tenkorang, *British Slave Trading Activities on the Gold and Slave Coasts in the 18th Century*', unpublished M.A. thesis, London University, 1964, p. 36

2 See Philip D. Curtin, *The Atlantic Slave Trade: a Census*, Madison, 1969

3 Curtin, *Atlantic Slave Trade*, p. 86; Georg Nørregard, *Danish Settlements in West Africa 1658–1850*, Boston, 1966, pp. 50, 80 and 87; Donnan, *Documents*, ii, p. xv

4 Johannes Postma, 'The Dimension of the Dutch Slave Trade from Western Africa'. *J.A.H.* xiii, 2, 1972, pp. 246–7   5 *Ibid.*

Region	1711–20	1721–30	1731–40	1741–50	1751–60	1761–70	1771–80	1781–90	1791–1800	1801–10	Total
Senegambia	30,900*	22,500	26,200	25,000	22,500	21,400	17,700	20,300	4,400	800	191,700
%	16·5	10·0	8·2	7·4	7·6	5·5	6·0	3·4	1·1	0·3	5·8
Sierra Leone	5,900	15,000	14,900	18,400	9,900	5,300	3,700	17,700	12,200	9,600	112,600
%	3·2	6·7	4·7	5·4	3·4	1·4	1·3	3·0	3·2	3·6	3·4
Windward Coast	30,600	47,600	55,200	65,300	29,800	67,600	49,700	24,400	14,700	11,200	396,100
%	16·4	21·2	17·3	19·3	10·1	17·4	16·9	4·1	3·8	4·2	12·1
Gold Coast	44,000	54,200	65,200	67,000	41,800	52,400	38,700	59,900	29,400	22.100	474,700
%	23·5	24·2	20·5	19·8	14·2	13·5	13·2	10·1	7·7	8·3	14·4
Bight of Benin	72,500	48,400	59,400	30,900	35,600	48,400	41,400	120,400	15,100	5,300	477,004
%	38·8	21·6	18·6	9·1	12·1	12·5	14·1	20·3	3·9	2·0	14·5
Bight of Biafra	—	4,500	45,100	71,300	100,700	139,300	100,000	114,800	137,600	110,400	823,700
%	—	2·0	14·2	21·1	34·1	35·9	34·0	19·4	35·9	41·5	25·1
Central and south-east Africa	3,200	32,000	52,500	60,200	54,600	53,200	42,900	234,400	170,400	106,700	810,100
%	1·7	14·3	16·5	17·8	18·5	13·7	14·6	39·6	44·4	40·1	24·7
Total	187,000	224,200	318,500	338,100	295,000	387,700	294,000	591,800	383,800	266,000	3,286,100
%	100·0	100·0	100·0	100·0	100·0	100·0	100·0	100·0	100·0	100·0	100·0

* Figures and totals have been rounded.
Sources: Tables 43, 49 (through the 1740s), and 60 (1751–1810) leaving aside category of 'other' or 'unknown'.

1 Curtin, *The Atlantic Slave Trade*, p. 221

11

The slave trade pattern on the Gold Coast, like that of other parts of West Africa, responded to local supply. However, with the castle trade and European traders around to buy slaves at all times the Gold Coast reacted to the demand of European traders more than others without castles. Curtin has suggested that certain peaks existed in the slave trade because of large numbers of prisoners for sale. The slave export peaks of Sierra Leone in the 1720s and 1740s are rationalised this way. The case of trade fluctuations in the Bight of Benin in the early decades of the eighteenth century was the result of political change.[1]

The steady increase in the slave trade on the Gold Coast from the beginning of the eighteenth century to the 1740s coincides with the rise and expansion of Asante. Thus it is possible to conclude that the slaves exported during that period were from the wars waged in the wake of the expansion during the first half of the eighteenth century. Of course it must be borne in mind that figures by decades are too general to relate to particular events unless one is dealing with a period of severe war or anarchy. Despite Curtin's claim that one cannot correlate the rise and fall in the slave trade figures after the 1740s with wars in Asante and the hinterland, nevertheless Asante's internal political situation and pattern of wars may partially explain what, admittedly, is a complicated problem. Thus, the 1750s, which were marked by the lowest export figures yet in the century, also correspond roughly to the reign of the unwarlike Asantehene Kwasi Obodum (1750–1764). For the increase in the sixties one might adduce civil disturbance in Asante, their great defeat of 1764 and their invasion of the coast in 1765. The decline in the seventies was because of the greater stability in the reign of Osei Kwadwo (1764–1777) and the new peak in the eighties could represent the reign of Osei Kwame (1777–1801) which was marked by continuous instability, disunity and civil wars. The sharp decline after 1790 could be due to external factors, especially war in Europe.

It has been estimated that only about 25% of the slaves exported from the Gold Coast came from the coastal region, and by the middle of the eighteenth century the *Donkos*, people from the north, had replaced Fante slaves.[2] There is documentation to suggest that the Asante were obtaining their slaves from the north as early as 1715.[3]

The bulk of the people sold in the Atlantic slave trade were the victims of wars and raids. The connection between wars and slavery is well known, but has often led to the static picture that Africans fought wars solely for the purpose of obtaining slaves.[4] Acquiring slaves, however, was only incidental to the conduct of warfare. Furthermore, wars were detrimental to trade items like gold and did not always yield slaves. European traders therefore stood to gain most from wars after major conflicts where one side was routed.[5]

Raiding was especially calculated to secure slaves for sale. Asante raided

---

1 *Ibid.*, p. 226

2 Tenkorang, *British Slave Trading Activities*, p. 60

3 T.70/1464: Komenda Fort Diary, entry dated 4 August 1715

4 This attitude of fighting wars for economic purposes as applied to Asante is what Kwame Arhin has attacked as 'a barbarous view of Ashanti history'. See Kwame Arhin, 'The Structure of Greater Ashanti (1700–1824)', *J.A.H.* viii, 1, 1967.

5 Rodney, 'Gold and Slaves on the Gold Coast', 23

northern areas and during the early decades of the eighteenth century Akyem, Kwahu and Krepi villages often became the victims of Akwamu raiders. Asante received slaves, too, from subject peoples like Dagomba which at one point supplied Asante with 400 slaves a year.[1] Of course some of Asante's slaves were also obtained through peaceful trade with northern markets like Salaga in exchange for kola. Other groups sold into slavery were those convicted of witchcraft, people panyarred and those caught committing adultery with a wife of the chief. A recent study of the notes on the 179 informants supplied by S. W. Koelle in his *Polyglotta Africana* of 1854 shows that 34% were war captives, 30% were kidnapped and the remaining third were mostly people sold by relatives or superiors for debt or condemned by the judicial process.[2] The external and internal slave trade existed side by side, but the external recruitment invariably took priority everywhere[3] with the slave trade largely in the hands of the ruling class and the chiefs. It was they who were engaged in a partnership of exploitation with the Europeans: they made wars, sanctioned raids and, by their traditional legal authority, condemned people accused of certain crimes to slavery.[4]

Slaves employed in European castles, known as 'castle slaves', were often obtained from the Slave Coast or the Niger Delta region. Whenever the supply of castle slaves dwindled, vessels were sent to get more from these regions.[5] To be sure some castle slaves were obtained from the Gold Coast, but it seems that the reason for bringing some of them from the outside was to avoid fraternisation with free Africans on the coast. British castle slaves were, in a way, a privileged group. While domestic slaves on the Gold Coast were liable to be sold for misdemeanours, it was the order of the Company of Merchants Trading to Africa that they could never be sold off the coast whatever their crimes.[6]

Mode of trade

Trade on the Gold Coast until the end of the seventeenth century was supplemented by the barter trade and to some extent replaced by what came to be

1 Bowdich, *Mission from Cape Coast Castle*, 320–1; Jack Goody, *Technology, Tradition and the State in Africa*, Oxford, 1971, p. 52

2 P. E. H. Hair, 'The Enslavement of Koelle's Informants', *J.A.H.* vi, 2, 1965, pp. 193–203. Among those condemned by the judicial process were witches. In 1811 Henry Meredith wrote in reference to this practice: 'Since the abolition of the slave trade, we have heard of no conviction of this sort and we may suppose that the severity of the laws, as they regard trifling and imaginary offences, will be mitigated, if not absolutely altered, in consequence of that humane act'. *An Account of the Gold Coast of Africa*, London, 1812, p. 29. He also pointed out that trade-boys and gold-takers 'were not backward in stimulating a disposition for quarrels and encouraging palavers, or lawsuits, which tendered to the slavery of their countrymen'. *Ibid.*, p. 104.

3 Rodney, 'Gold and Slaves on the Gold Coast', p. 25

4 Rodney, 'Impact of the Atlantic Slave Trade on West Africa', p. 37, in R. Oliver, *The Middle Ages of African History*, Oxford, 1967

5 Postma, 'The Dimension of the Dutch Slave Trade from Western Africa', pp. 30 and 53

6 Eveline C. Martin, *The British West African Settlements 1750–1821*, London, 1927, p. 52

known as the commodity currency, the ounce trade or sorting.[1] As Africans were reluctant to part with their gold, this system came to provide a basis of exchange on the principle of a 1:1 ratio. Commodity currencies were expressed in ounces and ackies but their real value did not correspond to that of these units in gold.[2] The introduction of the ounce in the eighteenth century represents an attempt to bring about a gradual implementation of a monetary system into what once had been basically a barter trade. Goods sold on the coast were normally reckoned to be double their cost price in Europe.[3] As a trader wrote at the beginning of the nineteenth century:

> The value of goods in gold, on the Gold Coast, is estimated, pro forma, to be half the trade price, or half the price at which they were valued when bartered for ivory . . . The prices in gold are, nevertheless, governed by the demand, and the qualities and patterns of the articles on sale . . . At one period I have sold a hogshead of tobacco, which cost £30 in England, for £260 sterling in gold.[4]

Trade on the Gold Coast involved certain risks, and precautions had to be taken to guard against fraud and to select items for trade. One of the dishonest practices of the Guinea trade was the adulteration of goods, especially gold and ivory. Brass and copper filings were often mixed with gold and to avoid being cheated most ships trading on the Gold Coast engaged a professional gold assayer.[5] Large ivory tusks had to be examined very carefully because traders had a trick of pouring melted lead into the hollow part to increase the weight. A brass rod was usually employed for sounding the tusks to detect the lead and the filling was discovered when the lead in the ivory was struck.[6] In trading on the Gold Coast, items had to be carefully selected and goods on the whole had to suit seasonal changes and demands. Occasionally, by the time certain goods reached the coast, there would be no demand for them, while at other times the colour of the goods might not appeal to the people.[7]

Another risk of the trade was the credit system that developed and seems to have been extended on both sides. Sometimes the African advanced the European trader goods and at other times the European supplied the African with

---

1 K. Polyani, 'Sortings and "Ounce Trade" in the West African Trade', *J.A.H.* v, 3, 1964, pp. 381–95: Johnson, 'The Ounce in Eighteenth Century West African Trade', pp. 197–214

2 Johnson, 'The Ounce in Eighteenth Century West African Trade'; Daaku, *Trade and Politics*, p. 36

3 Tenkorang, *British Slave Trading Activities*

4 Captain John Adams, *Remarks on the Country Extending from Cape Palmas to the River Congo; including Observations on the Manners and Customs of the Inhabitants*, London, 1823, pp. 236–7; see pp. 235–6 for some comparisons of cost price in England and trade value in Africa.

5 Lars Sundstrom, *The Guinea Trade*, Oslo, 1966, p. 59

6 W. F. Hutchinson, 'The Gold Trade of the Gold Coast 1826–1890', *E.D.M.* xiii, 4, 1925, p. 9

7 Wyndham, *Atlantic and Slavery*, pp. 66–67; Daaku, *Trade and Politics*, p. 39

goods beforehand.[1] Although this credit system, commercially called the 'trust', was often abused by both sides, it continued. It has been suggested that the system might have originated as an attempt to secure the goodwill of important chiefs and merchants but became a necessary evil in the face of rivalry between competing Europeans.[2] On the Gold Coast, as in other places in West Africa, trade depended upon the goodwill of the people. Europeans, therefore, sought and cultivated the friendships of local potentates with gifts, a major feature of the trade, being sent to coastal rulers as well as to those inland. It even became customary for newly arrived governors of European castles to send presents to the rulers.[3]

Middlemen were essential for the conduct of trade on the Gold Coast, but they did not seem to have complete control of the coastal area. Asante seems to have had an outlet to the coast at Elmina from at least the beginning of the eighteenth century, and although the Fante and other states periodically closed the routes to the interior during times of conflict, they apparently never totally denied the interior people access to the coast to trade. The Accra coast also appears to have been open to interior traders for most of the time of European trade. Of course it is true that the coastal people established interior markets where they met and traded with people from inland, but this did not preclude the interior people's coming to the coast to trade. At one time or another, most of the important trading nations like Assin, Denkyera, Fante, Akwamu and even Asante acted as middlemen. For example, by the 1630s Assin, renowned throughout the seventeenth century as a trading nation, had established a middleman position between the interior and the littoral strip between Elmina and Winneba. Denkyera also assumed a middleman position between the interior and the western region of the Gold Coast when it conquered Assin. Denkyera apparently lost her middleman position when conquered by Asante in 1701. Fante became the principal middleman for the central region after Denkyera conquered Assin. By 1702 in the east Akwamu, which controlled the coast between Apam and Whydah in Dahomey, maintained a monopoly of trade with that section and the interior until her collapse in 1730.[4] Asante could be said to have played a middleman role between the coastal and the interior trade. Further one might say that the Portuguese and other Europeans who followed them also played a middleman role as carriers in the coastal trade between the Gold Coast and other sections of West Africa. The Portuguese, for example, participated in a carrying trade between the Gold Coast and Benin.[5]

The emergence of a new class

The role of the coastal states acting as a liaison between European traders and those of the interior resulted in the emergence of a broker class through whom inland traders had to operate in their dealings with the Europeans. These brokers knew the trading language and many of them were found around all the

1 Daaku, *Trade and Politics*, pp. 42–43

2 Sundstrom, *Guinea Trade*, p. 39   3 Daaku, *Trade and Politics*, pp. 33 and 54

4 K. B. Dickson, *A Historical Geography of Ghana*, Cambridge, 1969, pp. 107–8

5 See Wilks, 'Medieval Trade Route'; Blake, *European Beginnings in West Africa*

European settlements.[1] Merchants on the coast often contracted with coastal chiefs to act as brokers for them. Chiefs from the interior also, from time to time, assigned traders from their territories to coastal chiefs who received a brokerage fee on the merchandise traded.[2] The chiefs seem to have received a brokerage fee from European traders when inland traders came to the coast to trade. The practice, which dated from the time of the Portuguese, persisted well into the nineteenth century.[3]

In fact the position of the coastal states and trade led to the rise of a new class,[4] which was both a response and a by-product of the European trade, especially the Atlantic slave trade. Dr Daaku, amplifying the roles of some of them, says there were those

> ... who may be described in modern parlance as the advertising agents or market researchers. Not only were they to popularise the European goods and to induce inland traders to trade with their employers, but it was these agents who watched the trend of demand by the consumers.[5]

Among the new class names like Edward Barter, John Konny and John Kabes stand out. Barter was probably one of the most influential mulattoes on the Gold Coast during the seventeenth century whose main duty seemed to have been to collect debts due to Europeans from Africans.[6] John Kabes became a broker from whom the British and the Dutch sought services. In the 1680s he was trading for the Dutch and when he broke with them he invited the British to Komenda in 1695. He became the most important person in Komenda and often played the English and the Dutch against one another. Engaged in many business enterprises besides his extensive trade, he had maize farms and kept a flotilla of canoes which he hired out to Europeans. Because of his economic position he was able to wield far-reaching social and political influence at his base in Komenda. Kabes could even boast of friendship and influence with the Asante hene.[7]

John Konny was born around the 1660s and early 1670s. He virtually became the ruler of Ahanta and with a large force at his disposal was able to disrupt trade. Because of his influence European companies sought to avert confrontations with him that might disrupt trade. Like his contemporary Kabes, Konny achieved wealth and power. Daaku dubbed both men 'the Merchant Princes'.

The social and economic impact of European trading on the Gold Coast, felt both on the coastal states and the inland states of the country, was far-reaching. European trading on the coast transformed many former fish or salt extraction coastal villages into thriving commercial centres and urban markets.

1 Daaku, *Trade and Politics*, pp. 96–114

2 Meredith, *Account of the Gold Coast*, p. 96; Bosman, *New and Accurate Description*, p. 191

3 C.O. 96/94: D. P. Chalmers to Acting Administrator, 28 Oct. 1872; C.O. 96/96: Pope-Hennessy to Earl of Kimberley, 8 Feb. 1874; C.O. 96/94: Representative of F. and A. Swanzy to Pope-Hennessy, 4 Nov. 1872; C.O. 96/94: Salmon to Colonel Harley, 30 Nov. 1872 and C.O. 96/94: Pope-Hennessy to Kimberley, 28 Dec. 1872

4 For more information of the rise of the new class, see Daaku, *Trade and Politics*, pp. 96–114

5 *Ibid.*, p. 104   6 *Ibid.*, p. 98   7 *Ibid.*, pp. 15–27

Inland trade and economic institutions

Despite the activities of Europeans on the coast, the internal trade of the Gold Coast continued to remain important. The importance of the northern interior markets to the people is shown by the trading patterns and in the direction of the expansion of the Gold Coast states during the seventeenth and eighteenth centuries. Akyem's trade during the early decades of the seventeenth century, for instance, was mainly directed north and not to the coast. The farthest south they came at that time was the Accra inland market of Abonce.[1] Adansi traders also directed their commerce north and the establishment of Europeans on the coast simply added to their trade.[2] The initial expansion of Denkyera was to the north for the purpose of controlling the trade routes leading to the markets of Bono-Manso and Begho. It was not until after her northern expansion that Denkyera began to penetrate south.[3] Asante expansion, which gave it the enviable control of the sources of gold, slaves and kola-producing regions, was along the northwest and northeast trade routes.[4]

There is evidence that during the last four decades of the eighteenth century when the gold trade on the coast was at a low ebb, considerable quantities were reaching North Africa. This indicated that the flow of gold was being reversed and commercial contacts with the interior were not unimportant.[5] The interior trade was always important to the Gold Coast economy despite the trading activities of Europeans on the coast and by 1800 indigenous trade had neither disappeared nor completely yielded to the external trade; it was strong and viable enough to function when the slave trade which formed the basis of the foreign trade was removed. Although the internal trade of the Gold Coast was still important at the time of abolition, the slave trade era had been a significant phase in the long-term economic evolution of the Gold Coast and had affected its social and economic institutions by the nineteenth century.

Domestic slavery, together with the associated practice of panyarring, was a common feature of all Gold Coast societies. It dated back at least to the fifteenth century when the Portuguese were selling slaves from Benin on the Gold Coast. Professor Fage has shown in his recent study which sums up the current thinking and scholarship on the slave trade, that what might be called a 'slave economy' developed along with the foreign trade with its demand for slaves. According to Fage the 'slave economy' which had been established in the western and central Sudan had spread to the Senegal and the Lower Guinea coasts by the fifteenth century.[6] The practice of slavery was universalised and the number of slaves greatly increased during the period of the Atlantic slave trade.[7]

---

1 *Ibid.*, p. 145   2 *Ibid.*, p. 148   3 *Ibid.*, p. 157

4 *Ibid.*, p. 162; J. K. Fynn, *Ashanti and Her Neighbours 1700–1807*, Ph.D. thesis, University of London, 1964, pp. 124–64; and see Ivor Wilks, *The Northern Factor in Ashanti History*, Legon, 1961

5 Johnson, 'The Ounce in Eighteenth Century West African Trade', p. 204

6 J. D. Fage, 'Slavery and the Slave Trade in the Context of West African History', *J.A.H.* x, 3, 1969, pp. 393–404

7 Tenkorang, *British Slave Trading Activities*, pp. 25–26. On the Gold Coast a class of domestic slaves who emerged concurrently with the Atlantic slave trade were the unacceptable slaves who were left over. They were known locally as *waw-waw* slaves, meaning unacceptable ones. *Ibid.*

Domestic slavery

Domestic slavery was still an important institution in the country at the beginning of the nineteenth century, but, as is well known, it differed considerably from the plantation slavery of the Americas. Slaves were often regarded as part of the family on the Gold Coast. A nineteenth-century resident on the coast described the system thus:

> The condition of the slaves in the countries under our protection is by no means one of unmitigated hardship. In ordinary cases, the slave is considered as a member of his master's family, and often succeeds to his property, in default of a natural heir. He eats with him from the same dish, and has an equal share in all his simple enjoyments. He intermarries with his children, and is allowed to acquire property of his own, over which, unless under very extraordinary circumstances, his master exercises no control. He sometimes even acquires wealth and consideration far superior to his master, who may occasionally be seen swelling his importance by following in his train. They address each other as 'my father' and 'my son', and differ in little in their relations from the respect and obedience implied in these endearing epithets.[1]

The whole question of slavery is the more difficult to understand because there were many varying degrees of servitude. Asante had at least five terms describing different conditions of slavery. First, there was the *Akoa* which, although it could mean slave, is best translated as subject and originally referred not to a condition of servitude but to a state of dependence such as all men and women in the society stood in relation to some other persons or groups.[2] Although Brodie Cruickshank might have overstated his case, his words, to some extent, do convey the concept of *Akoa*:

> . . . the acknowledged head of a family possesses the unquestionable right to dispose of his descendants, and collateral relations, in any way that he may think fit; that they are in fact so much property, which he can sell, pawn, or give away at his pleasure.[3]

Even where the position of the *Akoa* was one of servitude, there was surely a distinction between the 'favoured' domestic slave, virtually a member of the family and the slave labourer employed in mining, porterage and the like. The relative use of the word slaves as applied to people who worked for European companies and who were called castle slaves might be interjected here. Some of these people performed skilled tasks, were handsomely paid by the standards of their day and often felt superior to the free people outside the castle.[4]

Secondly, there was *Awowa*, which in essence was a pawn, a pledge, a mortgage or a security for what a person owed. Thus, if a person needed to borrow

1 Brodie Cruickshank, *Eighteen Years on the Gold Coast of Africa*, London, 1853, 2 vols., ii, p. 240

2 R. S. Rattray, *Ashanti Law and Constitution*, London, 1929, pp. 34–46

3 Cruickshank, *Eighteen Years*, i, p. 313

4 Tenkorang, *British Slave Trading Activities*, p. 27

or owed another person he could take a member of his family or a slave to his debtor as pawn. The pawn worked for the creditor who fed and clothed him and to all intents and purposes he was a slave until the debt was paid. Other valuable items such as expensive cloths, silk and gold ornaments were also pawned.

A third term, *Odonko*, which could mean a person from the North, was applied to people who had been purchased for the express purpose of enslavement. Prisoners of war and people given in the form of tribute from subjugated powers were often used as *nnonko*. The fourth term, *Domum*, denoted enslaved war captives. The last term, *Akyere*, referred to people living in designated villages who were looked upon as a human reservoir for sacrifices.[1]

To these categories could be added the practice of panyarring – the forcible seizure of a person for debt. If a person became involved in debt and was, either from the want of ability or from whatever motive, dilatory in the discharge of it, the creditor was at liberty to seize and confine, or according to their phrase 'panyar', any person or persons belonging to the family of the debtor or even to the same country, state or town; and if an opportunity were presented they were sold, without delay or ceremony. This destructive practice was carried to such an extent during the slave-trade that many innocent persons were reduced to servitude or sold overseas.[2] Although panyarring must have originally been practised in relation to established customary law, the impact of the Atlantic slavery led to the abuse of the traditional law when individuals were 'panyarred' and sold overseas.

Slavery existed in many forms and was put to different uses. This was realised by the slave trader Don Theodore Canot who astutely observed:

> . . . the financial genius of Africa, instead of devising bank-notes or the precious metals as a circulating medium, has from time immemorial declared that a human creature – the true representative and embodiment of labour – is the most valuable article on earth. A man, therefore, becomes the standard of prices. A slave is a note of hand that may be discounted or pawned; he is a bill of exchange that carries himself to his destination and pays a debt bodily; he is a tax that walks corporeally [*sic*] into the chieftain's treasury.[3]

Slavery indeed formed a basic part and played a vital role in the economic life of the people, but the part it played was to be in the larger context of the economic life of the people at the beginning of the nineteenth century. Many of the economic activities pursued by the people were affected by European contact and specialisation brought about by the process of economic change and development.

Occupations

The occupations that engaged the people were diverse and varied with a large number of the inhabitants involved in the economic activities of collecting,

1 Rattray, *Ashanti Law and Constitution*, pp. 34–46

2 Henry Meredith, *Account of the Gold Coast of Africa*, pp. 29–30. Also T. E. Bowdich, *Mission from Cape Coast Castle to Ashantee*, p. 257

3 Theodore Canot, *Captain Canot: or Twenty Years of an African Slaver*, London, 1854, p. 105

19

farming, livestock rearing, fishing, hunting, salt extraction and gold mining. There were also metal workers, potters, wood-workers, cloth-makers, not to mention priests, 'doctors' and other such 'professional' men.[1] Most inhabitants of the coastal region earned a living by fishing, salt or canoe-making. The fish they caught were often dried, cured, packed in loads and carried inland for sale or exchanged for other products. In the interior, fishing activities were carried out along inland rivers and streams and on Lake Bosomtwe in Asante. It was reported that 'upwards of thirty small crooms were reckoned situated around it supported by fishing' and that 'fish were forwarded thence daily for the King's table, by relays of men'.[2] Canoe-making was a necessary appendage to fishing and was widely carried out on the coast.

Salt extraction was another economic activity of consequence for the coast people, enlisting the support of most of the small coastal villages. Although there was a salt deposit in the interior beyond Asante at Daboya in Dagomba the people of the Gold Coast seem to have preferred salt from the coast.[3] Salt was obtained by two methods – salt boiling and salt pits. Salt water was boiled in earthen pots until the water evaporated leaving a residue of salt. By the salt pit or pans methods, a technique supposedly introduced by the Portuguese, sea water was normally allowed to run into the pits to be evaporated by the extreme heat of the sun, leaving the salt.[4]

Although most of the people produced their own food, the sale of agricultural produce was nevertheless an integral economic activity. For the people of Akuapem, for example, agriculture was their chief means of support and they supplied the Accra and Adangbe people with food. In return the Akuapems received salt, dried fish, gunpowder, iron, guns and cotton manufactures.[5] Such a place as Yomoho, in Akyem, supplied the markets of Juaben, Begua, Sarasu, Dumpasi and other places with corn and yams.[6] The villages near Cape Coast must have also supplied the town with agricultural goods as 'few indeed attended to the labours of the field'.[7]

Profitable gold-washing and mining were carried out in Akyem, Denkyera, Wassaw, Assin and Asante.[8] Gold was regarded as sacred and life-giving and the people had a propensity to hoard it. Because of its alleged life-giving property it was interred with crops.[9] Normally when a nugget of gold was dis-

---

1 Carl Christian Reindorf, *The History of the Gold Coast and Asante*, 2nd ed., reprint, Accra, 1966, pp. 261–4; Meredith, *Account of the Gold Coast*, p. 182

2 Bowdich, *Mission from Cape Coast Castle*, p. 163   3 *Ibid.*, pp. 173 and 176

4 Reindorf, *Gold Coast and Asante*, p. 263. George MacDonald, *The Gold Coast, Past and Present*, London, 1898, pp. 56–57

5 Meredith, *Account of the Gold Coast*, p. 227

6 J. Beecham, *Ashantee and the Gold Coast*, London, 1841, p. 137; Joseph Dupuis, *Journal of a Residence in Ashantee*, 2 vols., London, 1824, ii, p. xxxi

7 Meredith, *Account of the Gold Coast*, p. 96

8 Reindorf, *Gold Coast and Asante*, p. 263

9 Eva L. R. Meyerowitz, *The Sacred State of the Akan*, London, 1951, p. 197; Marcus Allen, *The Gold Coast or a Cruise in West African Waters*, London, 1874, p. 117; Meredith, *Account of the Gold Coast*, p. 32

covered it was taken to the chief who divided it into three parts and gave a third to the finder.[1] In some places two thirds of the gold dug went to the chief.[2]

Most gold-bearing states owned some gold mines that were worked principally by slave labour. When gold was found in a new mine pit the chief had to be notified whereupon he provided a sheep for sacrifice while the discoverer supplied fowls, eggs and drinks for libation.[3] Menstruating women were not allowed where gold was mined and in some areas plantains and bananas, regarded as phallic symbols, were forbidden.[4]

Gold pits about two to three feet in diameter and up to fifty feet deep were often dug in auriferous gravel.[5] Besides such pits, upright or steeply sloped shafts were usually sunk in mountainous regions until the miner struck dark and coloured rock which contained gold. The shafts varied in depth and like the pits were neither timbered nor reinforced at the mouth. The miners worked with a palm oil lamp and cut the ore loose with a pickaxe, hoe or iron chisel. The bottom of the mine was reached by a rope ladder, by foot holes in the side of the shaft or by 50 to 60 annular steps on which men stood to pass up trays full of soil. Shafts located close by each other were often connected by tunnels.[6] It is likely that quartz mining was introduced on the Gold Coast by the Portuguese in 1630 when they began operations in Aboasi, near Kommenda. The underground workings of these mines were destroyed in 1636 by an earthquake.[7] Probably following the Portuguese example, local people were working auriferous reefs as well as alluvial deposits by the early eighteenth century.[8]

Alluvial gold occurred freely in many places and the simplest way of obtaining the metal was by gold-washing. This activity was often carried out by women on river banks and other places, especially after a heavy fall of rain:

> . . . a quantity of soil is collected near a stream, or at the sea-side, in which gold is known to be, a portion of which is filled with water, and then mixed together; and while the soil is held in solution, a quick rotary motion is given to the calabash, by which means the mixture is made to fly over its side, and the gold, by its specific gravity, sinks to the bottom.[9]

Dupuis relates that eight to ten thousand slaves were employed during the rainy season on the banks of the Bana stream in Banda to wash for gold.[10]

1 Meyerowitz, *Sacred State of the Akan*, p. 197

2 Rattray, *Ashanti Law and Constitution*, ch. 3, and K. A. Busia, *The Position of the Chief in the Modern Political Systems of Ashanti*, London, 1951, p. 81

3 Meyerowitz, *Sacred State of the Akan*, p. 198

4 *Ibid.*, p. 199   5 *Ibid.*

6 *Ibid.*, p. 200. Also, Junner, *Gold on the Gold Coast*, p. 12; W. Rodney, 'Gold and Slaves on the Gold Coast.'

7 Junner, *Gold on the Gold Coast*, p. 6   8 *Ibid.*, p. 10

9 J. Adams, *Remarks on the Country Extending from Cape Palmas to the River Congo, including Observations on the Manners and Customs of the Inhabitants*, p. 47; see also Meredith, *Account of the Gold Coast*, p. 119.

10 Dupuis, *Journal*, ii, p. lvi

Hunting on the Gold Coast usually provided game for meat. But the killing of elephants provided more than food: it yielded ivory tusks which were used as ornaments at the courts of chiefs and furnished a readily marketable item of trade in the European commerce on the coast. Although ivory was a staple trade on the Gold Coast and West Africa, until the nineteenth century there is not much information about the manner in which elephants were hunted. In general animals hunted on the Gold Coast are classified into two groups: those spiritually dangerous, *sasammoa*, and those that are not.[1] Of all the *sasammoa* most people consider the elephant as the most dangerous. When these animals were killed they were accorded funerals so that the hunter could cleanse himself of all possible harm from the spirit of the animal.[2]

The hunting of the elephant was not undertaken lightly. A hunter would not normally commence killing animals that were spiritually harmful until he acquired a charm (*suman*) for guidance, safety and success in hunting *sasammoa*. The *suman* was not bought, but was discovered in the bowels of animals the hunter had killed. After acquiring a *suman* the hunter killed several lesser kinds of *sasammoa* before he felt himself capable of pursuing the greatest of them all — the elephant. In places like Kwahu a hunter was not admitted to the innermost circle of his profession until he had killed at least three elephants. Although the elephant hunter was accompanied by a group he usually left it in camp in the forest and sought the animal alone. It was after shooting the animal that he reported the matter to his companions at the camp, and they helped with the elaborate ritual surrounding the killing of an elephant.[3] Guns were used in hunting, but it is likely that other means (spears, bows and arrows, etc.) were employed before the introduction of firearms on the Gold Coast. By tradition the hunter who killed an elephant had to send the foreleg (*basa*) and one of the tusks to the chief.[4] Although the Gold Coast did produce a fair amount of ivory, most of it came from the Gyaman area.[5] Ivory was also obtained from other animals such as hippopotami. This kind of ivory, which was often very white and brittle, averaged about sixteen inches in length and weighed from four to fifteen pounds.[6] Small quantities of ivory were referred to as *scrivelloes*.[7] Besides elephant hunters, other professional hunters acted as protectors against certain predatory animals. Furthermore, collecting snails and various medicinal and edible plants can be classified as hunting.

Far from having disappeared under the impact of European trade, local indigenous industries were still very important in the nineteenth century. As late as 1865 Elias Schrenk of the Basel Mission said, 'If we come to the interior, six days' journey, people make their iron and make their own cloth.'[8] According to J. Beecham, iron was manufactured to a great extent in Asante and their swords

1 Some of the spiritually harmful animals are the elephant (*esono*), the bongo (*trom*), the bush-cow (*eko*), the yellow-backed duiker (*kwaduo*) and the roan (*oko*).

2 A. G. Fraser, 'The Cult of the Kwahu Hunter on the Question of *Sasa* Animals, especially the Elephant,' *G.C.R.* iv (2), 1928, pp. 155–6

3 *Ibid.*, pp. 157–65

4 Busia, *Position of the Chief*, p. 49   5 Dupuis, *Journal*, p. 49

6 Walter Rodney, *A History of the Upper Guinea Coast*, Oxford, 1970, p. 157

7 *Ibid.*   8 *Parl. Papers*, Evidence of Elias Schrenk 3295, 1865, pp. xxxvii and 170

Cape Coast Castle

The Castle of Elmina

Port of Christiansborg, near Accra

were said to show very fine workmanship.[1] Even though iron works in the interior survived, it seems that iron smelting had almost disappeared on the Gold Coast in the nineteenth century. However, the techniques and traditions used survived well into the twentieth century across the Volta at Akpafu.[2] Iron ore often occurred near the surface and consequently shafts or galleries were usually not necessary for mining. Akpafu provides us with one of the few instances of elaborate works of iron mining. To obtain the ore, the people dug vertically sloping or horizontal shafts and hacked it out with socketed iron celts.[3] Undoubtedly, iron obtained locally was supplemented by imports from Europe.

Weaving was one of the more vital industries. The simplest cloth available on the Gold Coast was the bark cloth, locally called *kyenkyen*, made from the bark of the *kyenken* tree (*Antiaris toxicaira*). Long narrow pieces of bark about a foot wide were stripped off the trees, softened in water, then laid over a fallen trunk and beaten out with wooden mallets until the original width was trebled.[4] Grass cloths were also made at places like Apollonia.[5]

Weaving was probably first introduced in Asante from the north some time during the seventeenth century. The first loom, a Mande cultural feature, was reported to have been set up near Kumasi at Bonwire, the centre of weaving in Asante. According to Bonwire tradition, when Salaga came under Asante suzerainty the inhabitants were engaged in growing and spinning cotton for the Bonwire weavers.[6] Besides Bonwire there were other important weaving centres. It was said that almost the entire population of Asiminia in Asante was engaged in weaving.[7] The towns of Agotime, Dumpasi[8] and Moisy in Assin,[9] Datchanso[10] and Saresso[11] all subsisted by weaving. On the Gold Coast the men did the weaving while the women did the spinning. The loom was employed in weaving with the web from the loom about four inches in width and the finished cloth normally consisted of narrow strips sewed together.[12]

The pottery industry – the source of cooking utensils, water pots, pipes and other wares – was also essential. In Asante, Tafo, Pankrono, Obuokrom, Dataise[13] and Ekwea there were important centres of the pottery industry. Nearer to the coast Shai was perhaps the best known area for pottery with its people supplying all their neighbours. The Krobos, who lived near the Shai people, also manufactured pottery. In other areas, Moisy in Assin and Osino in

1 Beecham, *Ashantee and the Gold Coast*, p. 146

2 Walter Cline, *Mining and Metallurgy in Negro Africa*, Mensha, 1937, p. 26

3 R. S. Rattray, *Religion and Art in Ashanti*, Oxford, 1927, pp. 309–10. Celts are bronze, stone or iron chisel-edged prehistoric implements.

4 *Ibid.*, p. 220   5 Cruickshank, *Eighteen Years*, ii, p. 271

6 Rattray, *Religion and Art*, pp. 220 and 234. Also, see Marion Johnson, 'Ashanti East of the Volta', *T.H.S.G.* viii, 1965, p. 39.

7 Bowdich, *Mission from Cape Coast Castle*, p. 30   8 *Ibid.*, p. 28

9 Dupuis, *Journal*, i, p. 50   10 *Ibid.*, p. 59   11 *Ibid.*, p. 68

12 Bowdich, *Mission from Cape Coast Castle*, p. 29 and Rattray, *Religion and Art*, pp. 301–2

13 Bowdich, *Mission from Cape Coast Castle*, p. 311; Beecham, *Ashantee and the Gold Coast*, p. 147 and Cruickshank, *Eighteen Years*, ii, pp. 11 and 270

Akyem were important. Nineteenth-century travellers were impressed by the quality of Gold Coast pottery.[1]

Tanning and leather work figured prominently in local industry. Although leather was prepared and worked in Asante, leather goods from countries behind Asante were considered superior. From this industry emerged items like sandals, cushions, belts, pouches, saddles and cases for knives or swords.[2] Goldsmiths were also found throughout the country manufacturing trinkets, chains and other ornaments.[3] Carving, another common industry, produced canoes, stools, drums, wooden spoons, pestles and mortars for pounding the popular *fufu*.[4]

Occupational specialisation was the result of many factors and was sometimes regional. For example, a region addicted to waging war and raiding for the purpose of securing hostages for the slave trade might often depend upon a peace-loving sedentary people devoted to agricultural pursuits. Akwamu at the height of its fame was devoted to warfare and yet had to obtain food supplies from neighbours engaged in agricultural pursuits. Again, when gold-mining states like Akyem directed most of their energy to gold digging they had to buy quantities of foodstuffs from neighbouring states.[5]

Economic specialisation and markets

It would appear from the occupations and economic activities prevalent on the Gold Coast that by the beginning of the nineteenth century a remarkable degree of specialisation had been attained. For example, trading activities on the coast had brought about certain occupational specialisation which not only produced skilled and semi-skilled workers like masons, carpenters, bricklayers and other types of work associated with trade, but also stimulated local industries like canoe-making and agricultural production to feed those engaged in other pursuits.[6] Furthermore, in places inland like Asante, as the Asante Empire grew, many artisans converged upon the capital and groups of villages were organised into what could be termed as guilds to carry on with the pottery, weaving, metalwork, carving and other crafts for the Asantehene.[7] This shows a level of specialisation with a shift from the primary to secondary economic activity.[8] It is this economic specialisation as well as economic surplus that brings markets into existence. Belshaw has observed:

1 Bowdich, *Mission from Cape Coast Castle*, p. 311

2 *Ibid.*, and MacDonald, *Gold Coast*, p. 56

3 Dupuis, *Journal*, ii, p. lviii and Bowdich, *Mission from Cape Coast Castle*, p. 311

4 Bowdich, *Mission from Cape Coast Castle*, p. 313 and Beecham, *Ashantee and the Gold Coast*, p. 147

5 Dickson, *Historical Geography of Ghana*

6 Daaku, *Trade and Politics*, p. 103   7 Rattray, *Religion and Art*, p. 310

8 P. T. Bauer and B. S. Yamey, *The Economies of Under-Developed Countries*, London, 1957, p. 40; Bert F. Hoselitz, *Sociological Aspects of Economic Growth*, Chicago, 1960, p. 55. In his book Hoselitz has pointed out that apparent specialisation of occupations can be deceptive because while the economic role performed in developed economies tends to be specific those in societies on a lower level of economic advancement are normally diffuse.

The market does not come into existence to enable persons to dispose of surpluses. It comes into existence as a function of the division of labor, so that those who concentrate on production of one sort may obtain the produce of others. Division of labor has economic exchange implications, but it is a social phenomenon . . . The notion of economic surplus is a red herring because only chance accident can produce a surplus over and above the planned expectations of the producer, who markets to obtain specific, needed, goals.[1]

Markets formed an important part of the economic landscape of the Gold Coast in the nineteenth century. The use of the term market is two-fold in this context: first, as an institution or a place where people meet at appointed times to trade and exchange goods;[2] second, in relation to the principle of market exchange where price or exchange is determined by the forces of supply and demand.[3] It is significant that a fair amount of goods traded never found their way to markets but were sold privately, as frequently happened with the sale of ivory and slaves.[4] As institutions, markets served two major functions: 'to move consumer goods through exchange cycles between areas that were not self-sufficient in their economy; and, more particularly, to serve as bulking and wholesale centres for professional long-distance traders dealing in rarer and more valuable commodities'.[5]

Three types of markets delineated on the Gold Coast were indicative of stages in their evolution. In the first place, there was the traditional site where foodstuffs and locally manufactured tools (pots and other goods) with an almost age-old position in the local subsistence economy could be obtained. While the use of 'currency' on this level did exist, exchange might be based on the principle of reciprocity. Secondly, there was the regional or specialised market where goods locally unobtainable could be secured. Abonce, for example, was an early regional market of the people of Accra where they used to trade with Akyem, Akwamu and Kwahu.[6] There were also markets like Fosu and Mansu which owed their rise and former importance to the slave trade.[7] Thirdly, there were market towns or emporia like Salaga which were major termini of long-distance trade. The growth of the second and third categories were indices of the differentiation of subsistence economy and the emergence of what could be described as a 'money' factor or the market principle, by which means exchange took place on the basis of the interplay of the forces of supply and demand.

1 C. S. Belshaw, *Traditional Markets and Modern Exchange*, New York, 1965, p. 78; see also B. W. Hodder and U. I. Ukwu, *Markets in West Africa*, Ibadan, 1969, p. 19

2 See Polly Hill, 'Notes on Traditional Market Authority and Market Periodicity in West Africa', *J.A.H.* vii (2), 1966, pp. 295–311 and Belshaw, *Traditional Markets*, pp. 6–8

3 Paul Bohannan and George Dalton, eds., *Markets in Africa*, Northwestern African Studies, 9, Evanston, 1963, p. 1

4 Belshaw, *Traditional Markets*, p. 75 and Sundstrom, *Guinea Trade*, p. 31

5 Colin W. Newbury, 'Trade and Authority in West Africa from 1850–1880', in L. H. Gann and P. Duigan, *The History of Colonialism 1870–1914*, p. 67

6 E. Tilleman, *En Liden Enfoldig Beretning om det Landskab Guinea*, Kobenhavn, 1697, pp. 32–33

7 Dupuis, *Journal*, i, pp. 17 and 59

Salaga was a market which was the terminus of a long-distance trade. The former coastal villages which European commerce turned into important commercial centres were also markets of importance resorted to by the people of the interior. Besides market centres, there were 'moving markets' consisting of traders buying and selling merchandise as they went up and down the country.

Periodicity was an important element of local African markets. It has been observed that 'at the lowest level, periodicity may well have been the necessary result of a relative lack of specialisation among women farmers and food processers'.[1] In West Africa, except for the large urban centres, markets were held only periodically. The standard market week in most places in West Africa was often three, four, five, six, seven or eight days in length. Four- and seven-day markets were the most common, the latter being more prominent on the Gold Coast.[2] Periodic markets have the economic function of collecting, bulking and distributing local products.

Trade routes

Communications were essential if trade items were to reach their destined markets and numerous routes provided links with all the important centres of commerce in every province of the country. These routes were, for the most part, mere narrow bush paths through the forest, often overgrown with weeds or blocked by fallen trees. During the rainy season some became small water courses. Trade along the paths depended almost entirely upon the peaceable condition of the country and were frequently closed through the exigencies of war and coastal politics.[3] The only means of practicable transportation of goods along the routes depended upon expensive head porterage.

Our knowledge of the trade routes at the beginning of the nineteenth century derives mainly from the travels of T. E. Bowdich and Joseph Dupuis to Asante in 1817 and 1820, respectively.[4] Kumasi, the capital of Asante, with its large share of the commerce of the early nineteenth century was the focal point from whence radiated four major routes southward. The first route running southward was the most westerly route, the Aowin path which passed through the forest leading to Apollonia, Assin and Grand Bassam. A second western route was the Wassa path which went through Denkyira to Wassaw and thence branched into two directions: one to the Elmina, Komenda and Shama area while the other branch went through Ahanta to Cape Three Points and the European settlements like Dixcove and Akwida in that area. A third track was the Assin route which led to the Fante coast. This route bifurcated at Dunkwa with one branch leading to Anomabo and another going to Mouree in the vicinity of Cape Coast Castle. The fourth link with the coast was the Accra route which went through Akuapem to the coast at Accra.[5]

1 Newbury, 'Trade and Authority', in Gann and Duigan, *History of Colonialism*, p. 67

2 Hill, 'Notes on Traditional Market Authority and Market Periodicity in West Africa', pp. 300–4

3 Dupuis, *Journal*, ii, p. xxvii

4 Bowdich, *Mission from Cape Coast Castle*, p. 162; Dupuis, *Journal*, ii, p. xxvii

5 Bowdich, *Mission from Cape Coast Castle*, pp. 162–9. See Dupuis' *Journal*, ii, appendix III, pp. 482–3

The routes to the coast provided communication not only for the province through which they passed, but also for the coastal area and the European settlements located there. The commercial significance of these routes is underlined by the fact that most of them went through the rich gold mining districts of the western region and Akyem and then to the areas with heavy concentration of European forts. European goods as well as indigenous produce penetrated the interior markets along these routes.

Another network of four main tracks led northwards out from Kumasi.[1] One major inland road from Asante was the Bonduku path. It led northwest from Kumasi to Isuta and Nkwanta and westward to Bonduku and beyond. A second route led west through Nkoranza to Kintampo at which point the route intersected the Salaga Bonduku road. From Kintampo the route crossed the black Volta near the Gonja market town of Buipe and thence to Daboya. A third route, the 'old road' to Salaga, was a path also known as *Amanianpong Temporn*, Amanianpong's highway,[2] which passed through Mampong, Ejura and Atebubu crossing the Volta near Yeji to Salaga. Another route rarely used and described as hazardous that linked Kumasi and Abomey passed through Kwahu and Brong country and transversed the Volta at Odente near Kete Krakye. Apart from the major routes, there were numerous others that criss-crossed the country joining various sections.[3] Besides those routes a road was cut between Kumasi and Gaman in 1819 when Asante was fighting against the latter.[4]

The Volta provided communication too for the interior. Boats carrying salt normally destined for Salaga from Ada plied their trade along the Volta. Upon leaving Ada at the mouth of the Volta River the people sailed up the river on what was reckoned to be an eleven-day journey to Odentee where it became too rocky for canoes. From Odente traders journeyed four days on foot to Salaga.[5]

East of the Volta on the Anlo coast there were tracks radiating from the coastal towns eventually connecting with the great long distance routes of the interior. The first of these trade paths linking Anlo with Krepi in the interior and beyond was the route going from Keta northwards which led from Sadame on the Keta lagoon through Adaklu, Waya, Peki, Ho, Kpando, Nkonya and Buem to Salaga. A branch of this path went from Kpene and Ho through Abutia and crossed the Volta to Akyem country. Further east another route led from Begida and later Lome to Agome – Palime, Kpando, Krakje and Yendi.[6] Despite the network of communication in the country, the Gold Coast was not well served by its river system as a means of transport, and it lacked good natural harbours. The difficulty of unloading cargo on surf-bound coasts, where ships had to stand out far from the beach, was going to be a real factor in the slow development of the country's economy right up to the building of Takoradi harbour in the 1920s.

1 See Bowdich, *Mission from Cape Coast Castle*, pp. 482–3 and Dupuis' *Journal*, ii, p. xxviii

2 Kwame Arhin, ed., *Ashanti Northeast*, Legon, 1970, p. 1

3 Dupuis, *Journal*, ii, pp. xxvii–xxix   4 *Ibid.*

5 Bowdich, *Mission from Cape Coast Castle*, p. 177. Also, see Marion Johnson, *Salaga Papers*, Legon, Institute of African Studies, 2 vols., 1968

6 D. E. K. Amenumey, 'Geraldo de Lima: a Reappraisal', *T.H.S.G.*, ix, p. 67, 1968: D. E. K. Amenumey, 'The Extension of British Rule to Anlo (South-East Ghana), 1850–1890', *J.A.H.* ix, pp. 1, 99–117, 1968 – see map on p. 100.

It is obvious from the wide network of trade routes at the beginning of the century that the interior trade and markets were of vital significance. Along the littoral, the coastal people exported inland via the land routes and the Volta River dried fish, salt and European goods. Salt imported by Asante from the coast was re-exported to Kong, Bonduku, Salaga and beyond.[1] Salt secured from the inland deposits at Daboya was exported mainly to Dagomba and Mamprusi.[2] European goods like liquor, firearms and cloth reached Asante, and were sent from there to interior markets. Items like kola and gold found their way to the northern markets. The kola nut, a stimulant, was the staple commodity of Asante trade with the north and was in popular demand as far afield as Tripoli and the Fezzan. The famous interior market of Salaga owed its reputation as a trading centre to the kola trade.

From the interior markets along the southward routes came slaves, shea butter, cloth, leather goods and other products. A large number of the slaves required for domestic purposes, normally referred to as Donko (*nnonko* in the plural), were secured from the northern markets. According to Bowdich 'Most of the slaves in Coomassie were sent as part of the annual tribute of Inta, Dagwumba and their neighbours to Ashantee; many were kidnapped, and for the few who were bought, I was assured by several respectable Ashantee, 2,000 cowries, or one basket of *Boossee* (kola) was the greatest price given.'[3]

Shea butter imported from the north was used in cooking and for oiling the skin. Cloth was a significant item of export from the interior originating from Dagomba and Inta countries,[4] as well as from Kano and Bonduku.[5] Leather goods like sandals and pouches of fine workmanship were brought to Salaga by caravans from Kano, Marawa, Sokoto and various countries on the banks of the Niger and on the shores of Lake Chad. Such diverse items as girdles of silk manufactured by Africans, farming implements, sheep and cattle all found their way from the African interior to markets of Greater Asante like Salaga. It was even said that 'when the road to the coast is closed, it is possible to procure from this market (Salaga) powder and guns, but only at a very high price'.[6] The importance of the interior routes cannot be over-stressed: intra and inter-state trade which provided the various necessities of life also moved along these routes. It is not known to what extent trade among the coastal people and other West African peoples was carried out by sea, but traders from Dahomey were reported at Anomabo late in the nineteenth century.[7]

Tolls were levied on traders using the trade routes.[8] In Apollonia it was said

1 L. G. Binger, *Du Niger au Golfe de Guinée*, Paris, 1892, 2 vols., i, p. 375 and ii, pp. 51, 100 and 140; Bosman, *New and Accurate Description of the Coast of Guinea*, p. 321; Donnan, *Documents*, ii, p. 188

2 Binger, *Du Niger au Golfe de Guinée*, i, p. 315

3 Bowdich, *Mission from Cape Coast Castle*, pp. 332–333

4 *Ibid.*, p. 334 and Binger, *Du Niger au Golfe de Guinée*, ii, p. 168

5 M. J. Bonnat, *L'Explorateur*, Paris, 1876, iii, pp. 1–3, quoted in Marion Johnson, *Salaga Papers*, Sal/34/1

6 *Ibid.*   7 P. Labarthe, *Voyage à la Côte de Guinée*, Paris, 1803, p. 71

8 Beecham, *Ashantee and the Gold Coast*, p. 101; Bowdich, *Mission from Cape Coast Castle*, p. 320 and Meredith, *Account of the Gold Coast*, p. 69

that before a trader commenced activities he gave the chief an annual gift, after which he was free to carry on his trade to any extent.[1] Often tolls could possibly have taken the form of gift exchange between host and guest. In this way while travelling through a country a trader might show his appreciation by giving a present to the man providing him with accommodation as well as to the sovereign offering him a safe conduct through his territory. In a recent collection of oral traditions by a Ghanaian historian the people of Assin Nyankumasi denied they ever paid tolls to anyone on their way to the north to trade, but they showed gratitude for hospitality by presenting a gift: 'Nobody paid anything to anybody. If you wanted to sleep in any town you just went to any house and asked for a place to sleep and food to cook and eat. In the morning nothing was demanded but you showed your gratitude by offering some of your salt.'[2] Although this quotation underlines the propensity to hospitality, the salt given in gratitude was a valued commodity and was no mean present for a night's accommodation.

When Dupuis suggested that the Asantehene make his capital the depot for British manufactured goods and African produce in addition to levying customs on goods passing through Asante, the king refused, saying that Asante custom was different:

> None but kings and great men trade here, the same as myself. Sometimes I lend them gold, if they are good people; and then I cannot say, give me the gold back. If they come from another country to trade in Coomassy, they make friends, and give me a present; then, to be sure, I cannot tell them to give me gold, when they buy and sell the goods. Besides, some traders are kings sons and brothers and great captains: I must not say to them, give me gold, but I must give them gold and provisions, and send them home happy and rich, that it may be known in other countries that I am a great king, and know what is right.[3]

It has been suggested that the Asantehene's (Osei Bonsu) attitude towards the toll signified his intention of offering favourable conditions of trade to Muslims for the development of the trade north of Asante.[4] However, this attitude may point to the fact that there was nothing rigid about toll collection.

Despite the Asantehene's disclaimer of collecting tolls, there is ample evidence at various points on the Gold Coast of Asante toll posts reported at Ahenkro,[5] Ansa[6] and Mamfe in Akuapem. Probably the payment represented a recognition of sovereignty of the ruler through whose region a trader was passing and the toll, whatever form it took, was a tribute to the ruler. Once a local chief accepted tolls he was bound by the laws of hospitality to give the trader every

---

1 Meredith, *Account of the Gold Coast*, p. 69

2 K. Y. Daaku, *Oral Traditions of Assin-Twifo, Traditions of Assin-Nyankumasi*, p. 13 and *Traditions of Assin-Nyanter-Kyikrom*, p. 3

3 Dupuis, *Journal*, i, p. 167

4 Ivor Wilks, 'Asante Policy towards the Hausa Trade in the Nineteenth Century', in Claude Meillassoux, ed., *The Development of African Trade and Markets in West Africa*, p. 6

5 C3386, 1882   6 Bowdich, *Mission from Cape Coast Castle*, p. 320

possible protection. It is even said that chiefs who contemplated robbing traders often refused toll payments.[1]

The amount of road toll paid might have been based on the value of goods and the standing of the chief of the territory, but the tolls were probably affected by the fighting potential of the collector and the person paying. Traders sometimes paid tolls in both directions between the coast and the inland country, but tolls were levied more often in only one direction.[2] Bowdich mentioned a tax paid in gold on all slaves purchased for the coast. Furthermore, customs levied near Ansa in Assin[3] were paid in gold by all traders returning from the coast. Tolls were not only paid on routes, but also on ferrying across the rivers. In the Asante kola trade north, the duty was 25 kola nuts.[4]

State and trade

Trade on the Gold Coast was state-oriented and was often a royal monopoly. Rattray wrote that ' A fruitful source of revenue in the olden days was trading, in which some stools had a kind of temporary monopoly'.[5] It has been suggested that the reason for this was not the result of a state policy, but rather of the heavy outlay needed to fit out trading expeditions; engaging carriers to head-load the goods, hiring men to protect the party and paying tolls along the routes.[6] Chiefs and rulers could take a larger part in trading activities because of the wealth and purchasing power accumulated from their stool estates.[7]

Asante trade to the north was mainly in kola and imports from the north consisted of slaves, livestock and shea butter. Asante exports to the coast consisted primarily of slaves and gold dust in return for liquor, firearms, metal rods and salt. In Asante trading for the chief on the coast and north was conducted by such groups as the *Akyeremadefo* (drummers), the *Asokwafo* (horn-blowers), the *Asoanifo* (hammock-carriers) and the *Agwarefo* (bathroom attendants). In the kola trade these groups carried the king's kola in loads consisting of between 1,500–2,000 nuts. Each carrier was allowed any extra amount of kola he could carry in addition to the king's. This extra load was called *nsitiri* (place on top). The trade routes to the north were first thrown open by the Omanhene's men to the king's traders and then closed for twenty days until the traders had disposed of the king's kola. Because of the carriers' access to the early market for any surplus kola they could bring, there was often competition to convey the chief's kola. After reopening the routes all other traders going north had to pay twenty-five kola nuts of which twenty went to the king and five to the heralds who collected it, whereas no toll was levied on imports from the north.[8]

In the Asante division of Asumegya, trade in kola was carried out by the Asokwafo after the Asantehene opened the road.[9] In another division, Bekwai,

1 Sundstrom, *Guinea Trade*, p. 9   2 *Ibid.*, p. 10

3 Bowdich, *Mission from Cape Coast Castle*, p. 320

4 Rattray, *Ashanti Law and Constitution*, pp. 109–12

5 *Ibid.*, p. 109   6 Dickson, *Historical Geography*, p. 106

7 Daaku, *Trade and Politics*, pp. 32–34

8 Rattray, *Ashanti Law and Constitution*, pp. 109–11   9 *Ibid.*, p. 140

which had no kola, the Asokwafo were the chief's traders. They went to the coast to purchase cloth, beads and salt which were sold in Bontuku and Salaga. In return they bought slaves, shea butter, cloth and cotton to be retailed at Kumasi with profits from these transactions going to the stool. Although the Asokwafo were not paid, they often became rich from profits they reaped from each transaction for the king.[1] In Juabin kola trade was carried out by the Asokwafo and Akyeremadefo who profited by carrying extra kola to sell on their own behalf.[2] In Kokofu and Kumawu the trade for the stool was carried out by the Asokwafo.[3]

While the bulk of the population was free to participate in trade in places like Asante access to the coast and inland markets was often controlled. Reasons for this, no doubt, were to prevent both the acquisition of firearms by the states in the hinterland of Asante and the rise of a rich merchant class. As Bowdich observed, Asante placed these restrictions on commerce

> ... lest their genius for war might be enervated by it, and lest, either from the merchants increasing to a body too formidable for their wishes to be resisted, or too artful from their experience to be detected, they might sacrifice the national honour and ambition to their avarice, and furnishing Inta, Dagwumba, or any of their more powerful neighbours (who have yielded to circumstances rather than force) with guns and powder (which are never allowed to be exported from Ashantee,) break the spell of their conquests, and undermine their power.[4]

Bowdich further wrote:

> Were they to encourage commerce, pomp, the idol of which they are most jealous, would soon cease to be their prerogative, because it would be attainable by others; the traders growing wealthy, *would vie with them*[5]; and for their own security, stimulated by reflections they have now too little at risk to originate, they would unite to repress the arbitrary power of the Aristocracy; and even if they did not, inevitably (as the chiefs conceive) divert the people's genius for war.[6]

Although Bowdich may have exaggerated his case, the underlying point was clear that most of the trade was in the hands of the ruling class and that advancement in the state was achieved through military prowess and not through trade.

Asante, however, encouraged rising captains to trade and it was probably for this reason that the king distributed gold every forty days to enable them to trade, to acquire wealth, to experience the positions of responsibility to be conferred upon them and to bind them closer to him.

1 *Ibid.*, p. 160   2 *Ibid.*, pp. 185–6   3 *Ibid.*, pp. 211 and 228

4 Bowdich, *Mission from Cape Coast Castle*, p. 335

5 Compare this statement with the rise of the African merchant class and the decline of the power of chiefs in ch. 4.

6 *Ibid.*, p. 295

It is a frequent practice of the King's, to consign sums of gold to the care of rising captains, without requiring any from them for two or three years, at the end of which time he expects the captain not only to restore the principal, but to prove that he has acquired sufficient of his own, from the use of it, to support the greater dignity the King would confer on him.[1]

In Asante the very considerable revenue that accrued to the state from trade and other sources like tribute and tolls led to the establishment of an elaborate bureaucracy of finance.[2] This system seems to have been introduced under the rule of the Asantehene Osei Kwadwo (1764–1777). The key position in this bureaucracy was the Gyaasewa stool, and the Gyaasewahene assumed both the financial responsibility of the Asante Empire and the keeping of the treasury.[3] Bowdich has left a description of the function of a Gyaasewahene:

Apokoo is the keeper of the royal treasury, and has the care of all the tributes, which are deposited, separately, in a large apartment of the palace, of which he only has the key . . . Apokoo holds a sort of exchequer court at his own house daily, . . . to decide all cases affecting tribute or revenue, and the appeal to the King is seldom resorted to.[4]

Under the Gyaasewahene were a number of lesser officials including the Sanahene who saw to the actual payment to and from the treasury. Below the Sanahene in rank were the *Fotuosanfo* who were the 'cashiers' or 'weighers' and groups responsible for collecting tributes. Then there were the *Batafo* made up of Asokwafo and Akyeremadefo who were responsible for state trading. There were also the *Nkwansrafo* consisting mainly of road wardens who exercised control over the passage of traders and over immigration.[5] It is evident that chiefs and kings achieved considerable wealth but they could not accumulate the capital they amassed for their own personal use. Whatever they received was in turn redistributed as presents to the elders and their subjects.[6] It would seem that

1 *Ibid.*

2 On sources of revenue to chiefs, E. J. P. Brown writes that:
Among the Akan tribes the king's revenue was raised in kind, from war indemnity taxes, called *Adanprantuw*; from slaves (prisoners of war), some of whom were enlisted as soldiers or sold; from the swearing of oaths, the fines in connection therewith were collected by the King's *Nhinkuwa* – that is, personal servants of his household. Outside Asianti, in the old days, *Abayin Nyir* (male wives) . . . were created by the kings of Asianti to collect their fines and war indemnity taxes. Revenue was also raised from ferries and land tributes in various forms; besides court fees, death duties and oral bequests by chiefs and other noblemen, to the kings.
The Gold Coast and Asianti Reader, 2 vols., London, 1929, i, pp. 185–6.

3 Wilks, *Ashanti Government*, p. 214

4 Bowdich, *Mission from Cape Coast Castle*, p. 296

5 Wilks, *Ashanti Government*, pp. 217–18

6 Busia, *Position of the Chief*, pp. 50–51. The distribution of wealth by chiefs among their subjects was a common practice in West Africa. C. W. Newbury writes, 'It must be remembered that much of the accumulated wealth of West African States was disbursed in hospitality, ceremonies and rewards. 'Trade and Authority', in Gann and Duigan, *History of Colonialism*, p. 75.

the substantial revenue derived from fines, trade and other sources necessarily implies a differential as opposed to subsistence economy. The whole treasury system of Asante and gold weights shows a sophisticated economic system. In this context, it is legitimate to speak of Asante economy as a national economy.

Currency

Although slaves could be regarded as a form of money other forms of currency were also used in the commercial activities of Gold Coast society. Beads (*bota*) seem to have been one of the original currencies and even when they ceased to be used as currency, they continued to be of great value.[1] A report of 1883 noted that:

> What are known as Aggri beads are usually met with among the tribes on the Gold Coast, are highly valued by them, and form part of the royal jewels of the Kings of Ashantee; their manufacture is a lost art, and generally supposed to be of ancient Phoenician origin; they have probably been given in barter for slaves, gold dust and nuggets; they fetch at the present day an equal weight in gold, and the rarer sorts one-and-a-half to twice their weight in gold dust.[2]

An iron currency, called *nnaabo*, had also been in use before the 1700s but after this period gold and cowrie shells came into use.[3] Some 25 pieces of these iron currencies were discovered on the Gold Coast in 1935 in Odumase, 40 miles south-east of Kumasi. These currencies were in the form of a disc and were described thus: 'The discs are roughly circular with a diameter varying from $2\frac{5}{8}$ inches to $2\frac{7}{8}$ inches. Their thickness varies from $\frac{1}{8}$ to $\frac{3}{16}$ inch.'[4] Before this discovery, a district commissioner had noticed pieces of iron, about two inches by two and a half inches, stored away within the precincts of the 'palace' of the Omanhene of Juaben. The officer was informed that they were iron currency, formerly made at Juaben and issued under the authority of the Omanhene.[5] Gold dust also passed as currency in Asante and in the western region, while cowrie shells passed for currency east of Accra. Although some writers would prefer to call the currencies described above as 'primitive money', 'special purpose money' or 'substitute money', such categorisation can no longer be acceptable in the case of the Gold Coast.[6]

1 Meyerowitz, *Sacred State of the Akan*, p. 203

2 John Edward Price, 'On Aggri Beads', *J.A.I.* xii, p. 64, 1883

3 Meyerowitz, *Sacred State of the Akan*, p. 203

4 R. P. Wild, 'Iron Disc Currency from Ashanti', *Man*, No. 99, p. 78, 1936

5 *Ibid.*, p. 79; Paul Einzig, *Primitive Money*, London, 1949, p. 154

6 Money used to be viewed as serving at least five basic functions: (1) a medium of exchange and/or store of value; (2) purchasing power; (3) liquid or short-term capital; (4) liquid reserves in general; (5) units of value and where currency did not meet all the general functions of money it was often called 'special purpose money', 'substitute money' or 'general purpose money'. Belshaw, *Traditional Markets*, p. 9; Paul Bohannan, 'The Impact of Money on an African Subsistence Economy', *J.E.H.* xix (4), p. 491, 1959; Bohannan and Dalton, *Markets in Africa*, pp. 11–12.

The common denominators of gold used in trade were as follows:

12 takus = 1 ackie = 5s
16 ackies = 1 ounce = £4
2 ounces = 1 benda = £8 [1]

By this reckoning gold dust was valued at £4 an ounce until it was changed to £3 12s; this was subdivided into sixteen ackies which amounted to 5s each. This was further divided into 12 takus of 5d each. The common denominators of gold weights of cowries were:

40 cowries	= 1 string
5 strings	= 1 bunch
10 bunches	= 1 head = 1 ackey
2000 cowries	= 1 ackey of gold
16 ackies	= 1 ounce of gold
1 ounce of gold	= £4 [2]

According to Meredith during the plentiful season from September to April or May a labouring man 'may subsist abundantly on two strings of cowries or twopence farthing a day'.[3] In areas where gold was in use the weights of the chiefs were one third heavier than those belonging to the people. Bowdich explained this:

> It is to be observed that the King's weights are one third heavier than the current weights of the country; and all the gold expended in provision being weighed out in the former, and laid out in the latter, the difference enriches the chamberlain, cook and chief domestic officers of the palace, as it is thought derogatory to a King avowedly to pay his subjects for their services.[4]

Although gold, cowries and other forms of currency served a monetary purpose, surplus amounts seem to have been invested in slaves as a form of capital. A recent study points out at least seven functions that a slave as capital could fulfil: 1) He was a unit of labour who could be used as a canoe hand, fieldhand, a servant or trade for his master; 2) As a capital investment, he was necessary for trading or farming; 3) Representing a store of wealth, he could in some cases be resold when necessary; 4) As an object of speculation, the slave had the potential of becoming a valuable trader or farmer and could also command a resale price higher than his purchase price; 5) He could be used in a sacrifice as consumer good; 6) As wealth he could be used as a status symbol in the way

1 Meredith, *Account of the Gold Coast*, p. 183; Daaku, *Trade and Politics*, p. 36; Robert Chalmers, *A History of Currency in the British Colonies*, London, 1893, p. 212. See also K. Polanyi, 'Sortings and "Ounce Trade" in the West African Slave Trade', pp. 381–95; M. Johnson, 'The Ounce in Eighteenth Century West African Trade', pp. 197–214.

2 Meredith, *Account of the Gold Coast*, p. 183; Bowdich, *Mission from Cape Coast Castle*, p. 330

3 Meredith, *Account of the Gold Coast*, p. 183

4 Bowdich, Mission from *Cape Coast Castle*, p. 293

that cows are used in other parts of Africa; 7) He could be used as a unit of defence expenditure to defend his master and trade.[1]

The Gold Coast economies at the beginning of the nineteenth century were not static, but were highly developed with commercial organisation, a system of trade, trade routes and markets. Although the market principle was present in the economy, land which was communally owned was not actively involved in this principle. The use of currencies and the sale of labour, even though limited, were present. There was also some trade by barter, but even then it was often based on established rates of exchange.[2]

The often painted picture of a static African economic development which used to be perceived in sharply contrasting terms of an inward-looking subsistence economy – as opposed to the world-wide market economy – does not hold true for the Gold Coast.[3] This view distorts the nature of the economic situation of the Gold Coast which was between a subsistence and a fully-fledged modern market economy. Attempts to place it rigidly at a given state of development are very misleading. 'The concept of non-monetary economics is hardly applicable to pre-colonial Africa, with the possible exception of certain hunting groups of minimal importance,' writes Jack Goody. 'In West Africa the medieval empires of the Niger bend were built up on the trade which brought salt, cloth and beads south from the Sahara across to West Africa and took gold and ivory and slaves back to the Barbary Coast and from there into medieval Europe.'[4] Goody further submits:

From the point of view of mercantile economy, parts of Africa were not dissimilar to Western Europe of the same period. Metal coinage was in use on the East African coast. In the West, currencies consisted of gold, brass, salt, but more especially cowrie shells which, coming as they did from the Maldive Islands off the south of Ceylon, filled most of the necessary attributes of money. In certain respects this was a monetary economy. Trade was highly organised and in kingdoms such as Dahomey and Ashanti important sectors of the economy were under state control, whereas in the savannah regions exchange was left largely in private (Muslim) hands. Most of the kinds of economic operations that were found in pre-industrial Europe were also to be found in Africa: even in the stateless societies of the interior, barter had been superseded by more complex forms of exchange, and production was rarely limited to subsistence alone; the extensive use of cowries from the Maldives

---

1 A. J. H. Latham, 'Currency, Credit and Capitalism on the Cross River in the Pre-Colonial Era', *J.A.H.* iv, 1971, p. 604

2 For more on this exchange, see Johnson, 'The Ounce in Eighteenth Century West African Trade', pp. 197–214.

3 For such a picture, see Bohannan and Dalton, *Markets in Africa*. This view has been challenged in J. H. Gray and David Birmingham's *Pre-Colonial African Trade Essays on Trade in Central and East Africa before 1900*, London 1970. Another book that questions the static picture of non-Western economies is Cyril S. Belshaw, *Traditional Markets*. See, too, Jack Goody, *Technology, Tradition, and the State in Africa*, pp. 23–24.

4 Goody, *Technology and the State in Africa*, p. 23. See also Wilks, 'A Medieval Trade Route from the Niger to the Gulf of Guinea'.

and carnelians from Gujerat shows that they were all in some degree part of the economic system of the Old World.[1]

Thus the idea of regarding the Gold Coast economy at the beginning of the nineteenth century as one solely of subsistence must be rejected. Elements of a modern economy were already present and as Dr Newbury has observed: 'It is difficult to think of any West African community which relied solely on subsistence crops and lacked the simplest surplus for gifts, tribute and trade'.[2]

This is not to suggest, however, that the majority of the people derived a livelihood from the market principle; but the development of the internal trade as well as the impact of the Atlantic slave trade had brought about significant changes and the removal of the latter commerce was going to leave a serious gap in the economy of the Gold Coast.

1 Goody, *Technology and the State in Africa*, p. 24

2 Newbury, 'Trade and Authority', in Gann and Duigan, *History of Colonialism*, p. 67

CHAPTER TWO

Abolition and its aftermath, 1807–1828

Abolishing the Atlantic slave trade was a gradual process; Britain's abolition act of 1807 and the acts of other nations outlawing the trade rarely meant an end to the trade which persisted through the 1860s. The illegality of the trade led slave dealers to keep most of their activities concealed, with the result that it is a subject on which historians can never be clearly informed.

Before 1793, when the maritime war began in Europe, slave trading between the Senegal River and the Volta River on the Gold Coast was wholly in the hands of the English, French, Dutch and Americans. In 1795 during the war the French and the Dutch were almost driven from the trade in this area; thus, when it was abolished in 1807 England and America were the major participants. The abolition of the slave trade by these two nations diminished the exports from this area and consequently affected Portuguese activities. Before abolition Portugal's slaving activities were confined to the Bight of Benin and the area south of it, but as a result of the diminution of the number of slave ships and the reduction in prices on the Windward and Gold Coasts following abolition, they were drawn to this area.[1]

When the British Abolition Act of 25 March, 1807 took effect, the slave trade had been declining for almost twenty years.[2] Preceding Great Britain a Danish royal ordinance of 1792 had made the trade illegal for Danes after 1 January 1803.[3] Other countries to outlaw it were the United States in 1808, Portugal in 1815 and Spain in 1817. The last two countries agreed to confine their activities to South of the Equator. When the British Act became effective, subjects who participated in the trade were liable to a £100 fine for every slave found on board their ships and to the forfeiture of their vessels. In 1811 the United States declared the human traffic an act of piracy and made it a capital crime, but this law was not enforced until 1861 during the Presidency of

---

1 African Institution, 13th Report, 1819, Appendix A, pp. 56–60. Queries proposed by Viscount Castlereagh to, and Answers of, the African Institution in London: Dec., 1816. Answer to Questions 3 and 4.

2 Curtin, *Atlantic Slave Trade*, p. 221. For the period 1781–1790 the French and English slave exports from the Gold Coast amounted to 59,900; from 1791–1800, 29,400 and from 1801–1810, 22,100. See chart on p. 11 in ch. I.

3 Nørregard, *Danish Settlements in West Africa*, p. 183. Although there was no large-scale shipment of slaves in Danish ships some vessels exceeded the 1803 time limit. It was not until 1805 that the Danish coastal authorities declared that the slave trade was no longer allowed.

Abraham Lincoln. Britain passed a similar act in 1824, but in 1837 the sentence of death was reduced to that of transportation.[1]

The persistence of the slave trade

From the time of British abolition in 1807 to 1810 the slave trade was carried on by American and Spanish ships, but after 1810 and for the greater part of the century the slave trade was, for the most part, carried on in Portuguese and Spanish ships.[2] The number of slaves taken from the Gold Coast from the time of abolition to the end of the Napoleonic Wars was probably not large because during this time British dominion over the sea enabled enforcement of the abolition act and prevented most Europeans from participating in the traffic.[3] At the end of the war it was said that 'the return of peace will now restore, to states possessing settlements on the Coast of Africa, the power of renewing the trade in slaves; and our present object is to prevent, if possible, the injurious consequences likely to result from this change to the British settlements on the Gold Coast'.[4] For the sixty years or so following Great Britain's abolition of the Atlantic slave trade, sustained attempts were carried out by way of diplomatic and naval pressures to induce other nations to renounce the slave trade and to maintain abolition. The reluctance of Spain, Portugal, Brazil, France and the United States to comply readily with treaties designed for the total eradication of the trade made its suppression extremely difficult; but war in Europe and British abolition reduced the outlet for slaves from the Gold Coast. Consequently, many slaves brought from the interior could not be sold, and some were either sent back to the interior or disposed of as domestic slaves.[5] The Asantehene settled some of these around Lake Bosomtwe to fish.[6]

At the end of the war in Europe it was reported that except for 200 slaves taken from Dutch Accra in November, 1815, the slave trade on the Gold Coast was at an end.[7] Just when slave traffic was thought to have been stopped on the Gold Coast, it began to revive. Although by this time most of the slave trading activities were confined to the area beyond the Volta River, they were far from dead as evidenced by the fact that in late 1816 servants of the Company of Merchants were writing to request a man-of-war to be stationed between Apollonia and Whydah in order to stop the trade.[8]

By 1818 the Governor of Cape Coast Castle was lamenting that slave vessels

1 James B. Bandinel, *Some Accounts of the Trade in Slaves from Africa as Connected with Europe and America*, London, 1842, p. 305

2 *Ibid.*, p. 145

3 T.70/73: George Barnes to Earl of Bathurst, 23 April 1814; George E. Metcalfe, *Great Britain and Ghana, Documents of Ghana History 1807–1957*, London, 1964, p. 26

4 *Ibid.*   5 African Institution, 6th Report, 1812, p. 67

6 Dupuis, *Journal*, i, p. 61

7 T.70/74: African Office to Viscount Castlereagh, 1 Nov. 1816; Answer to Questions 1, 8 and 15

8 T.70/36: John Hope Smith to the African Committee, 5 Nov. 1816; *Ibid.*, Dawson to the African Committee, 3 Nov. 1816

under the Spanish flag, but owned mostly by Americans, had ended all prospects of abolition. He said that the people had begun to give up any hope of the restoration of the slave trade and were confident that considerable progress in commerce would have been made if the slave traffic had not reawakened.[1] In March, 1818, the slave trade on the Gold Coast was reported to be almost as active as it had been at any time before abolition. As an eye-witness reported: 'I found the trade almost as active in the neighbourhood of our forts as at any time of the slave trade, and before my arrival, rows of poor wretches in chains were to be seen even in the very streets of our town of Cape Coast.'[2] Between December 1817 and April 1818 no fewer than 30 slave vessels were reported to be trading on the Windward and the Gold Coast.[3] Said to be fast sailing ships, they could not be intercepted easily by the older and slower British cruisers.[4]

The Dutch and Danish settlements were instrumental in the resurgence of the slave trade. By 1817 the English were charging the Dutch with aiding and abetting the slave trade with Dutch forts reputedly supplying traders with canoes and water, and permitting the local people to sell slaves openly.[5] James Bannerman, a leading merchant at Accra, also reported that between 1816 and 1820 the slave trade was carried on 'with great activity by the natives being in the abandoned Dutch settlements' particularly at Dutch Accra. The slave trade proceeded without interruption in the Danish settlement as well until 1821. In that year when P. S. Steffens came to be installed as the Danish governor, free mulatto traders claimed that they had not been informed of the abolition of the slave trade.[6] The general problem of British readiness and that of other legitimate traders to deal with slavers must have aided the revival of the trade. In 1817 a merchant wrote that 'the grand focus of the slave trade on the Gold Coast lies 20 leagues (perhaps) to leeward of Accra, and as near to Annamaboe as vessels dare anchor with impunity'.[7]

The historian Carl Reindorf has described the renewal of the slave trade after the Asante army left the coast in 1816:

> After General Amankwa had left for Asante, the country enjoyed peace, but the Portuguese slave trade prospered. All the leading chiefs were concerned in it; and Chief Ankra was the general broker. Dutch Town was made the Depot. Slaves were sold at night, and Ankra had them in charge till a slaver arrived; and the poor creatures were shipped in the darkness to avoid detection by the English and Danish Governments.[8]

1 T.70/36: John Hope Smith to Committee of Merchants, 23 Feb. 1818

2 T.70/1604/1: James Lucas Yeo to J. W. Croker, 12 March 1818

3 T.70/36: A. G. Nicolls to the African Committee, 27 April 1818

4 T.70/1604/1: John Hope Smith to the African Committee, 15 June 1818

5 T.70/36: John Hope Smith to the African Committee, 5 March 1817; 18 July 1817 and 30 July 1817

6 Nørregard, *Danish Settlements in West Africa*, p. 184

7 T.7041: Hutchinson to Smith, 11 Oct. 1817

8 Reindorf, *History of the Gold Coast*, 2nd ed., pp. 144–5

Because of Ankra's slave trading activities in August 1819, an English man-of-war bombarded Dutch Accra where slaves were harboured.[1] In February, 1820, seven English men-of-war arrived at Accra with a view to suppressing the slave trade. At this time the people of Accra moved their property to Christiansborg and their plantation villages to Kaneshi; marines from the men-of-war removed Ankra's property and took all fishing and landing canoes to James Town. The British asked that the slave dealers at Accra be delivered to them, but the king of James Town was unwilling to give up the offenders. The bombardment of Dutch Accra did not bring an end to his operations; he and other slave dealers retired only for a time to other places to carry on the trade.[2]

In 1820 reports from Accra said that 'to put down the slave trade at Accra, we must contrive to remove the man Anchra and his brother from the Dutch Town, they are the agents for the trade'.[3] In 1821 Ankra was involved in a slave trading incident when a slave ship, pursued by British cruisers, landed 160 slaves at Tema. Before rescue by either the British or the Danish authorities an army headed by Ankra's brother went to Tema to remove the slaves into the bush. Throughout the 1820s Ankra continued his slave trading activities, as confirmed in 1827 by the governor of the settlements, who wrote that 'the increase of the slave trade may be ascribed to the open manner in which a man named Ancra has been permitted to carry on this traffic for the last two or three years, and in which the British Accras now participate more openly'.[4]

After the defeat of Asante at the 1826 battle of Katamansu there appears to have been a great deal of slave trading. The Commandant of Anomabo Castle described the situation:

> The Accras, British, Dutch and Danish by their example and advice have completely unsettled the minds of the natives along the coast and the interior. During their stay in Fantee they have been indefatigably purchasing slaves to the amount of several hundreds – all slaves that have been guilty of anything to displease their masters have been seized, parties of from 6 to 10 have been met on their way to Accra chained together, to be sold to the vessels that now constantly call there for slaves and canoes. 'Old Palavers' have been brought up among the natives and accusation of alleged adultery and witchcraft at all times the excuse for slavery on this coast have been resorted to as a pretext for dragging people from their homes, and the unhappy people are constantly coming to this town for protection against their more powerful enemies.[5]

Although it is known that the slave trade on the Gold Coast revived after 1816, no definite figures exist for the number leaving the coast. The records of the Gold Coast give us only isolated instances of figures for slave exports. The

1 F.C., letter of 2 Sept. 1820

2 Reindorf, *History of the Gold Coast*, 2nd ed., p. 145

3 C.O. 267/54: Gordon to John Hope Smith, 5 Nov. 1820

4 C.O. 267/82: Neil Campbell to Goderich, 14 July 1827

5 *Ibid.*, W. Hutchinson to Captain Ricketts, 17 Feb. 1827

acting British Consul at Bahia gave the following figures of slave exports from the Gold Coast to Bahia in Brazil between 1 January 1815 and 1 January 1816:[1]

Date	Number of slaves exported	Origin of slaves
9 February 1815	345	Axim
13 February	527	Akwida
31 March	437	Akwida
20 June	2 shiploads of 498 and 449	Axim
24 September	234	Axim
27 September	211	Akwida
18 November	130	Accra
18 December	393	Axim

The following exports were also recorded:[2]

Date	Number of slaves exported	Nationality of vessel used	Origin of slaves	Destination
November 1815	200	Portuguese	Dutch Accra	Brazil
January 1817	600	Unknown	Elmina	Cuba
February 1817	400	Spanish	Apam	Unknown[3]
1817	1,000	Spanish or American	Asante	Unknown[4]
September 1820	300*	Unknown	Gold Coast	Unknown[5]
July 1820 to February 1821	1,200	Unknown	Accra	Unknown
July 1820 to February 1821	800	Unknown	Kita	Unknown[6]

* Prisoners of the Asante

Thus the total number of slaves exported from the period between January 1815, and February 1821, amounted to at least 7,724.

According to Curtin, the total number of slaves imported from African territories for the period 1811–1820 was 394,500.[7] The known total of the slave exports from the Gold Coast would therefore be equal to 1·95% of the total.

1 C.O. 267/44: A. Cunningham, Acting Consul at Bahia to Viscount Castlereagh, slave trade to Bahia, 1 Jan. 1816. This list also included the number of slaves shipped from Calabar, Price Islands and Angola to Bahia.

2 T. 70/74: the African Committee of Merchants to Castlereagh, 1 Nov. 1816

3 T. 70/36: Smith to Committee of Company of Merchants, 5 March 1817

4 Bowdich, *Mission from Cape Coast Castle*, p. 339

5 C.O. 267/73: Hingston to Neil Campbell, 1 Nov. 1820

6 F.O. 84/9: Her Majesty's Commission under the Treaties for Preventing Illicit Traffic in Slaves, Freetown, 8 March 1821

7 Curtin, *Atlantic Slave Trade*, pp. 234 and 258

Curtin, basing his data on the British Foreign Office information from the Parliamentary Papers of 1845, does not list any percentage of slaves from the Gold Coast for the period between 1817–1820 and 1821–1830. From 1831–1840 he gives a figure of 0·5% and no percentage for the period 1841–1843. For 1817–1820, 1821–1830, 1831–1840 and 1843 he gives a percentage of the unknown origins of slaves, respectively, as follows: 4·0%, 8·3%, 17·7% and 51·0%. With a figure as high as 1·95% from isolated instances of slave export it is probable that the slave trade on the Gold Coast between 1817–1820 was more than has been thought. So far, the documents have not revealed any definite numbers of slave exports from the Gold Coast between 1821–1830, but there is ample evidence that a good deal of it was going on.[1] In 1829 E. H. Collier, a Dutch factor at Accra, reported slave trading at Accra[2] and just two years later in 1831 it was alleged that it had ceased to exist on the Gold Coast. For the period 1831–1840, however, we have 0·5% of the total number of slaves coming from the Gold Coast, according to British Foreign Office data quoted by Curtin. If this be the case, it is probable that the exports from the Gold Coast between 1821–1830 were not negligible, but far greater than the 0·5% quoted for 1831–1840.

The apparent increase in the slave trade led to a renewal of panyarring on an unprecedented scale. The Governor of Cape Coast Castle reported its suppression in 1817, years before the re-establishment of the slave trade, but now it had been revived with vigour.[3] The Dutch Governor-General Daendels summarised this when he said:

The Spanish slave trade has given birth to this calamity . . . The uncertainty of not any day being seized and sold to the ships extinguished the courage for all peaceful labour, and made the negro into an armed and restless robber who laid snares for his fellowman to catch and sell him, as he feared and expected for himself . . . One ever hears of murders and house breakings, that had brought the wild-tempered negro to such a state that he lived in a continual quarrel with his neighbours, so that soon there existed no kroom which had no palaver, claim or dispute with its nearest neighbour from which resulted the panyaring off of men, women and children.[4]

The trade was going to continue as long as it was possible and as long as there was an outlet for it. As the Committee of the Company of Merchants wrote, not without a little prejudice:

Can the wildest theorist expect that a mere act of the British legislature should be in a moment inspired with wisdom and refinement of the unenlightened natives of the vast continent of Africa, and persuade them, nay

---

1 *Ibid.*, p. 258. While the persistence of the slave trade at this time cannot be denied, it must be recognised that those who reported it sometimes had an axe to grind and might have exaggerated.

2 F.C.: 15 April 1829; F.C.: 28 June 1829 and F.C.: 23 March 1830

3 T. 70/36: John Hope Smith to the African Committee, 16 July 1817

4 H. W. Daendels, *The Correspondence of Daendels*, Legon, 1964, entry for 6 Dec. 1816, p. 250

more, make them practically believe and feel that it is for their interest to contribute to, or even to acquiesce in the destruction of trade not inconsistent with their prejudices, their laws, or their notions of morality and religion and by which alone they have been hitherto accustomed to acquire wealth and to purchase all of the foreign luxuries and conveniences of life?[1]

The Governor of Cape Coast Castle also declared that slavery was 'the only object they are actively disposed to. They will cling to it to the last moment, they may be deprived of it, but cannot be diverted from it. They will quit it but from necessity'.[2] With the profits to be derived from the slave trade, the interest of the people was obvious. Many of the people had a stake in it, and the prosperity of the coastal people depended upon it:

The people of the coast are the brokers of those of the interior who supply the slaves; and as they are established from necessity as the sole medium betwixt the vessels and the sellers, they have every facility of adding to their regular profit by impositions which can neither be noticed by one party nor detected by the other. This trade is consequently beyond all comparison so indolent and lucrative that even were there any appeal to their feelings, it would not influence in competition with such inordinate gain. Every other trade requires, comparatively, activity and exertion, and yields very inferior profit. It is unreasonable, therefore, to expect any conduct on the part of natives but such as may be auxiliary to the slave traders.[3]

Passing the abolition act was one thing; getting the local people and other nations to abide by it was quite another.

The renewal and the persistence of the slave trade indicated that the Act of 1807 was not wholeheartedly embraced by the people of the Gold Coast; indeed, some Gold Coast rulers wished for its abrogation.[4] In 1817, when Thomas Bowdich was in Kumasi he found the Asantehene very anxious for the re-establishment of the slave trade and was most importunate in his inquiries concerning it.[5] During Bowdich's negotiations with Asante to secure a treaty signed for the promotion of peace and trade one of the principal chiefs of Asante proposed the reinstatement of the slave trade as a *sine qua non*.[6] At the time one of the Asantehene's captains said that there were too many slaves in the country and he wanted to be rid of some of them.[7] The question of the renewal of the trade was still being discussed when Joseph Dupuis went to Kumasi as the English Consul in 1820: 'I think, that the great king will do me much good, if

1 T. 70/73: the African Committee to Lord Castlereagh, 5 May 1817

2 T. 70/36: John Hope Smith to the African Committee, 25 May 1817   3 *Ibid.*

4 T. 70/35: Governor to the African Committee, 26 Dec. 1809

5 T. 70/36: John Hope Smith to the African Committee, 16 July 1817; *Ibid.*, 21 Feb. 1818 and Bowdich, *Mission from Cape Coast Castle*, p. 381

6 T. 70/40: Bowdich to John Hope Smith, 29 Aug. 1817

7 Bowdich, *Mission from Cape Coast Castle*, p. 381

he likes to make a proper trade for slaves as before,' the Asantehene told Dupuis.[1]

While the slave trade persisted, intermediaries between the coast and the interior maintained secret contacts with the inland rulers in order to obtain slaves to sell to slave ships.[2] Sam Kanto Brew was one of the more important middlemen about whom something is known.[3] Described by Governor John Hope Smith as 'a great slave merchant', he was banished for a time from Cape Coast.[4] Smith had hoped to deport him from the Gold Coast but the help of Spanish slave traders enabled him to avoid deportation.[5]

Brew was reputed to be the chief connection of the slave trade between Asante and the coast. A British trader wrote of Brew: 'This insolent mulatto man, by presents to the king and his principal men, and being the chief support of the slave trade between this nation and the coast, has made the king interest himself in his favour in an improper degree.'[6] He allegedly pleased the Asantehene when he said he was personally responsible for bringing so many Spanish ships to purchase slaves on the coast. He also maintained he was being prosecuted by the English because of his attachment to the slave trade and consequently solicited the protection and the assistance of Asante to empower him to establish a regular system of trade between the interior and the coast.[7]

By sending the Asantehene and his principal men guns, gunpowder and other presents, Brew was able to secure slaves.[8] This kind of activity must have been helped by the fact that firearms were restricted on the coast by the British Government's prohibition of the arms trade because they encouraged indigenous wars and produced captives for the slave trade. During Bowdich's mission to Kumasi two Spanish slave ships, one at Apam and the other at Beraku, sent presents by way of Brew to the Asantehene, his chief linguist, and one Kwamina Bwa who was purported to be the agent for the purchase of slaves in Kumasi.[9]

In January, 1817, Brew promised the Captain of a Spanish ship, *La Fama Africana*, to deliver slaves to Kormantine. Although Governor Dawson was attempting to stem the flow of the slave trade as much as possible and even managed to seize some of Brew's canoes, the ship succeeded in departing with 500 slaves.[10] According to Joseph Dupuis, most of the disorders he witnessed in the Gold Coast – and which the term 'Bad Palaver' with the Asantehene served

1 Dupuis, *Journal*, i, p. 171

2 *Parl. Papers*, 1826–1827, p. 30–31

3 See Margaret Priestley, *West African Trade and Coast Society*, London, 1969, pp. 129–42

4 T. 70/36: John Hope Smith to the African Committee, 23 Feb. 1818

5 Priestley, *West African Trade*, p. 131

6 T. 70/41: Hutchinson to Hope Smith, 11 Oct. 1817

7 T. 70/36: John Hope Smith to the African Committee, 23 Feb. 1818

8 T. 70/41: William Hutchinson to John Hope Smith, 11 Oct. 1817

9 T. 70/40: Bowdich to Hope Smith, 29 Aug. 1817

10 Daendels, *Correspondence*, 10 Jan. 1817 and 31 Jan. 1817

to cover – were directly or indirectly connected with slaves, who were kept for the most part in the 'bush' in readiness for the arrival of slave ships to take them quickly from the coast.[1]

While the slave trade in West Africa continued, the coastal people were able to make profits selling canoes and hiring themselves out as canoemen because they were important for the prosecution of the slave trade for use in communication between the ships and the coast. Slave vessels normally called at the settlements which were not under the control of the British to make arrangements to purchase and to hire canoes and canoemen. These men and boats were employed in ferrying slaves from the coast to the slave ships or transporting slaves along the coast to be loaded at some convenient spot beyond the reach of British cruisers.[2] The best canoemen were reputed to be obtained from the Gold Coast.[3]

The Abolition Act of 1807, coupled with the Asante invasion, disrupted the pre-1807 economic and trading activities. Both the coastal states in their brokerage role and the interior chiefs as suppliers of slaves had derived profits from the trade. Certainly the once apparent prosperity of the Fante was partly due to the slave trade. Early nineteenth century travellers like W. Huydercooper, Thomas E. Bowdich and Joseph Dupuis journeyed through Fante and Assin to Kumasi and saw the remnants of a country that once seemed to have thrived. Bowdich described Mansu as originally a great Fante market for slaves from the interior.[4] Dupuis also described Mansu in similar terms and said it was formerly a wealthy town which owed its importance to the slave trade.[5] When Huydercooper passed through Mansu he stated that it was uninhabited and partially burnt.[6] A large town, Fosu, 'formerly the market of the exchange between the Fantees and the Ashantees', was now destroyed.[7] A once flourishing country lay in ruins and with the trade that had once given that country its prosperity now abolished there were no immediate prospects for recovery. Furthermore, the wars of this period established a new position for Britain as protector of the coastal states. Without the source of revenue to maintain the states and to buy arms and ammunition for defence, abolition would, in the long run, affect the political structure of the coastal states.[8]

Consequently, agricultural pursuits, so interwoven with the physical demands of the slave trade on the Gold Coast, especially those near the coastal areas, must have suffered a severe setback from abolition. Slaves brought from

1 C.O. 96/63: Joseph Dupuis to Duke of Newcastle, 31 July 1863

2 Sir G. R. Collier, *West African Sketches Comprised from the Reports of Sir G. R. Collier, Sir Charles MacCarthy and Other Official Sources 1824*, Legon, 1967, p. 243

3 C.O. 96/14: W. Hutton to Palmerston, 6 March 1848

4 Bowdich, *Mission from Cape Coast Castle*, p. 19

5 Dupuis, *Journal*, i, p. 17

6 Huydercooper's *Journal of His Missions to Kumasi*, 7 May 1816

7 Bowdich, *Mission from Cape Coast Castle*, p. 22

8 Kwame Arhin, 'Diffuse Authority among the Coastal Fanti', *G.N.Q.* 9, pp. 66–70, 1966

the interior had to be fed along the way as well as upon their arrival at the European castles and forts on the coast while awaiting transportation; they had to be given food there as well as for the long journey across the Atlantic.[1]

During the slave trade agriculture thrived on the Gold Coast and in some places in West Africa slaves waiting for ships had been employed in agricultural labour. According to Governor White of Cape Coast Castle, large quantities of yam, plantain, corn and cassava were purchased during the days of the slave trade.[2] The people in the vicinity of Accra made considerable progress in agriculture and provided great quantities of agricultural produce and provisions.[3] The port of Komenda was deemed a good place for stopping before proceeding to the Windward Coast because it furnished corn and yams,[4] but in 1814 progress in agriculture in Komenda had decreased since the abolition of the slave trade because there was not 'that vent for commodities, which was when shipping had frequent recourse here'.[5] Tantumquerry also had an 'abundance of provisions'. The Akuapems were primarily agriculturalists and, according to Henry Meredith, traded in agricultural products 'which always met with a ready sale'.[6] With abolition, the outlet for agricultural products was reduced, and it is likely that the unresponsive attitude of the people to European entreaties to cultivate agricultural exports was related to the diminishing outlet for farm products.

The Asante invasion coming at the same time as abolition was a coincidence even though such invasions had been rumoured as early as 1768.[7] The invasion came when Asante was stable and peaceful at home after the reign of Osei Kwame (1777–1801) which was marked by 'instability, disunity and civil wars'[8] while internecine wars prevailed among the Fante during the late eighteenth and early nineteenth centuries.[9] Reindorf, describing the coastal states at the time of the Asante invasion, said 'Pillage, manstealing and murder was the rule of every district. If the European Governments had not been weakened and demoralised through the slave trade, such terrible disorders could have readily been checked'.[10] A rapid decline in the slave trade in the Gold Coast had coincided with the breakthrough to the coast after almost fifteen years of European war. Undoubtedly the decline and abolition of the slave trade weakened the Fante and other coastal states and broke the precise and complex politico-econo-

1 Dickson, *Historical Geography*, p. 120

2 *Parl. Papers* 1816, VII, 2 (405), Reports of Commission of Enquiry into the African Forts 1810. Quoted in the Report of the Select Committee on African Forts.

3 *Parl. Papers* 1826–1827, VI, Report of Commissioners into Sierra Leone 1826

4 *Parl. Papers* 1816, VII, 2 (405), Report of the Committee Relating to the African Forts; the African Committee to the Treasury, 9 April 1812

5 *Ibid.*, 26 April 1814   6 Meredith, *Gold Coast of Africa*, p. 227

7 Martin, *British West African Settlements*, pp. 54 and 151; Margaret Priestley, 'The Ashanti Question and the British: Eighteenth Century Origins', *J.A.H.* ii, p. 1, 1961

8 Boahen, 'Asante and Fante A.D. 1000–1800', in *Thousand Years of West African History*, p. 183

9 *Ibid.*, p. 345   10 Reindorf, *History of the Gold Coast*, 2nd ed., p. 138

mic equilibrium, thus allowing Asante pressure at last to prevail. People like the Fante had been not only brokers for the inland states in the slave trade, but also had been active participants themselves. In 1753, for example, the Danes reported that there were over 300 Fantes in Akwamu buying slaves. The report said that Fantes travelled with goods to Akwamu in hundreds in order to buy all the slaves they could get.[1]

The loss of income from the diminution of the slave trade after abolition must have reduced the ability of the coastal states to maintain their defences against Asante aggression. In fact, after the Asante invasion of 1807 the coastal peoples, unable to defend themselves, had to rely for protection upon the European powers on the coast. The armed conflicts between Asante and her southern neighbours in 1807, 1811, 1814–1816, 1823–1824, 1826, 1863, 1873 and 1874 as well as the narrowly avoided conflicts in 1820, 1844 and 1853, all served to indicate the weak and vulnerable position of the coastal states and their rulers after abolition. These conflicts with Asante hindered the peace necessary for trade and economic change on the Gold Coast.

From 1807 until Asante was defeated at the battle of Kantamansu in 1826, a *de facto* suzerainty was established over the coastal states. This period of Asante rule has been described by Reindorf (probably not without some bias) at a time when 'the people suffered from the most barbarous tyranny'. Sovereignty over the people was exercised by Asante chiefs and headmen residing in the principal towns. Asante rule at the time was described by Reindorf thus:

> Everybody, merchants, mechanics, clerks, canoemen, the poor, the rich; in fact, high and low, were subjected to a system of cruel extortion on every possible occasion, and on pretences ludicrous and unheard of. People were deprived of their wives when they were handsome; if one had any words with an Asante, inadvertently touched, or even alluded to an Asante, he was punished. In Fante as well as in Akra, several chiefs were made to pay enormous fines under various pretences.[2]

European traders and abolition

Abolition was also to have a significant impact upon European trade and merchants on the Gold Coast. In 1807, the Danes, the Dutch and the British were the only European concerns on the coast. Great Britain had a major share of the slave trade and consequently British merchants and traders on the Gold Coast were concerned about the results of abolition. Governor George Torrane of Cape Coast Castle wrote that he feared little or nothing would remain for them to do on the Gold Coast, and without the profits to be made from the slave trade he felt that no man's pay on the coast would be sufficient even for maintenance and his own salary would not pay half his expenses.[3]

1 Vestindish-guineisk Kompagni 1671–1755, Breve og Dokumenter fra Guinea 1751–1754, Engman, Schmidt, Hessen, Christiansborg, 3 May 1753

2 Reindorf, *History of the Gold Coast*, 2nd ed., p. 162

3 T. 70/35: Torrane to the African Committee, 21 Sept. 1807 and T. 70/73: S. Cock to E. Cooke, 26 Sept. 1808

In July, 1807, British merchants on the Gold Coast complained to the Committee of Merchants that due to deprivation of the sources of profits that existed during the days of the slave trade their salaries were less than half the sum adequate for their support.[1] The African Committee argued that during the existence of the slave trade they were able to secure the services of competent people at low salaries for the Gold Coast settlements because of the commercial advantages to be derived from slavers' vessels. Now that the slave trade had been abolished they feared that their servants in Africa were unable to support themselves on their present salaries and might leave Africa for Europe and abandon the forts.[2] As a result of these submissions in 1808 the salaries of British merchants on the Gold Coast were at least doubled and the annual Parliamentary grant to the Gold Coast was increased from £13,431 to £23,000 per annum. In spite of the claims of the African Committee after abolition there remained a vested interest in continued British presence on the Gold Coast. This was evident from the committee's representing to the government that 'several of their forts, being situated in that part of Africa in which gold (in any quantity) and ivory are to be procured, will still be found of the utmost importance, as the means of keeping up a secure intercourse with the Africans, in trading for those articles'.[3]

In 1811, a request from John Hope Smith and Henry Meredith to the African Committee for an increase in their salaries was an indication of the changes that had taken place in the Gold Coast trade. Smith and Meredith, Governors of the Tantumquerry and Winneba forts, argued that before abolition, the forts of Anomabo, Winneba and Tantumquerry in particular and other leeward forts had been prosperous because many slaves were sold through them. They said that the situation had changed and the windward forts that had been more remarkable for the gold rather than the slave trade before 1807 were now the profitable ones. Since the relative advantages of the different settlements had been reversed by abolition and the Governors of the windward forts were 'approaching to affluence whereas the chiefs of Tantumquerry and Winneba with difficulty are supporting the respectability of their situation', they asked that their salaries be increased.[4] The Governor supported the claim and justified it on the grounds that it was with great difficulty that Smith and Meredith maintained themselves in moderate comfort.[5]

In 1808, in response to the demands of those abolitionists who wanted to extend British interests and to promote legitimate trade and civilisation in Africa, the British Government sent a Commission of Inquiry to the coast for the purpose of obtaining information about the situation on the Gold Coast and its probable future after abolition. The commission found the number of European forts on the Gold Coast 'very considerable, compared with the extent of coast

1 T. 70/1586: Merchants on the Gold Coast to the African Committee, 1 July 1807; *Parl. Papers* 1816, VII, p. 21, S. Cock to Castlereagh, 4 Oct. 1807

2 *Ibid.*

3 *Ibid.*; Martin, *British West African Settlements*, p. 150; J. J. Crooks, *Records Relating to the Gold Coast Settlements 1750–1874*, Dublin, 1923, pp. 104–6

4 T. 70/1593: Meredith and Smith to African Committee, 22 June 1811

5 70/35: Dawson to African Committee, 1 July 1811

which they occupy'. The settlements were regarded as 'very trifling, unproductive concerns' which could be considered as 'small private factories supported, at the public expense' and that if any of them were relinquished there would be no loss to British commerce. The government had hoped the commission would recommend abandoning the forts, but they suggested that only Sekondi, Komenda, Tantumquerry, Winneba, PramPram and Whydah should be given up.[1] British merchant interest in Africa persuaded the government to continue maintaining the forts, however, arguing that they were necessary for the persons and property of the traders. Furthermore, the commerce of Africa was made so insignificant by the abolition of the slave trade that 'before any material improvement can be expected to take place in any district of Africa, the slave trade must be completely annihilated, or at least driven from that part of the coast'. Justification was found for retaining all the forts recommended for abandonment. Sekondi was said to have 'a good landing place and considerable trade in gold'; Komenda had 'some gold and ivory trade'; Tantumquerry was 'a valuable point of communication'; Winneba was 'useful in many respects and although PramPram and Whydah had weaker claims, they were not to be rashly given up'.[2]

A Parliamentary Select Committee was appointed in 1816 and 1817 to examine the Gold Coast settlements and to consider the future policy which it might deem expedient for Parliament to adopt towards the African Company, which was responsible for them. The committee considered whether the settlements should be abandoned or maintained under the direction of the African Company and, if so, whether a new management was needed. It recommended that a Governor-in-Chief should be appointed by the government with supreme authority over all the Gold Coast settlements and that the number of the forts would be reduced. It also suggested that the Parliamentary grant to the settlements should be increased to enable the company to 'establish a regular intercourse with the great interior kingdom of the Ashantees'. The committee also wanted the crippling import duties on African produce reduced and an end brought to the revived slave trade which was 'absolutely incompatible with and destructive to the legitimate commerce of Africa'.[3]

Back on the Gold Coast, the realisation that the greatest potential for legitimate trade was with Asante led the British to follow the example of the Dutch who had sent W. Huydercooper on a mission to Asante in 1816. In 1817, a British mission reached Kumasi and concluded a treaty encouraging trade and peace between England and Asante. This treaty was never ratified by the British Government.[4] T. E. Bowdich negotiated the treaty which allowed for the appointment of a British Consul to Kumasi; consequently Joseph Dupuis was appointed to the post in 1818.

Dupuis arrived on the Gold Coast in 1819, but due to bickering between him and the authorities at Cape Coast Castle, it was not until 1820 that he reached

1 *Parl. Papers* 1816, VII, pp. 135–6; Crooks, *Records*, pp. 109–10

2 *Parl. Papers* 1816, VII, pp. 135–6, African Committee to Treasury, pp. 104–8; also, T. 70/73, Liverpool Traders to Treasury, 26 April 1812

3 *Parl. Papers* 1817, Report from the Committee on African Forts, 25 June 1817

4 Bowdich, *Mission from Cape Coast Castle;* Crooks, *Records*, pp. 118–20

Kumasi and entered into another treaty with Asante. This treaty contained clauses undertaking to keep the peace, promote trade, protect traders and keep the routes open. It also declared that all of Fante was part of the Asante Empire. The government on the coast refused to recognise the treaty as they refused to acknowledge Asante suzerainty over the Fante country.[1] Neither the mission of Bowdich nor that of Dupuis brought peace or prosperity to the Gold Coast settlements. Thus, with the decline of trade on the Gold Coast, the revival of the slave trade, and the criticism of the management of the forts, the government introduced a bill to abolish the African Company in 1821.[2] This bill embodied the provisions of an earlier measure of 1819 entitled a 'Bill for the Better Regulation of the African Company'.[3] The Gold Coast settlements came under the direct control of the government as of July 1821, and were made dependencies of the colony of Sierra Leone. The forts were also reduced to those of Cape Coast Castle, Anamabo, Dixcove and Accra and officials were prohibited even at these settlements from trading. Direct Crown rule was short-lived, lasting only seven years until 1828.

On the other hand, Dutch trade on the Gold Coast had greatly decreased since the last decade of the eighteenth century, and during the Napoleonic Wars had been almost driven out altogether. After abolition Dutch trade recovered only briefly under the tenure of Governor H. W. Daendels from 1816 to 1818.[4] A letter to the secretary of the African Committee testified to this:

> The Dutch settlements you know to have been entirely neglected for many years by the mother country. Consequently, the amount of the articles of trade which accompanied General Daendels that year for the payment of arrears, the establishment of the Forts and the recovery of the trade, was very heavy and as this large supply comprehended scarcely any articles but guns and powder, the importation of this was considerable.

The trade in firearms immensely helped Dutch trade, and Asante traders who could not procure these items when their imports from the British forts were limited, resorted to the Dutch settlements in great numbers.[5] After Governor Daendels' period of office the forts were reduced to Elmina and Axim.[6]

The Danish establishments on the Gold Coast were not profitable even during the days of the slave trade, and their commercial value further declined after

---

1 William E. F. Ward, *History of Ghana*, rev. 3rd ed., London, 1966, p. 173; Crooks, *Records*, p. 121

2 Martin, *British West African Settlements*, pp. 164–6

3 T. 70/1605/2: Treasury to African Committee, 27 Oct. 1819

4 African Institution, 13th Report, 1819, Appendix A. Queries proposed by Viscount Castlereagh to, and answers of, the African Institution in London, Dec., 1816. Q. 4, p. 60; Albert Van Dantzig, 'Dutch Recruitment in Kumasi', *G.N.Q.* 8, Jan., 1966, p. 21; J. T. Lever, 'Mulatto Influence on the Gold Coast in the Early Nineteenth Century: Jan Nieser of Elmina', *A.H.S.* iii, 2, p. 254, 1970. Also see Douglas Coombs, *The Gold Coast, Britain and the Netherlands 1850–1874*, London 1963, p. 196

5 T. 70/36: Bowdich to Cock, 20 Aug. 1816

6 C.O. 268/56: MacCarthy to Bathurst, 18 May 1822

abolition. The European War from 1807–1814 prevented Denmark from sending ships to the Gold Coast to supply her forts and after a disastrous war she did not have the money to equip ships for the Danish West African settlements. After the war, visits of Danish ships to supply her possessions on the coast became annual or biannual affairs.[1] In relation to trade at the Dutch and Danish settlements, it was written in 1822 that for the last three years there had been an average of only one vessel from Holland to the Gold Coast with cargoes valued at approximately £1,500 each, and only one from Denmark.[2] By 1816 Denmark was seriously contemplating giving up the forts and the Danish Government considered exchanging all its settlements on the Gold Coast for the two Portuguese islands of Sao Thomé and Principe. However, this never occurred probably because of the hopes of Denmark to develop plantations on the coast. In 1817 reports from the coast indicated that there was no possibility of the Danes making such a transaction with the Portuguese. As the report stated:

> No compensation could be given on this coast, to the [Danish] settlers in the island equivalent to their plantations, the Portuguese being prohibited from trading in slaves to the northward of the line, the Danish settlements would consequently be useless to them.[3]

In addition to European commerce, there was American trade to Africa[4] which until the end of the eighteenth century was confined to slaves. During the Napoleonic Wars, which precluded Europeans from fully supplying their West African settlements, American merchants were given the opportunity to carry out profitable trade on the Gold Coast which became especially important after the American war of 1812. From 1821–1828 when the Crown assumed direct control of the forts, however, trade at the British settlements was closed to them and they were confined to dealing with Dutch and Danish forts and the areas between them.[5]

Alternatives to the slave trade

The success of European trade activities on the Gold Coast after abolition depended, to a large degree, upon the extent to which they were able to shift indigenous subsistence production into production for exchange. This, in a sense, implied a commercialisation of indigenous resources and an enlargement of the resources of the country dedicated to money-earning activities, all of which essentially meant that more resources would have to be devoted to subsistence surplus production to allow for cash crop specialisation.

1 Nørregard, *Danish Settlements in West Africa*, p. 191

2 C.O. 267/56: Memorial of Cape Coast Merchants, 30 Sept. 1822; Metcalfe, *Documents*, pp. 80–82

3 T. 70/36: John Hope Smith to the African Committee, 5 March 1817

4 See George E. Brooks, Jr., *Yankee Traders, Old Coasters and African Middlemen*, p. 70; Norman Bennett and George E. Brooks, Jr., eds., *New England Merchants in Africa*, Boston, 1968

5 Brooks, *Yankee Traders*, pp. 65–72

European trade interests during this period considered developing trade resources of a country about which they were so little informed. In 1807 Governor Torrane made inquiries of various chiefs about the interior of the Gold Coast, but he said that it was impossible to get any correct information from the people as they thought the questions were put with a view to gaining advantages of the interior trade to their prejudice.[1] Again, in 1811, Governor White of Cape Coast Castle admitted that despite the years of intercourse between England and the Gold Coast, they were not well informed about the resources of the area. He wrote that some knowledge of the interior was necessary before one could estimate the capabilities of the country.[2]

Despite the inadequate knowledge of the resources of the region, it was hoped that trade in gold dust, ivory, cotton, indigo, rice, corn, palm oil and timber could replace the trade in human beings.[3] Yet the enumeration of the Gold Coast's known resources was not a true guide to its economic prospects. As has been observed, 'such an inventory cannot be translated into terms of commercial values or of potential economic development without importing assumptions about quantities and prices of complementary resources and about markets for the products arising from the use of the resources'.[4] Henry Meredith, the Governor of Winneba Castle, asserted that the way to increase trade was to establish free intercourse with the Gold Coast interior.[5] He suggested that substantial sums would be needed to extend European influence into the interior for trade purposes, and unless additional grants were made for these purposes all efforts to increase trade would prove abortive.[6] He felt that alliances should be formed with rulers and residents placed in principal towns for the purpose of ultimately reaching the resources of the country, extending manufactures among the people and encouraging confidence and friendship.[7] Governor Torrane's policy of friendship with Asante was influenced by the desire to exploit the interior trade. Writing after the invasion of 1807 that he had received a message from the Asantehene asking that the two of them meet in order to arrange the 'future welfare' and 'the regulation of the trade', Torrane reported:

> Let me observe that an intercourse securely open with Ashantee, offers prospects of the highest advantage, and the more so as the slave trade is now at an end. The Ashantees have ivory and gold in great abundance, and the Fantees have ever thrown impediments in the way.[8]

At the time of British abolition the only significant items of export from the Gold Coast were gold and ivory. These products, although not exclusively con-

1 T. 70/35: Torrane to the African Committee, 1 Feb. 1807

2 *Ibid.*, Governor to the African Committee, 13 Oct. 1811

3 T. 70/73: S. Cock to E. Cooke, 26 Sept. 1808

4 Bauer and Yamey, *Economics of Under-Developed Countries*, p. 48

5 Meredith, *Gold Coast of Africa*, pp. 183–4

6 *Ibid.*, p. 207   7 *Ibid.*

8 T. 70/35: Torrane to the African Committee, 20 July 1807

fined to the inland country, came mainly from the interior or were produced in greater quantities inland.[1] It was said that 'gold dust has hitherto been imported into this country in very inconsiderable quantities, it being the policy of the natives to prevent the export', and that 'elephants' teeth have long been an article of import from Africa, but hitherto as an appendage to the slave trade, the ordinary methods of conveying them from the interior having been by means of the slaves on their way to the coast'.[2] The hope of making ivory a viable export from the Gold Coast was nothing new. Ivory was scarce on the Gold Coast and yet despite the difficulties involved in obtaining it Europeans had since the eighteenth century been optimistic about improving the ivory trade.[3]

Trade after abolition

In this period following the abolition of the slave trade there were two kinds of trade on the Gold Coast, namely, 'native' and 'factory' trade. What was called 'factory' trade was carried on at the European forts and settlements and was said to yield an average profit of between 75% and 100% over gross outlay. 'Native' or 'floating' trade, supposedly dangerous and difficult but more lucrative, was carried out where there were no factors.[4] This trade consisted primarily of gold and ivory from the interior in exchange for East Indian and Manchester goods, guns, powder, lead and iron.[5] In the floating trade a merchant house put on board ship a certain quantity of goods under the charge of a captain to sell on the African coast for the products of the country. The captain sailed along the coast going from port to port selling his goods out of his vessel to the indigenous people.[6] In the factory trade, commercial houses in England established trading posts on the coast with a resident merchant who opened a store where the Africans could come to sell and purchase goods. These merchants had fixed salaries plus a commission and were thus assured of a steady income, any risks and losses falling upon the merchants in England.

Most of the handling of the legitimate trade in the British settlements after abolition was in the hands of the servants of the Company of Merchants, and, in 1816, it was reported that there were only five private traders at Cape Coast.[7] Those interested in free trade resented the company monopoly, saying that it was injurious to British commercial interests. Matthew Forster wrote that he considered the annual grant to the Company entirely wasted, and 'only beneficial to the servants of the company who of course monopolise the whole of the trade'. He said that in Cape Coast, for example, the Governor was the chief

1 Meredith, *Gold Coast of Africa*, pp. 106–7; Cruickshank, *Eighteen Years*, ii, p. 41

2 T. 70/73: S. Cock to E. Cooke, 26 Sept. 1808

3 Daaku, *Trade and Politics*, p. 28

4 Samuel Swan to Benjamin L. Swan, 'Atlantic Ocean', Nov. 1910, MS Swan letter book in Bennett and Brooks, *New England Merchants*, p. 30

5 *Parl. Papers* 1816, VII, 2 (405), Report from the Select Committee on Papers Relating to the African Forts, pp. 15–18

6 *Parl. Papers* 1842, XIII, Q.3340 and Q.3345

7 *Parl. Papers* 1817, Report from the Committee on African Forts, 25 June 1817

trader and since he had such influence free traders in the town could not compete with him.[1] Company servants enjoyed their advantageous trade position not only because of their posts but also because of the cheap goods assigned to them for their salaries that enabled them to undersell free traders.[2] Although governors of the forts during the Crown period were traders, free-trading became the practice in the British settlements after 1821. In 1826 it was said that all of the merchants on the Gold Coast 'traded on their own account'.[3] At this time there were five merchants at Cape Coast, one at Anomabo and three at Accra – two of whom were Africans.[4] There were no European merchants at the abandoned forts but in some of them and in villages nearby, some traders had indigenous factors who disposed of European goods by barter. This kind of operation was limited because of the floating trade, which enabled some traders to obtain their goods directly from the supercargoes.

Dutch and Danish trade after abolition was official but since the reduction in their establishments and the increase in the floating trade some independent or private traders emerged at these settlements as H. Richter and W. Lutterodt did at Christiansborg. The floating trade and the decreasing scope of official trading helped to augment the direct participation of the indigenous people as they began to trade directly with merchant vessels. This increase of indigenous participation was not welcomed by the European private traders and the coastal local government. In 1819 the Council at Cape Coast Castle wrote that:

> the trade carried on by natives with foreign vessels to the great detriment of the free trader had arrived at such an alarming height, that the President considered it a matter of duty to interfere, and to revive a regulation which was formerly in force here prohibiting it.[5]

If there had been a regulation limiting the direct dealings of the people with foreign vessels it does not appear that it was successfully renewed and the trend continued, as an official testified in 1826:

> Some vessels bring out all their cargo for barter direct with the natives, and none for the merchants. It is difficult to ascertain what proportion of the whole trade is carried on by each mode, but I am led, after every possible enquiry, to think that one fourth or one fifth only is carried by the merchants. The collector thinks only one-tenth, but his estimate is probably erroneous.[6]

1 C.O. 267/55: M. Forster to Earl Bathurst, 4 Jan. 1821   2 *Ibid.*

3 C.O. 167/74: Campbell to Bathurst, 12 Nov. 1826

4 *Ibid.* These African merchants were J. Hansen and James Bannerman. By 1819 these merchants were exporting large quantities of corn and palm oil from Accra. In 1828, it was said that the 'Bannerman house at Accra consumed 1,000 puncheons of rum during the last 17 months. 34,000 oz (an exaggeration no doubt) of gold have been collected during the same period and in the last six months, 10 tons of ivory and £7,000 worth of palm oil have been sent to England'. C.O. 267/94: Denham to Hay, 1 Feb. 1828.

5 T. 70/1604/1: Governor Smith and Council to the Africa Committee, 11 Jan. 1819

6 *Ibid.*

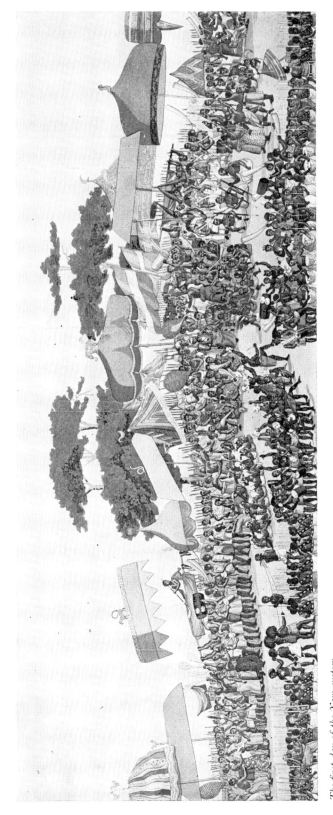

The first day of the Yam custom

The growth of free trade on the Gold Coast owed some of its impetus to Matthew Forster, of the merchant house of Forster and Smith. In about 1817 he introduced a new system of trading which became popular with some merchant houses in London until the introduction of the steamship in 1852. By this plan the London houses became agents and wholesalers to merchants on the African coast. The system involved sending out goods on commission and the distinguishing feature of this new method was that the merchants in London were absolved of all risks and losses.[1] Under this arrangement any person who wished to go to Africa to seek his fortune applied to a house which supplied him with goods on credit and was charged a commission. By having many correspondents on the coast, great profits accrued to the merchant houses; yet at the same time the correspondents often suffered losses when there were accidents or misfortunes.[2]

This new system of trade must have influenced to some extent the formation of the Gold Coast Mining and Trading Company, numbering among its membership such well-known merchants interested in Africa as Matthew Forster and John George Nicholls. The company aimed at providing help and encouragement to merchants involved in carrying on trade on the Gold Coast and in making arrangements with chiefs to introduce better mining methods.[3]

> This company has been formed with a view to obviate the impediments to individual enterprize; and it is proposed to extend the intercourse now subsisting with the Native Chiefs and Princes and to make arrangements with them to introduce better methods of working the Mines and Pits in the Dinkara, Warsaw, Ahantah, and Fantee Territories on the Gold Coast, and at Grand Bassam and Assinee on the Windward Coast. Individuals in the Directions of this undertaking are already provided with Agents at different points, who, with other Agents and Factors to be employed, will enable the Company to carry its objects into immediate effect, and to secure the power of working those Mines, which are the richest and most accessible.[4]

The company, however, confined its activities to trade. The sources that have come to the present writer's attention reveal little that is directly connected with the activities of this company, but the emergence of correspondents of about half a dozen London houses on the Gold Coast might have been connected with it.[5] These companies provided jobs for a growing number of African traders acting as local correspondents for the European importers. The large capital involved in the Gold Coast trade until 1852 eventually led to the commerce being chiefly in the hands of three London houses: Messrs Forster and Smith, Swanzy and T. Hutton (the latter firm disappeared from the coast after 1843).

The lack of complete and reliable trade figures for the Gold Coast makes it

1 *Parl. Papers* 1842, p. xii, Qs. 3319–3320   2 *Ibid.*, Qs. 3325–3327

3 *Gold Mining Company Prospectus*, London 1825

4 Junner, *Gold on the Gold Coast*, p. 14

5 Included in the houses that were to operate on the Gold Coast were: Forster and Smith; F. and A. Swanzy; King of Bristol and Banner Brothers.

difficult to evaluate the level on which trade was being maintained after abolition; however, more accurate figures than are presently available could probably not be assembled. Abolition, for example, made about 90% of the trade of the Company of Merchants Trading to Africa illegal.[1]

The bulk of the Gold Coast trade immediately following abolition was mainly in gold dust and ivory was brought to England during the European conflict and for a short period after that in men-of-war. In certain instances passengers from the Gold Coast to England brought their own gold dust and ivory with them – such cases are not included in the figures below:[2]

GOLD DUST EXPORTS

Year	Ounces	£
1807	*	*
1808	3,852	15,408
1809	2,573	10,494
1810	6,742	25,968
1811	**	**
1812	1,090	4,360
1813	16,976	67,908
1814	20,059	80,350
1815	4,885	*
1816	5,876	21,904
1817	7,911	31,644
1818	4,108	16,434
1819	*	*
1820	*	*
1821	*	*

* Figures not available.   ** No exports those years.

IVORY EXPORTS[3]

Year	Cwt	Approximate value in £
1807	254	4,826
1808	82	1,558
1809	279	5,301
1810	204	3,876
1811	–	–
1812	317	6,023
1813	995	18,905
1814	1,355	25,745
1815	1,209	22,971

1 Metcalfe, *Documents*, p. 3

2 T. 70/1599, 1808–1815; T. 70/1604/2, 1815–1818; 27 Feb. 1819, Andrew Lendgren to Cock

3 *Parl. Papers* 1816, VII, 2 (405), Report from the Select Committee on Papers Relating to the African Forts, p. 12

Although the figures are incomplete, some attempt may be made to interpret them in light of events on the Gold Coast and correspondence to traders at the time. A comparison of the gold exports of the early nineteenth century and the last decades of the eighteenth century cannot be made since the figures for the latter period are lacking. However, it may be assumed that figures for the eighteenth century are low because gold exports from the Gold Coast had been declining since the middle of the eighteenth century.[1] Even though gold from the Gold Coast was usually in the form of gold dust, ornaments of gold were also exported intermittently. It was reckoned that gold remitted to England lost from 15% to 20% in value but gold received in direct trade with Asante lost only 10% to 12% of its value.[2] The loss of gold in trade with the Fante was the result of adulteration. This was formerly carried out by mixing the pure metal with copper and brass, but when it was found that *aqua fortis* was successfully used as a test, silver was used instead, and this often escaped detection until the gold reached England.[3] The ivory trade had been linked with the slave trade in the sense that ivory was transported by slaves on their way to the coast. Thus, abolition must have affected ivory export and probably other products as well.[4]

Stagnation of trade was often blamed on the wars and the disturbances on the coast.[5] In 1807, a war year, no figures are available for gold. However, it would seem that gold and ivory were becoming important exports during the period after abolition. In requesting an increase in salaries Hope Smith and Henry Meredith had pointed out in 1811 that the windward forts situated in the gold-producing areas were 'approaching to affluence'. Thus, they were apparently enjoying an amount of trade in gold they had not experienced previously.[6] No figures are available for 1811, when there was another clash between Asante and the coastal areas and it was reported that all trade at the forts, except at Accra and Apollonia, was nearly annihilated.[7] There was another war from 1814–1816 and this must have influenced the gold trade. In 1816 Elmina, which had not been involved in war with Asante, was engaged in prosperous trade. It was reported that Elmina received more Asante, Wassa and Fante traders' gold and ivory daily than all the other factories on the coast together. Of course this was in part due to the trade in firearms which had been prohibited at the English settlements.[8]

When the Asante army left the coast in early 1816 English merchants reported that trade with them was starting to flourish at their forts. In June, 1816, the Governor reported that for the past two months the Asante had brought

1 See Johnson, 'The Ounce in Eighteenth Century West African Trade'

2 *Parl. Papers* 1826–1827, VII, pp. 29–30   3 *Ibid.*, p. 30

4 T. 70/73: Cock to Cooke, 26 Sept. 1808

5 *Parl. Papers* 1816, VII, 2 (405), Report from the Select Committee on Papers

6 T. 70/1593: Meredith and Smith to the Africa Committee, 22 June 1811

7 T. 70/35: Governor White to Committee, 1 July 1811; Meredith, *Account of the Gold Coast*, p. 190

8 F.C., 23 Dec. 1816

down considerable gold dust and ivory.[1] Reporting on trade conditions in 1816, Dawson wrote that 'It is particularly gratifying to us to see an intercourse established which has not been known for sixteen years'.[2] In March, 1817, Governor John Hope Smith wrote: 'The commercial intercourse with the Asantes has been for the last ten months, extremely flourishing, and is now evidently daily improving.'[3]

From the correspondence of British merchants on the coast, it would seem that the revival of the slave trade terminated the progress that was reported after the Asante left the coast in 1816.[4] Since the figures quoted here represent those sent to England in men-of-war, some of the apparent drop in gold and ivory exports after 1814 can be accounted for by the fact that after the war most of these products were starting to go to England in merchant vessels instead of men-of-war. A letter to a commander of the West African Squadron in 1818 throws light on gold exports from the Gold Coast after the war. He said that during the last three years, 1815–1818, ships of war had not taken more than 8,000 ounces of gold to England. He calculated that about 12,000 ounces a year had gone home in merchant ships.[5] This estimate of not more than 8,000 ounces annually going to England in ships of war compares with the independent figures given in the table of 4,885 ounces in 1815, 5,876 ounces in 1816 and 7,911 ounces in 1817. Although by 1818 merchants were blaming the decline of trade on the revival of the slave trade, it would appear that causes for the rise and fall in the trade cycle were more complex. It must be pointed out here that produce from Africa fetched higher prices during the European war and this factor could not have been unimportant at the cessation of hostilities.

The prices during the war and in 1815 for various produce are given below.[6]

Article	War Price			Present Price		
	£	s	d	£	s	d
Palm oil	60	–	– per ton	35	–	–
Ivory	26	–	– per cwt.	19	–	–
Guinea pepper	25	–	– per cwt.	17	–	–
Guinea grains, or grains of paradise	15	–	– per cwt.	5	–	–
Barwood	24	–	– per ton	8	–	–
Camwood	35	–	– per ton	21	–	–
Ebony	50	–	– per ton	15	–	–
Beeswax	250	–	– per ton	140	–	–
Gum copal	–	3	6 per ton	1	6	–
Gum senegal	–	1	– per lb.	–	–	2
Hides	–	–	7 per lb.	–	–	2
Seahorse teeth	1	1	– per lb.	–	15	–
Gold dust	5	5	6 per ounce	3	18	–

Parl. Papers 1816, VII, 2 (405), Report from the Select Committee on Papers Relating to the African Forts, p. 12.

1 T. 70/36: Governor to Committee of Merchants, 1 June 1816

2 *Ibid.*, Dawson to Committee of Merchants, 4 Oct. 1816

3 T. 70/36: John Hope Smith to Committee of Merchants, 5 March 1817

4 T. 70/36: John Hope Smith to Committee of Merchants, 23 Feb. 1817

5 T. 70/1604/1: James Yeo to J. W. Crocker, 12 March 1818

6 The prices quoted were obtained in Liverpool.

According to Bowdich, Asante hoarded gold so that they could be prepared to buy firearms and gunpowder if a war suddenly broke out.[1] Guns and gunpowder which had been important items of trade during the seventeenth and eighteenth century[2] were still equally important.[3] Firearms, besides their use in wars, were widely used during celebrations, performances and observance of certain customs on the Gold Coast. However, in 1807, during the war in Europe, an Order in Council made the export of firearms to the African coast illegal because it was thought that it promoted contraband trade in slaves. When this Order expired on 6 June, 1809, it was deemed necessary to continue the ban.[4] In 1813, however, another Order in Council allowed a barrel of gunpowder to every ten tons of the vessel's burden, ten trading guns of blunderbusses and ten pairs of pistols for each barrel of gunpowder.[5] The Orders in Council banning or limiting firearm exports to Africa were repealed in May, 1817.[6] Despite restrictions on firearms, special permission was granted from time to time to export them to the Gold Coast allegedly for defence purposes.[7] Since the government had no objection to the export of firearms in large quantities to other places, some supplies were able to reach the Gold Coast markets by circuitous routes, some merchants exporting their firearms to Madeira and then re-shipping them to Africa.[8]

British merchants on the Gold Coast keenly felt the limitation of the export of firearms, complaining that they would lose trade to the Americans and other European merchants who could supply whatever quantities of firearms the people needed.[9] According to the merchants, without these articles it was impossible to carry on any trade, especially on the Gold Coast.[10] In 1816, a group of Birmingham gun and pistol manufacturers also asked for the lifting of the restrictions on the export of firearms, arguing that unless this were done, they would have to discharge most of the men they employed. Furthermore, they said, whatever might have been the expedience of preventing the Africans from obtaining any more than a limited supply during the existence of the slave trade or during the war, those considerations were at an end.[11]

---

1 Bowdich, *Mission from Cape Coast Castle*, p. 335

2 See Daaku, *Trade and Politics*, pp. 5 and 19

3 Bennett and Brooks, eds., *New England Merchant*, p. 41

4 T. 70/73: Committee of Merchants to Treasury, 24 April 1813

5 T. 70/74: African Office to Treasury, 20 Aug. 1816

6 *Ibid.*, 31 May 1817; also, Cock to Messrs. Pigon and Company, June 1817

7 T. 70/73: African Office to Privy Council, 15 Oct. 1812; *ibid.*, 30 Sept. 1816 (from African Office)

8 T. 70/35: Privy Council to Simon Cock, 31 Aug. 1814; T. 70/36: Harry Gill and 96 other Birmingham manufacturers of guns and pistols to S. Cock, 17 July 1816

9 *Ibid.*   10 T. 70/73: African Office to Earl Bathurst, 22 Nov. 1811

11 T. 70/35: London Traders to Committee of Merchants, 17 April 1813

There is conclusive evidence that the decline of trade at the British settlements was partially due to the prohibition on the sale of firearms and ammunitions. Traders who were unable to obtain these supplies at British settlements resorted to the Dutch forts.[1] The Parliamentary Committee of 1817 had 'reason to believe, from evidence laid before them, that the prohibition to export gunpowder and firearms has been a main cause of the depression of trade to the British settlements, and of its transfer, in part, to foreign nations, to whom it has furnished increased facilities for reviving the slave trade'.[2]

After its apparent drop in 1816, trade did not recover for some time and by 1819 the gold trade was reported to be so trifling that servants of the Committee of Merchants were recommending the abandonment of Dixcove, Cape Coast and Accra.[3] The cause of much of the decline in the external trade was the result of a conflict between Asante and the British Government about sovereignty over the Fante. In 1821 when both treaties included by Bowdich and Dupuis in 1817 and 1820 failed to settle the dispute, the Asantehene broke off negotiations with the British and suspended trade with the coast.

In 1822, when the new Governor of the British settlements arrived on the Gold Coast, trade was at a standstill, and much of the trade left at the British forts was driven from them when they came under the Crown. By placing the Gold Coast under Sierra Leone the settlements came under the British Trade and Navigation Acts and as such the forts were closed to foreigners and a duty was also payable on all trade carried out there. Merchants at the British forts were quick to complain:

> We allude to the peculiar circumstances which have tended to fetter the commerce of the British settlements, and materially to further increase that of the Dutch and Danes, who draw their trade from the same source, and have all their ports free, without any duties whatever being levied. The plain fact is that ships, not only of all foreign nations, resort to Elmina but British vessels make a practice of doing their trade at that port in preference to Cape Coast, by which means they avoid paying any duties, and by which the Dutch are enabled to undersell us by 8 per cent, and some articles 12 per cent, which unintentionally makes the regulations of the Colonial Government a bounty to the foreign trade.[4]

Considering the law and even non-existent level of Asante trade with the British establishments MacCarthy sought permission from England to suspend the Navigation Acts to admit some foreign vessels at their forts so that the merchants could sell 'their inferior African produce, such as the lowest class of ivory and palm oil'.[5] Before MacCarthy could get a reply to his request he was killed in a war with Asante.

1 T. 70/36: T. E. Bowdich to S. Cock, 20 Aug. 1816; T. 70/36: John Hope Smith to Committee of Merchants, 5 and 7 March 1817; T. 70/1602/2: 5 March 1817 and T. 70/36: Governor to Committee of Merchants, 16 July 1817

2 *Parl. Papers* 1817, 25 June 1817

3 T. 70/1605/1: Smith, Mollan and Adamson to the African Committee, 22 March 1819

4 C.O. 367/56: Memorial of Cape Coast Merchants, 30 Sept. 1822

5 C.O. 267/58: MacCarthy to Bathurst, 11 Feb. 1823

This trade depression was, of course, further prolonged by the war between Asante and her southern neighbours in 1823–1824 and 1826. The main exports are given in the table below.[1]

ABSTRACT OF THE AMOUNT OF EXPORTS FROM THE SETTLEMENTS OF CAPE COAST, ACCRA, ANNOMABOE AND DIXCOVE UPON THE GOLD COAST FROM THE PERIOD OF THEIR TRANSFER TO THE CROWN ON 1 APRIL 1822 TO 30 JUNE 1826

Year	Gold dust oz.	Silver coin	Ivory ton	cwt	Palm oil puncheons	ton
1822 1 April– 31 December	10,896	168	18	15	1,202	480
1823	600		4		95	38
1824	2,011		20		638	255
1825	17,063	7,950	59	10	650	260
1826 1 January– 30 June	5,071	6,834	29	15	590	217
Total	35,641	14,952	130	40	3,175	1,250

Compared with the period before 1818 the main change in the trade figures seems to be the addition of appreciable quantities of palm oil exports. It appears that palm oil was beginning to figure prominently in the exports from the Gold Coast, but its production in comparison with the total from West Africa was very low as can be seen from the table below.

PALM OIL EXPORT

Year	Gold Coast* Tons	Total from West Africa** Tons
1822 1 April–31 December	480	3,188
1823	38	3,270
1824	255	3,699
1825	260	4,268
1826 1 January–30 June	217	4,953

* C.O. 267/93: Rowan Report.

** Figures from N. H. Stilliard, *The Rise and Development of Legitimate Trade in Palm Oil with West Africa*, unpublished M.A. thesis, Birmingham University, 1938, p. 185 and *Parl. Papers* 1844–1845.

The palm oil coming from the Gold Coast at this time came mainly from Krobo and Akuapem in the eastern part of the country. It was no surprise that the Krobos responded to the external demand for palm oil during this period, for they had been cultivating palm trees and engaging in local trade in palm oil long before it became important. A passage about the Krobos early in the nineteenth

1 C.O. 267/93: Custom House, Cape Coast, 21 Sept. 1826

century described them subsisting 'mostly by tilling the ground and cultivating the palm-tree'.[1]

Palm oil was a welcome addition to the staple exports of the Gold Coast, but wars with Asante affected exports like gold and ivory and must also have influenced gold supplies from Akyem and Wassa. The export of silver coin indicated in the table probably represents the profits of surreptitious dealings with the slave traders. In addition, 4,000 bushels of Indian corn were exported from Accra and varying quantities of tortoiseshell, coffee, camwood, beeswax, palm soap, ebony, gum copal and guinea grains.

The amount of recorded imports into the Gold Coast during the war (see table below) were not high, but these figures represent those imports upon which duties had actually been paid and with the propensity of traders to avoid duties it is possible that the actual import figures were slightly higher.

IMPORTS FROM 1 APRIL 1822 TO 31 DECEMBER 1822[2]

Cape Coast	£41,693	3s	3½d
Accra	£3,873	10s	2d
Anomaboe	£1,055	10s	3d
Dixcove	£52	3s	8d

IMPORTS FROM 1 JANUARY TO 31 DECEMBER 1825[3]

Cape Coast	£29,694	14s	8d
Accra	£2,627	12s	0d
Anomaboe	£606	17s	7d
Dixcove	£565	14s	4d

The total available imports for the whole period are given below.

IMPORTS INTO THE GOLD COAST FROM 1 APRIL 1822 TO 30 JUNE 1826[4]

	British	Foreign	Total
1822 1 April–31 December	£30,781 15s 8½d	£11,142 7s 4d	£41,924 3s ½d
1823	£27,101 2s 9½d	£3,591 0s 8d	£30,692 3s 5½d
1824	£13,898 5s ½d	£4,289 17s 8d	£18,188 2s 8½d
1825	£30,578 3s 4½d	£2,916 13s 2½d	£33,494 16s 7d
1826 to 30 June	£6,201 0s 11d	£2,653 15s 10d	£8,854 16s 9d

After 1822, until the end of the decade, there was a general depression in the whole trade except for a brief boom in 1825.

1 Meredith, *Gold Coast of Africa*, 221n

2 C.O. 267/93: Rowan Report　　　3 *Ibid.*

4 C.O. 267/93: Rowan Report. It would seem that this figure for 1822 represents only the imports to Cape Coast. The total for this period including imports to Accra, Anomaboe and Dixcove amounted to £46,673 17s 4½d. See also Metcalfe, *Documents*, p. 110.

The low level of trade development on the Gold Coast was partially dependent upon environmental factors and the fact that a successful substitute had not yet been found for the slave trade: it was this need to find a new basis of exchange for European products that led Europeans to start plantations and to encourage indigenous agricultural production for exports. These attempts were, of course, not only limited to the Gold Coast but were made in other areas of West Africa as well, especially Sierra Leone.[1]

Plantation agriculture

The idea of cultivating agricultural products on the Gold Coast for export was not new; experiments in plantation agriculture had been conducted and abandoned in the eighteenth century because of opposition to such enterprises in Africa from vested interests like those of West Indian planters.[2]

As early as 1689 the Dutch had started tobacco, indigo and cotton plantations near Shama on the River Pra.[3] And by 1700 there were other establishments at Axim, Burti, Sekondi and Elmina from which cotton was exported.[4] The British also attempted to cultivate cotton, indigo, pepper, ginger, tamarides, orange, lemon and palm trees in the 1680s and the early part of the eighteenth century. At this time, too, there was a regular export of corn from the Gold Coast for slave ships.[5] British plantation activities on the Gold Coast were opposed by the Board of Trade on the grounds that it was contrary to the national interest and that the British were only tenants of the land leased from Africans.[6]

By the middle of the eighteenth century there were suggestions in England for developing African agriculture on an extensive scale and for shifting the centres of production of tropical goods from America to Africa.[7] Then, towards the end of the eighteenth century, interest was renewed in plantations in Africa following the American Revolution, which seriously damaged the mercantilist system. By 1785 it was being suggested that to recover from the loss of the American colonies Britain should engage in agriculture instead of commerce on the Gold Coast.[8] The Danes had also been interested in plantations, ever since 1769 when the Danish Government invited the Moravian brethren to introduce plantations to the Gold Coast. These early attempts failed, probably because they were less rewarding than the slave trade.[9]

---

1 Curtin, *The Image of Africa*, Madison, 1964, pp. 68–71; John Peterson, *Province of Freedom*, London, 1969, pp. 55–56

2 Wyndham, *Atlantic and Slavery*, p. 23; Martin, *British West African Settlements*, p. 48

3 West Indische Compagnie 154 (at the Algemeen Rijksarchief in the Hague), letter from Elmina dated 15 Nov. 1689

4 *Ibid.*, letter from Elmina dated 10 Oct. 1703

5 Curtin, *Image of Africa*, p. 69

6 Wyndham, *Atlantic and Slavery*, pp. 22–23; Martin, *British West African Settlements*, p. 48

7 Curtin, *Image*, pp. 69–70   8 *Ibid.*, p. 102

9 Nørregard, *Danish Settlements in West Africa*, p. 173

For the new plantations to be successful, they had to be integrated into the existing farming patterns of the people. The method of farming, although conditioned by environment, was generally that of bush fallowing by which means plots of land were cleared and burned annually for cultivation. Farm production was primarily in the hands of indigenous smallholders, with labour provided mostly by slaves and women. This method of farming was different from the plantations system supported by foreign capital and maintained from outside. Plantations on the Western model required considerable labour distributed throughout the year and stringent supervision. Another difficulty was the use of land and its relation to indigenous social organisations. The introduction of an alien plantation system and increasing commercialisation was destined to bring about changes in traditional land tenure.[1] Furthermore, any efforts to establish plantations could not succeed without a rudimentary mastery of tropical agriculture as well as some botanical knowledge of the area.

Denmark was not the first country to see wastefulness in sending African slaves across the Atlantic to work plantations, but it was the first country to abolish the slave trade and to attempt to replace it by plantation agriculture. In 1787, following the work of a committee appointed to look into the Danish slave trade which was not self-supporting, plans were made to substitute plantations. Paul Isert, a Danish doctor and naturalist who had once visited the Gold Coast, seized this opportunity to go to Africa in order to establish plantations with public funds and the government's blessing.[2] Isert arrived on the Gold Coast in 1788 and proceeded up the Volta River to the island of Malfi, but finding the site unhealthy he proceeded to Akropong Akuapem where the chief, Obuobi Atiemo, leased him a piece of land. The plantation prospered, but Isert died in 1789.[3]

In 1792 the decree abolishing the Atlantic slave trade removed the economic foundation of the Danish settlements on the Gold Coast and caused suggestions in government circles that the possessions should be sold. Other interests favoured retaining them with the intention of cultivating the land and producing cotton, sugar, tobacco and other tropical produce. Consequently, in 1794 a number of Danes settled in the country to cultivate the land and to trade.[4] By 1797 J. P. Wrisberg, the Danish Governor, was urging the people in the Danish settlement to buy gold, cotton, coffee, indigo and other items that they produced rather than slaves.[5] Wrisberg himself began a seventeen-acre cotton plantation worked by slaves who lived in cabins on the property.

1 On traditional land use and agriculture, see S. la Anyane, 'Agriculture in the General Economy' and M. B. Wills, 'The General Pattern of Land Use', in J. B. Wills, ed., *Agriculture and Land Use in Ghana*, Oxford, 1962, pp. 192–200 and pp. 201–25, respectively.

2 Nørregard, *Danish Settlements in West Africa*, pp. 182–3. D. Adams, 'Activities of Danish Botanists in Guinea 1783–1850', *T.H.S.G.* iii, pp. 30–46, 1957 has an extended treatment of Danish plantation activities. Probably the best account of Danish plantation activities on the Gold Coast is H. Jeppesen's 'Danske Plantageaniag po Guldkysten 1788–1850', *G.T.* lxv, pp. 48–88, 1966.

3 Isert's activities are still remembered in Akropong traditions. See Bennett Akuffo's *Ahemfi Adesu Akanfo Amamere*, Akropong, 1950, p. 218.

4 Vestindisk-guineisk Rente-og Generaltoldkammer og Kommerce Sager til Guineisk Journales, No. 365, 1794

5 *Ibid.*, No. 365, 1798

By the beginning of the nineteenth century plantations had become widespread among Danish traders on the coast.[1] The work was performed by slave labour and the plantations were beginning to prosper when they were destroyed by the Asante invasions of the coast and the perpetual insecurity in the wake of the Asante incursions to the south. Although Denmark had suffered serious reverses in her efforts to establish plantations on the Gold Coast, she never lost interest. However, for the first two decades of the nineteenth century there was nothing to show for the Danish projects. According to H. C. Monrad, Danish chaplain on the Gold Coast, 1805–1809, nothing ever would come of the plantations as long as the Danish settlements remained in the hands of hardened slave traders.[2]

At the time when the Danes were trying to replace the slave trade with plantations, some efforts at cultivation were evident in the Dutch territory on the Gold Coast – for example, those of the mulatto, Jan Nieser, dating from 1784.[3] Dutch attempts to encourage plantation agriculture as a viable alternative to the slave trade began in earnest when Governor Daendels arrived on the Gold Coast in 1816 following Holland's abolition of the slave trade. The Governor suggested to the Dutch Department of Trade and Colonies that a number of Dutch families should come to the Gold Coast to undertake cultivation, but nothing came of this proposal.[4] Shortly after his arrival he secured land on which he cultivated cotton with his two sons, but the vigorous cultivation efforts of the Dutch under Daendels waned after his death in 1818 and were not to be revived until the 1840s.

The British also encouraged plantations as an alternative to the slave trade. During the days of the slave trade the Gold Coast settlements had fitted into the mercantilist economic philosophy of the day and had provided the labour for the West Indian plantations. However, when the slave trade was abolished the Company of Merchants trading with Africa urged British traders on the Gold Coast to promote the cultivation and export of agricultural products. Traders on the coast were asked to spend their leisure hours clearing small plots for cultivation.[5] To this end the Committee of the Company of Merchants in Britain periodically forwarded seeds to the coast to be planted and made persistent inquiries concerning their progress.[6] Because cotton grew wild on the Gold Coast it was felt that its systematic cultivation would yield greater quantities for export. In 1809, it was reported that the Governor had started a cotton and coffee garden five miles outside Cape Coast,[7] and in 1811 he was able to send samples of cotton grown in his garden to England.[8]

1 Nørregard, *Danish Settlements in West Africa*, pp. 181–3   2 *Ibid.*, p. 184

3 Daendels, *Correspondence*, 15 Nov. 1816, Jan Nieser to Daendels

4 Archief Van het Ministrie Kolonien, The Hague 3187, 6 Dec. 1816

5 T. 70/73: S. Cock to E. Cooke, 20 and 26 Sept. 1808

6 T. 70/73: African Office to Cape Castle, 4 Aug. 1809, 20 and 26 Sept. 1808, T. 70/74, T. 70/35: Governor to African Committee, 5 May 1809

7 T. 70/35: Governor to the African Committee, 5 May 1809

8 T. 70/35: Governor to the African Committee, 18 Jan. 1811

The Company of Merchants was not the only group to encourage cultivation; the African Institution also championed this cause. The African Institution believed that the wrongs suffered by Africa during the slave trade era could be redressed through the arts of civilisation and that the diffusion of information concerning agriculture and commercial facilities would influence Africa for the good.[1] But despite the efforts during the two decades following abolition very little progress was made in the development of plantations for export purposes.

Europeans normally blamed the lack of success on disputes among the 'natives',[2] the idleness of the people, the poor quality of the soil and destructive ants. According to a contemporary observer, agriculture on the Gold Coast was never going to flourish as long as the representatives of the companies on the coast made their own commercial pursuits the chief object of their attention.[3]

Not only were the merchants on the coast unenthusiastic about plantations; the local people were also slow to respond. As a Governor of Cape Coast Castle wrote:

> I, and so do many of your officers give encouragement to Industry and Agriculture, to what permanent good does it tend? If any Gentleman who has been in this country bears his memory, that the natives of Africa consider a fram-fram soup and a little corn a luxurious meal (as they do to this day and in my opinion to the last,) if such a gentleman will consider that a people so easily satisfied, so trained to idleness from their infancy to allot to females the labour they themselves ought to perform, so bigoted to the customs of their forefathers, I am inclined to think that he with all others possessed of a knowledge of Africa, will be of the opinion with me that unsuccessful will be all endeavours to civilise or dispose to Agriculture the natives of it.[4]

Although the Governor might have overstated his case, his assertion was not without grounds. Implicit in the difficulties was the basic problem of economic development and change, for in any growth from a traditional to an exchange economy, transformations in the institutional and cultural structures of the people are necessary. Evidently, in the Gold Coast, the process of growth involved more than a simple reshaping or altering of the economic structure. The degree of change differed from place to place according to the nature of available local resources, initiative, attitudes and aptitudes of the people.[5] The people did not have the incentive to work harder since most of them were not conditioned to want the things money could buy and which they could not produce or procure locally. They also had traditional uses for leisure – including major religious and social obligations – which they would be highly reluctant to curtail. In this context the often alleged laziness of the people coupled with the lack of labour on the Gold Coast should be viewed in terms of the social and economic institutions of the people. Bauer and Yamey have written that:

1 African Institution, 1st Report, 1809, pp. 1–3

2 T. 70/35: Governor to African Committee, 26 Dec. 1809

3 C.O. 267/48 and T. 70/1604/1; James C. Yeo to Wilson Crowther, 12 March 1818

4 T. 70/36: Governor to Committee of Merchants, 30 April 1814

5 Bauer and Yamey, *Economics of Under-Developed Countries*, p. 4

In subsistence agriculture in particular, as well as in many other farming pursuits, the demands on labour vary greatly with the seasons. Labour which appears to be idle during one season may be indispensable at times of planting or harvesting. There is thus a large element of part-time or seasonal employment. Agricultural production in some cases may be greatly reduced if the necessary supply is not on hand in times of peak demand for labour.[1]

A recent study of the traditional utilisation of labour in agriculture on the Lower Volta in Ghana has also concluded that:

The low level of labour input into farming is largely a function of the short seasonal demand for traditional farming. The main labour requirement is at planting season which lasts for some four to six weeks in April to May and labour requirements fall off after that since less labour is required for weeding.[2]

At the peak of the demand for agricultural labour, farmers worked an average of 3·25 hours a day and a total of 24 days in the month[3] Even today the average Ghanaian farmer is estimated to work only 160–200 days per year.

Thus the effort to find a production-based economy to replace the slave trade has to be viewed in context, both internal and external. Internally one must recognise that there is always resistance to a new money economy. As two economists have affirmed:

In economically backward societies there are difficulties in the way of developing and using the entrepreneurial qualities. The force of custom, the rigidity of status, and the distrust of new ideas and of the exercise of intellectual curiosity combine to create an atmosphere inimical to experiment and innovation.[4]

Obviously abolition did not encourage the people to engage in a plantation economy when it deprived them of part of the market for their surplus agricultural products.[5] The Asante wars hampered production and because of inadequate transportation the goods produced could not easily reach the market. The transportation problem moved a Danish Governor to urge his people to concentrate their plantations in the coastal areas and in locations near the Volta River.[6]

For Europeans who wanted to encourage plantations, the idea of merchants engaged in planting and normal trading activities was an uneasy combination.

---

1 *Ibid.*, pp. 32–33

2 Rowena M. Lawson, 'The Traditional Utilization of Labour in Agriculture on the Lower Volta, Ghana', *E.B.G.* xii, 1, p. 59, 1968

3 *Ibid.*, p. 60

4 Bauer and Yamey, *Economics in Under-Developed Countries*, p. 103

5 *Parl. Papers* 1816: Evidence of James Swanzy, p. 45; *Ibid.*, letter to J. Mollan dated 26 April 1814 and T. 70/1598, 1, 19 April 1814, Report of Diggles Bayless

6 Generaltoldkammer og Kommerce Indiske Koutor 1816–1841. Optegnelser og Akter til Borg for Kellige Kommissioner til Undersogelse af Forholdene i Guinea, p. 94

Both occupations demanded full-time attention and one could not succeed without the neglect of the other. Also, on the Gold Coast where most land was communally owned and where people who were not members of the society could not own land, securing land for plantation purposes was difficult. Furthermore, the attempt to make the Gold Coast a producer of tropical products also presented serious problems since the concept did not fit into the mercantilist philosophy of the day and, moreover, vested interests in the West Indian trade were not going to accept such developments unconditionally. They were bound to protect their interest. In view of these problems, plantation agriculture had made little headway on the Gold Coast by the end of the second decade of the nineteenth century. However, the plantation efforts did not stop there, but continued throughout the century.

The only plantation effort of note between 1828 and 1850 in the British sphere of influence was begun by James Swanzy in 1836. In that year he secured from the Governor of the settlements the old government farm near Cape Coast Castle and started a plantation called 'Napoleon'. Cotton flourished at 'Napoleon' but due to the shortness of the staple it fetched low prices and proved unprofitable. The coffee also grew well; however, as long as African coffee paid a duty of 1s 3d per pound while that from the West Indies paid 6d there was no hope for 'Napoleon' of making a profit. In 1841 Swanzy gave up his plantation and it was taken over by Methodist missionaries who set it up as the model plantation, 'Beula'.[1] According to Andrew Swanzy, one of the reasons for the decline of the plantation was the local government's interference with the use of pawn labour on the coast.[2]

The Dutch, too, renewed their half-hearted attempts at cultivation near Elmina in 1846. In that year a Brazilian named La Rocha Vierra was brought to the Dutch settlement to start cotton plantations. Vierra, a former schoolmaster accustomed to the system of slavery in Brazil, was unable to manage free unskilled labourers on the plantation and lost control of his workers. Frustrated by his failure and by the lack of cooperation from Dutch officials on the coast, Vierra embarked on a ship for Brazil, without even claiming his salary.[3] In 1848, further unsuccessful attempts were made to cultivate tobacco at Elmina and at Simbo. The Dutch blamed their failures on the indolence of the people claiming that:

> The laziness of the people, and their unwillingness to work, was a stumbling-block that no manager could get over. The Labourers were constantly running away, particularly after receiving the wage of a few days' labour. They then declared that they must go home and take their ease for a short time. On the slightest remonstrance or opposition to these resolutions, they ran away. Everywhere messengers were on foot to track out deserters and bring them

1 Henry Swanzy, 'A Trading Family in the Nineteenth Century Gold Coast', *T.G.C.T.H.S.* ii, Pt. 2, p. 97, 1956

2 *Parl. Papers* 1842, XI, Questions 4815, 4816 and 4826, Evidence of A. Swanzy. Obviously the attempt of Madden to enforce the abolition of domestic and pawn labour on the Gold Coast deprived Swanzy of the workers he employed on his plantation.

3 C. J. M. Nagtglas, 'What Must the Netherlands Do with Her Settlements on the Coast of Guinea' (pamphlet translated from the Dutch), p. 2, 1864, London

back to work; but all attempts were fruitless. All attempts to establish a tobacco culture were shipwrecked on the unwillingness, laziness and indifference
of the natives to stick to their work.[1]

As usual, instead of looking at the economic and cultural life of the people to ascertain why inhabitants were reluctant to sell their labour for rewards – monetary or otherwise – Europeans invariably placed the blame on what seemed to
them to be indifference and aversion to work.

The bulk of plantation efforts on the Gold Coast until the last two decades of
the nineteenth century yielded meagre results except for some coffee exports in
the 1830s, some cotton exports during the 1860s and palm oil export beginning
in the 1820s. Palm oil began to figure prominently in the exports from the Gold
Coast in the 1820s, and by the 1850s had replaced ivory as the second leading
export of the Gold Coast. The production of palm oil on the Gold Coast, however, was very low in comparison with the totals from other areas of West
Africa. The palm oil originating from the Gold Coast at this time came mainly
from the Krobo and Akuapem regions in the eastern part of the country and it is
clear that by the beginning of the nineteenth century the Krobos were buying
more land for their expanding palm oil plantations and population. The purchase
of land by the Krobos was to continue for the rest of the nineteenth century.[2]

The developing palm oil trade on the Gold Coast was limited by environmental factors. The palm oil from the Gold Coast was inferior in quality,[3] and
because of the difficulty of transportation the reproducing region of palm oil for
the overseas trade was confined to the area near the coast. Unlike the Gold
Coast the developing palm oil industry in the Oil Rivers on the Nigerian coast
had the advantage of reproducing good quality palm oil as well as having transportation provided by navigable waterways.[4] Although the production of palm
oil on the Gold Coast was never going to approach the level of that in the Niger
Delta, it was going to be a staple export on the Gold Coast to be replaced only
by cocoa at the end of the nineteenth century.

The progress of agricultural pursuits and the introduction of an agricultural
economy to the Gold Coast during the nineteenth century was slow and any
gains made were hard-won. Yet, the slow but gradual contribution that agriculture began to make to the larger world economy in producing palm oil (and
later cocoa) brought about important institutional changes in Gold Coast traditional society.

Asante and abolition

Since Asante was the major supplier for the Atlantic slave trade one would have
assumed that abolition would have affected her more than other states and that

1 *Ibid.*

2 Marion Johnson, 'Migrants' Progress', *B.G.G.A.* ix, 2, p. 7, 1964; *Heidenbote*, Basel,
Switzerland Mission Archives, pp. 6–7, 1867

3 Freda Wolfson, 'A Price Agreement on the Gold Coast – the Krobo Oil Boycott 1858–
1866', *E.H.R.* vi, Series 2 (I, 1953–1954), p. 70

4 For the development of the oil trade in the Niger Delta, see K. O. Dike, *Trade and Politics
of the Niger Delta.*

the loss of income from the trade might have had serious internal repercussions for Asante Union, but this did not happen. Besides the slaves that Asante sold in the overseas trade, she had another equally valuable produce – the kola nut which she sold in the markets of her hinterland. In fact, recent study has shown that the development of Asante trade with Hausa, especially at Salaga was in part a response to the decline and abolition of the slave trade.[1] Consequently, abolition was not very damaging to the Asante economy.

Several factors contributed to enhance development of Asante trade along the north-eastern route through Salaga that joined the major Hausa and Western Sudan trade routes. The moving of Hausa and other Muslim traders into Dagomba and eastern Gonja towards the end of the eighteenth and early nineteenth century stimulated the development of the north-eastern road. Furthermore, the Islamic reform that took place in Hausaland late in the eighteenth century, culminating in Uthman Dan Fodio's jihad in 1804, denied the use of alcoholic stimulants which served to encourage the demand for kola. Thus the development of the north-eastern trade route with Salaga evolving as a major commercial centre helped to meet the new demand for kola as well as provide an alternate market to Asante. With the outlet for slaves removed it was no wonder that Salaga, which was linked with the kola trade, was developed in accordance with Asante government policy.[2]

Bowdich noted the importance of the Asante trade along the eastern trade route and their preference for the markets of the Asante hinterland rather than the coastal markets when he wrote:

> The preference of the Ashantee for the Dagwumba and Inta markets for silk and cloth, results not merely from their having been so long accustomed to it, but because they admit of a barter trade. The Booseee or Gooroo nut, salt, (which is easily procured, and affords an extravagant profit,) and small quantities of European commodities, rum, and iron, yield them those articles of comfort and luxury which they can only purchase with gold and ivory from the settlements on the coast.[3]

While a state like Asante was not much damaged economically by abolition, other states like those on the coast had to make adjustments in relation to the overseas external trade and consequently the attempts to find other products to replace the slave trade were perhaps more important in trading with Europeans.

It is easy to dismiss the early attempts at finding a production-based economy for the Gold Coast as a failure, but it must be conceded, however grudgingly, that they were not without success. Gold exports from the Gold Coast, which had been drastically reduced since the middle of the eighteenth century, became important again after abolition. During their cultivation efforts the Danes learned what kind of soil and conditions were best for growing coffee on the Gold Coast.[4] Some attention was also being directed to the production of palm

---

1 See Ivor Wilks, 'Asante Policy towards the Hausa Trade in the Nineteenth Century' in Meillassoux, ed., *The Development of African Trade and Markets in West Africa*, pp. 124–39

2 *Ibid.*   3 Bowdich, *Mission from Cape Coast Castle*, p. 334

4 Nørregard, *Danish Settlements in West Africa*, p. 182; G. Tko K. K. Indiske Koutor 1816– 1841, Optegnelser og Akter til Brog for Kellige Kommissioner til Undersogelse af Forholdene i Guinea, p. 16

oil and, by 1819, some agricultural produce like corn was being exported from Accra and Secondi to Madeira and the West Indies.[1] Furthermore, it must be remembered that the two decades following abolition were not only a period of transition but a period of wars that hampered economic growth.

At the end of the third decade of the nineteenth century there were no far-reaching changes in the structure of trade, and the character of the imports and exports had remained basically unchanged since the era of the slave trade. Any changes could take place only as a result of the increasing participation in production for market of the traditional economy.[2] As long as the basic needs of the people are supplied from a near subsistence production with the incentive to earn cash limited to the need to acquire some luxury items,[3] the point is reached when leisure is preferred to cash incomes. Furthermore, the traditional interior trade and markets seemingly served the economic needs of the people adequately. Although by 1828, as at the beginning of the nineteenth century, there were elements of a modern market economy, the changes in the institutional structure of the people and the transformation needed in the traditional economy to bring about modernisation of the commercial life of the Gold Coast had not yet taken place.

1 Thomas E. Bowdich, *The British and French Expeditions to Teembo, with Remarks on Civilization in Africa*, Paris, 1821, p. 12

2 United Nations, *Enlargement of the Exchange Economy in Tropical Africa*, New York, 1954, p. 1

3 *Ibid.*, p. 38

CHAPTER THREE

The economy in transition, 1828–1850

The wars between Asante and her southern neighbours, supported by the English and the Danes, resulted in a victory for the allies in 1826 at the Battle of Katamansu. These wars (1823–1824 and 1826) had disrupted the peace and commercial life of the country, and prospects of trade were no more promising after the defeat of Asante than at the outbreak of hostilities. Rankling hatred between the British allies on the coast who were fighting and squabbling among themselves had severed communications with the interior and trade was almost annihilated.[1] This invariably led to retrenchment in some of the European commercial establishments on the coast.

Danes and the eastern region

Despite their reversals, the failure of their plantation attempts, and the diminishing returns from their settlements, Denmark showed remarkable resilience. Hoping to start a profitable trade between the West Indies and the Gold Coast, a Danish investigating committee which arrived in the country in 1827 constructed a mill to export maize flour. These attempts to export flour were unprofitable as it was fit only for pigs on arrival in the West Indies.[2] In 1827 the Danes also sent a mission up the Volta River to ascertain the economic value of the forests along the banks of the river. This expedition left Christiansborg in December and returned in February 1828. It reported that there was enough timber along the river banks to build between 200 and 300 ships, but the expense of transportation to Denmark was prohibitive. The mission also felt it would be unwise to establish settlements along the river because it was swampy and unhealthy. Nonetheless it intimated the Danes could profit from the salt production at Ada.[3]

It was no coincidence that these new attempts of the Danes to develop their settlements were simultaneous with the beginnings of the palm oil trade in the eastern region; the attitude of Danish officials at Christiansborg towards the peace treaty after the Asante war underlined a new economic interest in the eastern region. Since the Danish merchants had a number of high-ranking Asante prisoners, their cooperation was essential for the conclusion of any peace

1 Cruickshank, *Eighteen Years*, i, p. 170

2 Nørregard, *Danish Settlements in West Africa*, pp. 187–8

3 *G.J.* 1828, No. 141

treaty. When the question of a money deposit to ensure that Asante kept the peace in the future arose in 1827, the Danes demanded that half of the sum should be deposited at Christiansborg, but the British authorities declined to consider the request.[1] The Danish Governor, Broch, protested against the British attitude and informed the latter that they would make their own treaty with Asante. Another element of contention was the extent to which the eastern states of Akyem, Akuapem and Akwamu were under Danish authority.[2]

In March 1830, the Danes and the British signed an agreement forbidding separate treaties with Asante and bidding both nations to conclude peace with Asante on equal terms.[3] The peace treaty talks between the British and the Danes were interrupted by a quarrel between the British Commandant at Accra and the Danish Governor. Fry, the British Commandant, had been annoyed by the fact that when British ships anchored off Accra, traders from the Danish settlements had boarded them before their British rivals to the detriment of the latter. But as Metcalfe has pointed out, British captains would not have gone to Christiansborg to trade if it had not paid them to do so.[4] When the matter reached the Committee of Merchants they suggested that the ships calling at the Gold Coast should be visited first by their own nationals.[5]

Meanwhile, to get the peace talks going, Asante prisoners held by the Danes had to be released. H. Richter, the Danish merchant, held a number of the important Asante prisoners and it is surprising that he, together with James Bannerman, cooperated heartily with Maclean on the peace treaty.[6] Probably, to persuade him to give up his slaves, Maclean had to make a concession to Richter to enable him to trade with British ships on equal terms with British merchants. Such a concession to Richter would be the most likely explanation of the conflict between him on the one hand, and Governor Hein and the merchant Lutterodt on the other, which split the Danes into two parties in 1831.[7]

Despite this agreement with the Danes to sign a peace treaty with Asante on equal terms, the British made their own peace with the Asante in April 1831. This treaty prevented a major war until 1863. Under its terms the Asantehene gave two hostages, his son and nephew, to the British authorities and deposited 600 ounces of gold at Cape Coast Castle with the understanding that these securities were to remain in the castle for a period of six years. For the better regulation of commerce it was stipulated that 'the paths shall be perfectly open and free to all persons engaged in lawful traffic and persons molesting them in any way whatever, or enforcing them to purchase at any particular market, or influencing them by any unfair means whatever, shall be declared guilty of infringing this treaty and be liable to the severest punishment'. Another important provision was that 'panyarring, denouncing, and swearing, on or by any person or thing whatever, are hereby strictly forbidden, and all persons infringing this rule shall be rigorously punished and no master or chief shall be answerable for the crimes of his servants, unless done by his orders or consent, or when

---

1 Metcalfe, *Maclean*, p. 49   2 *Ibid.*

3 Nørregard, *Danish Settlements in West Africa*, p. 200 and Metcalfe, *Maclean*, pp. 80–81

4 Metcalfe, *Maclean*, pp. 82–84   5 *Ibid.*   6 *Ibid.*

7 *G.J.* 1832, Nos. 283, 285 and 300

under his contract'. The Asantehene also renounced his suzerainty over Denkyera, Assin and other coastal states.[1] This treaty accepted at Cape Coast by the
chiefs in the western region remained to be ratified by the people of the eastern
region,[2] but it seems that instead of signing a proper treaty, they only assented
to the terms on 27 April 1831.[3] The omission of the eastern region, especially
Akuapem and Krobo, from the treaty and the question of whether these people
were Danish allies or subjects inevitably resulted in a clash between George
Maclean and the Danish Governor Morch from 1835–1839.[4]

As early as 1821 English traders at Accra were reported to be sending presents to Akuapem in order to obtain trade, and by the 1830s there were rumours
of the British attempts to bribe Akuapem and Akyem to detach themselves from
the Danish interest. Undoubtedly the basis of British interest in Akuapem was
economic and at a time when the eastern region was becoming economically important because of the palm oil trade, conflict between the two powers was inevitable. The unavoidable dissention occurred after Frederick S. Morch became
the Governor of the Danish settlements in December, 1834. Morch made the
most redoubtable efforts to extend Danish influence and to gain control of the
eastern district. These were thwarted by the British, but Morch based his claim
on the treaty with the 'Republic of Krobo' that Isert in his ignorance of the area
had concluded in 1787 with Obuobi Atiemo, the Paramount Chief of Akuapem.
When Morch arrived on the coast he thought that the Akuapem were pro-
British and went there in 1835 to find out the true situation for himself.[5] While
in Akuapem he discovered that sub-chiefs there had revolted against Ado Dankwa, the Paramount Chief, and that there was a conflict between them and the
Krobos over Akuapem's claim over them. The Governor attempted to settle the
dispute between Akuapem and Krobo and invited the Krobos to come to Akropong. The Krobos politely refused because they felt their presence in Akuapem
would mean yielding to Ado Dankwa's claim over them. They told Morch they
would gladly do him homage in Krobo. Misunderstanding the situation, the
Governor sent a punitive expedition against the Krobos; the Akuapems, who
had a grudge against them, gladly participated. The expedition was quickly
over with the Akuapems destroying some of the palm oil plantations of their
enemies. The Krobos were fined 1,500 heads of cowries and because they had no
means of paying, had to relinquish their palm oil harvest. The Danish merchant,
H. Richter, farmed the fine and received the palm oil in compensation from the
Krobos.[6]

This meant that no oil was reaching the British merchants, and African traders
who had been advanced goods could not meet their obligations.[7] The dispute
over Krobo led to a conflict between Morch and Maclean. Initially, Morch received the support of the Danish Government in the matter, but later they came
to side with the British and asked their Governor not to do anything to harm

1 Reindorf, *Gold Coast and Asante*, 2nd ed., pp. 252–3

2 Metcalfe, *Maclean*, p. 88   3 *Ibid.*, pp. 92 and 95

4 Nørregard, *Danish Settlements in West Africa*, p. 207   5 *Ibid.*, p. 206

6 Metcalfe, *Maclean*, pp. 198–200 and M. A. Kwamena-Poh, *Government and Politics in the
   Akuapem State, 1730–1850*, Longman 1973, pp. 62–5, 104–5

7 *Ibid.*

British trade on the Gold Coast. In the meantime, devastated by his failures, Morch became an alcoholic and died in 1839. Although as late as 1842 Governor Edward Carstensen was attempting to involve the Danes in the palm oil trade,[1] it seemed that the days of the Danish settlements were numbered.

Meanwhile, however, the Danish invitation to the Basel Missionary Society of Switzerland to start mission work on the Gold Coast in 1828 was to have far-reaching consequences for the economy.[2] These missionaries who were always thoroughly trained in mission and trade methods at Basel were a valuable body of men, not only in their evangelical work, but also as pioneers in every kind of endeavour intended to improve and to promote what they considered to be the social interests of those among whom they laboured. Many of the early missionaries died, and the mission had achieved little by 1843. In that year Andreas Riis, who had arrived on the coast in 1832 and had in 1835 moved to Akropong Akuapem, went to Jamaica to recruit six West Indian families (twenty-four persons) to settle at Akropong as the nucleus of a Christian congregation to show the indigenous population that Christianity was not just for the white man.[3] Although some of the West Indians returned to Jamaica, others remained to leave a lasting contribution to the development of the Ghana Presbyterian Church. The names of some of them and their descendants like Hall, Clerk and Mullings are landmarks in the history of the Ghana Presbyterian Church.

The Dutch

After the Asante wars, the Dutch did not give up hope of making their Gold Coast settlements profitable. Between 1825 and 1828 attempts at mining were made in the neighbourhood of Elmina, but these failed. Apparently it was the wrong place to mine gold. The Dutch did not resume mining until 1843,[4] when they sent a German scientist, Housch, to the Gold Coast to pursue mineralogical research. Housch spent some time at Dobokrom, but fell ill and returned to Europe.[5] Some mining was done at Dobokrom until all the labourers ran away.[6] Housch returned to the Gold Coast in 1845 as the chief director of gold mines on the Gold Coast with three engineers, two assistant engineers, sixteen miners, smiths and carpenters. Two of the engineers and nine of the miners died before the work could begin.[7] To obtain sufficient labour and supplies for the miners the Dutch Government concluded an agreement with the chiefs of nearby Ahanta towns to supply the mines with workers and provisions.[8] There were a number of mining pits which had long been abandoned by the local people as they did not yield enough for the labour spent on them. It was at this place the Dutch chose to work; it proved to be an enterprise with little results. A second expedition was sent in 1847, but this was no more fortunate than the previous ones and

1 *G.J.* 1842, No. 347

2 The trading activities of the Basel missionaries are discussed in ch. 5.

3 N. T. Clerk, *A Short Centenary Sketch, the Settlement of the West Indian Immigrants on the Gold Coast 1843–1943*, Accra, 1943, pp. 1–8

4 F.C., 28 May 1828 and 6 July 1828   5 F.C., 16 and 26 Jan. 1843

6 *Ibid.*   7 F.C., 8 Jan. 1845   8 *Ibid.*, 23 Jan. 1845

the Dutch Government decided not to sacrifice any more lives or money on gold washing or mining.[1]

As Dutch efforts during this period to make their Gold Coast settlements profitable failed, Holland's interest in these settlements became secondary to those in the East Indies. To help build the necessary army for their expansion in this area, they decided to recruit troops from the Gold Coast. In 1831 Governor Last was asked to raise 1,800 people to form a colonial military corps for service in Java. The soldiers, who were to serve for six years, would be repatriated at the end of their term, when they would receive a pension payable either in the East Indies or in Elmina.[2]

Securing troops proved difficult. Local people were unwilling to volunteer for Java, and in six years only forty-four men offered their services. So the Dutch Governor decided to send people into the interior to purchase slaves to be used as troops. He offered an ounce of gold for valuable slaves and half an ounce for others.[3] The new scheme of recruitment was put into effect in 1836 when General Verver was appointed to head a mission to seek recruits in Asante.[4] He arrived in Kumasi in 1837, entered into an agreement with the Asantehene to provide 2,000 slaves, and W. Huydercooper was appointed the Dutch agent. After the agreement the Asantehene received substantial gifts from the Dutch, but the flow of slaves from Asante to Java proved irregular.[5]

The Dutch recruits who were slaves were brought down to the coast under the escort of soldiers, freed, given emancipation papers and then kept until ships were available to transport them to the East Indies.[6] Dutch authorities on the Gold Coast claimed that the difficulty of securing troops was due to the persistence of the slave trade. They said people preferred to sell their slaves for higher prices on the leeward coast.[7]

The first phase of Dutch recruitment on the Gold Coast terminated in 1842 because of serious attacks by the British.[8] It was resumed in 1855, but did not reach the earlier level. From 1837 to 1842, 1,887 slaves were sent to Java.[9] Although the British were opposed to the Dutch activities, their own 'voluntary' emigration from Sierra Leone to the West Indies in the 1840s, and the virtual conscription of recaptives into the British West Indian regiment, were hardly distinguishable from the abuses they attacked when committed by other powers.

George Maclean and the Gold Coast

The Asante wars and the diminishing trade at the British forts made Britain reconsider her commitments on the Gold Coast. The wars had been expensive for England and since it was believed that there was little to be gained from the con-

1 Nagtglas, *What Must the Netherlands Do*, p. 2

2 F.C., 4, 9, 17 and 24 Dec. 1831   3 F.C., 20 June 1836   4 *Ibid.*

5 Dantzig, 'Dutch Recruitment in Kumasi', p. 22

6 *Parl. Papers* 1842, Report of Select Committee in West Africa 1842, Evidence of F. Swanzy, Q.1543

7 F.C., 27 April 1835 and F.C., 7 Oct. 1840   8 F.C., 2 Feb. 1842

9 Some of these people later returned to Elmina on Dutch pensions.

flict, Britain speculated about giving up her forts.[1] By March 1827 Britain had decided to abandon the Gold Coast and the Governor was instructed to take immediate measures for withdrawing officers of the government stationed at the settlements.[2] Under pressure from local merchants, however, the government offered British resident merchants willing to leave the coast any assistance they needed; but those who wanted to stay were asked to embody themselves and their labourers into an armed militia. These merchants were to be given a sum not more than £2,000 for the first year, £1,500 the second year and £1,000 afterwards to support the militia. Beyond this help they were to remain on the coast at their own risk and could not expect any other assistance from Britain in protecting themselves and the forts against aggression.[3]

Meanwhile, in the course of 1828 proposals were made for the future administration of the Gold Coast forts which provided that the occupied forts, Cape Coast and Accra, were to continue as dependencies of Sierra Leone; the forts were to be regulated by a committee chosen by the government; five of the resident merchants were empowered to form themselves into a council of government, all of whom were to be appointed Justices of the Peace; an annual sum not exceeding £4,000 was placed at the disposal of the Committee of London Merchants on behalf of the resident traders for the maintenance and defence of the forts; and the ports of Cape Coast and Accra were to be open to all vessels without payment of any duty.[4] The first Committee of London Merchants included George Barnes, Robert Brown and Matthew Forster with a resident merchant on the coast, John Jackson, appointed as the first president of the Council of Merchants, but in 1835, a new committee consisting of J. G. Nicholls, Joseph Reid and William Hutton replaced the first one. George Maclean arrived on the Gold Coast in February 1830 as a full-time, non-mercantile president.[5]

Since conflicts in 1807, 1811, 1814–1816, 1823–1824 and 1826 had been devastating for commercial activities the principal task that faced Maclean was to secure peace between Asante and the coastal states. The prosperity on the Gold Coast for the years following the treaty was to a large measure due to the peace and the administration of Maclean. As Brodie Cruickshank wrote:

> The acknowledgment of the independence of the Fantees and other allied tribes, which the English government wrung from the Ashantees, relieved the country from its most oppressive load; and the consequent supervision of its general policy by the government, effected such a salutary improvement in the increased facility and security of communication, that such redress as the peculiar circumstances of the social condition of the people admitted, was open to all.[6]

1 C.O. 267/65: Turner to Bathurst, 24 March 1825

2 C.O. 268/26: Bathurst to Campbell, 21 March 1827   3 *Ibid.*

4 C.O. 268/27: Hay to Barnes, Brown and Forster, 30 Oct. 1828

5 For a good short summary of the work of Maclean, see J. D. Fage, 'The Administration of George Maclean on the Gold Coast, 1830–1844', *T.G.C.T.H.S.* i, part 4, pp. 104–20, 1955; and for an excellent biography, see Metcalfe, *Maclean of the Gold Coast.*

6 Cruickshank, *Eighteen Years*, ii, p. 5. This section relies heavily upon Brodie Cruickshank's books and letters. From 1835 to 1854 he was an agent of the Merchant House of Forster and Smith. He seems to have become a leading spokesman of the merchant community by

The presidency of Maclean marked a key period of transition in trade and economic change. As Cruickshank referring to the period of Maclean so rightly expressed it: 'From this time we are to date a new era in the history of the Gold Coast.'[1] And indeed it was a new era. The secret of his success lay in his use of an African force. When Maclean assumed office the whole physical force consisted of a local corps of 120 locally enlisted men, many of whom had served in the Royal African Corps that had fought in the Asante war and were eminently qualified for the services in which Maclean was to engage them.[2] Andrew Swanzy has aptly summed up the work of George Maclean for peace and commerce on the Gold Coast:

> During the life of Mr. Maclean commercial frauds or direct plunder were absolutely unknown . . . The decisions of the English magistrates were implicitly trusted, because they were founded by English notions of justice and humanity, and punishment both prompt and severe was dealt out to the wrong doer. Traders and travellers in the Protectorate were then as safe as in an English turnpike-road, and peace was effectively maintained.[3]

One of the significant developments that contributed to the spectacular economic growth that took place during the governship of Maclean was the extension of British judicial influence and the peace it brought to the country. Maclean's government had limited authority; strictly speaking, it did not have any jurisdiction on the Gold Coast beyond the towns and villages immediately lying under the guns of the different forts. But because of the disorganised and lawless state of the country the local government was induced to assume an authority not sanctioned by the British Government.

Judicial influence

When Goerge Maclean became Governor in 1830, the area between Axim and Elmina was claimed and controlled by the Dutch. Likewise, the Danes also claimed jurisdiction over the area from Christiansborg to Ada as well as the areas of Akyem, Akuapem and Krobo. Two types of areas came under the influence of the British areas where the English maintained forts and areas like Asin, Denkyina, Twifu and Wassa which had maintained no formal relations with the British prior to 1824.[4] In discussing the British jurisdiction under Maclean, G. E. Metcalfe writes:

---

the 1840s. When the Poll Tax Ordinance was passed in 1852 he was appointed the first Collector-General. From August 1853 to January 1854 he was the Acting Governor of the Gold Coast. He was assassinated in Lisbon in 1854. See Allen, *The Gold Coast, or a Cruise in West African Waters*, p. 16.

1 Cruickshank, *Eighteen Years*, ii, p. 15

2 C.O. 96/22: Cruickshank to Forster, 6 Feb. 1847; C.O. 96/4: Maclean to Stanley, 5 Feb. 1844; Cruickshank, *Eighteen Years*, ii, p. 15

3 Andrew Swanzy, 'On Trade in West Africa with and without British Protection, *J.S.A.* xxii, p. 479, 1874

4 Metcalfe *Maclean*, pp. 146–47

The attacks on kidnapping, human sacrifice, closing of the paths or actual warfare among the tribes were necessarily the first targets for the President's jurisdiction. Until they were eliminated, the possibilities of redress for private wrongs were remote; but all these tended to involve chiefly prerogative.[1]

In essence, the growth of the judicial influence of Maclean was the usurpation of the essential functions of local African government and a consequent reduction in the traditional power and influence of local African rulers. Illustrative of Maclean's extending power was the expedition he sent out in 1835 against Kojo Tsibu of Denkyena or Kweku Aka of Nzima for committing atrocities like the sacrifice of human victims at funeral customs.[2] An outcome of the expedition against Kweku Aka was the promulgation in February, 1835, of the *Rules for the Government of Apollonia* which revealed the nature of the relationship between Maclean and the people under the influence of the British. The document forbade chiefs to put to death any person under any pretext; those who committed crimes deserving death were to be sent to Cape Coast to be judged. Kidnapping and panyarring which were causes of constant strife were to be stopped and Maclean undertook to recover debts with all expenses if a debtor positively refused or evaded payment of his just debt.[3] Maclean's extension of British jurisdiction was going to have at least two important implications for trade and economic development on the Gold Coast. It would allow merchants to settle their trade problems and recover their debts. Furthermore, the Governor could prevent anything that would hamper the peaceful trade. Besides the benefits that the jurisdiction might have conferred, it afforded Africans a cheaper justice and in effect reduced the judicial role of African leaders.

To maintain peace and security for commerce as many of the African force as could be spared from garrison duty at the forts were distributed throughout the whole country on the main roads and in the principal inland towns to act as policemen in order to maintain order, keep the roads open and secure and report serious incidents that might rupture the peace.[4] In maintaining the peace which helped the prosperity of trade Maclean's own words describing his procedure are worth quoting at length:

> Ever since I succeeded in concluding peace with Ashantee, and in reducing to a state of tranquillity and order the whole of the extensive country denominated British Territory, I have invariably had a number of soldiers stationed, singly in various parts of the country, who, although entrusted with the exercise of no power, are yet charged with the execution of duties at once delicate and onerous. For example, I have three soldiers stationed at different points on the line of roads leading to the frontiers of Ashantee – a distance from Cape Coast Castle of one hundred miles. The duties of these men are to afford protection to all traders, to see that the traders themselves conduct themselves properly, and, generally to see that the roads are kept free from obstruction of every kind; while it is also their special duty, as well as the duty of all my other soldiers stationed at Out Posts in the interior, to give me the earliest information of any disputes having arisen, or likely to arise, betwixt

1 *Ibid.*, p. 151   2 *Ibid.*, pp. 151–68   3 *Ibid.*, pp. 166–7

4 C.O. 96/11: Cruickshank to Forster, 6 Feb. 1847

any two or more chiefs. By these measures I am enabled at all times, even with my limited means, to prevent any disturbances in the country, because I am enabled to bring my whole influence to bear on any particular point, before any overt acts of hostility have been committed by contending parties.[1]

The mode of trade during this period was described thus:

In those days the ordinary course of business was as follows:—The English merchants on the Gold Coast were supplied with credit with such goods as they required by their London correspondents principally by the well-known firms of Messrs. Forster and Smith and Messrs. W. B. Hatton and Sons, and as the transactions were very considerable and attended with much risk, great care was necessary in selecting the persons to whom advances were made, the consequence was that the resident English merchants, though few in number, were generally men of education and ability; and acting as magistrates and civil commandants in districts in which they resided, they exercised a great and beneficial influence over the natives. The native traders purchased their goods from these gentlemen, and also from British and Hamburg trading-ships, generally on credit, as they possessed but little capital, and they paid for the goods so advanced to them in three or four months, according to the state of trade. During my six years' residence on the coast, from 1844 to 1850, such debts were fairly met, and a very large business carried on; indeed, our outstanding accounts, due by the natives of Dixcove and that neighbourhood, amounted generally from £12,000 to £15,000.[2]

Probably one of the most significant developments in trade and economic change was the emergence of a number of African merchants who occupied the same position in commercial affairs as the European traders. According to Andrew Swanzy during this time a number of Africans were 'admitted to the same advantages as the resident English traders, and received their supplies direct from the London firms'.[3] Among the Africans who were to be given the opportunity of receiving goods directly from London firms on credit in the course of the period were James Bannerman, George Blankson Sr., Sam Kanto Brew, R. J. Ghartey, James Robert Thompson, Frank Cleland, Robert Hutchinson, F. C. Grant, John Sarbah, Thomas Hughes, Joseph Smith, Henry Barnes, J. C. Hansen, William Lutterodt, L. Hesse and J. E. Richter – to name but a few. In fact, most of these Africans who became prominent merchants in the country received goods on credit from London firms and exchanged the goods they received for produce of the country.[4]

Mass participation and changes in trade

While trading was restricted and the privilege of acting as brokers for the interior people was confined to the chiefs the mass of people were precluded from acquiring wealth. According to Cruickshank wealth was not within the reach of

1 C.O. 96/4: Maclean to Stanley, 5 Feb. 1844

2 Swanzy, 'On Trade in Western Africa with and without British Protection', p. 479

3 *Ibid.*   4 *Ibid.*

many and riches had been far from abundant in the country. At a time when pawning was very common, only the well-off could redeem their relations.[1] Cruickshank related that: 'While this state of matters continued, the general body of the people who felt most the pressure of their separate bondage, had no opportunity of acquiring means to purchase their own redemption, or that of their relatives.'[2] In situations where a pawn who had a bad master could not be redeemed, recourse was often made to a wealthy person who had the reputation of being a good man to purchase him from the cruel master.[3]

A second phase of development in trade could be said to have begun with the peace with Asante; this phase marks the inception of the participation in the trade by the masses of the people. 'No sooner was it fully apparent that protection was afforded to every one, than a new spirit seemed to pervade the general mass of the people,' wrote Cruickshank. 'It was like the awakening from a dream which had dissipated the senses, and left no tangible impression upon the mind, and required a process of careful reflection to arrive at a proper comprehension of their position.'[4]

After the peace treaty in 1831 the Asante realised that the chances of being molested on their way to the coast were at an end and the practice of being assigned to a chief on the coast for the sake of protection was no longer necessary. With peace and security established, Asante traders to the coast were relieved of the inconvenience of travelling in large numbers and paying exorbitant fees to the coastal chiefs for brokerage transactions. In place of the chiefs and rulers the inland traders found out that there were now thousands of people who were eagerly seeking to be employed as brokers willing to offer their services at a moderate fee.[5]

The people of the coastal towns who were largely dependent on the trade with the interior were interested in the traders' recourse to the towns. Inland traders to the coast brought with them trains of slaves to help carry back goods purchased on the coast. Since there was no accommodation for travellers, some coastal people made a living housing traders and their suites. Others lived by providing food for the strangers. Although no charge was made for lodging, an inland trader was expected to allow his host to act as his broker. In order to attract trade merchants paid a brokerage fee of about 3% on the amount of purchases made by the trader.[6]

It was customary for the host-brokers personally to introduce the inland traders to the merchants. Traders of relatively small purchasing power with 5 to 50 ounces of gold to spend were introduced together, but those with 100 ounces of gold to spend were accorded special treatment. They, with some of their slaves, were conducted by the broker to be presented on an individual basis to a given storekeeper and his gold-takers. This introduction was followed by polite conversation about the journey and health of the trader and his party. Drinks were then served, after which one or two clay pipes with tobacco leaves were usually presented. The broker then stated the amount of gold the trader anticipated spending and the trader specified the items of merchandise required.

1 Cruickshank, *Eighteen Years*, ii, p. 19   2 *Ibid.*, ii, p. 20

3 *Ibid.*, ii, p. 21   4 *Ibid.*, ii, p. 16   5 *Ibid.*, ii, p. 32

6 Hutchinson, 'The Gold Trade of the Gold Coast 1826 to 1890', *E.D.M.* xii, 3, p. 149, 1924

Then the storekeeper displayed samples of the desired trade items and the discussion would end with more drinks after which the traders and their slaves would return to their accommodation in the town.

The following morning the trader, accompanied by his broker, returned to the store with his principal attendant and porters with ivory or other goods. Each trader carried what was called a 'goldbook' in which the trader entered the amount due to him after appraising the value of his produce.

After the assessment of the goods came the careful task of weighing and testing the gold. Then the trader and his broker were again treated to drinks before they left the store. The trader normally spent a few days in the town visiting and inspecting various stores and before returning home he and his broker took the 'goldbook' to the storekeeper to begin the process of selecting purchases.

Trading methods in relation to one specific merchant, James Bannerman, were recorded by Sir Henry Huntley who observed:

> Mr. Bannerman transacted all the trading that came before him. His method of doing this had a singularity about it; the natives, perhaps twenty or thirty, would enter the town, each bringing a little gold dust, often under half an ounce; they sent to inform Mr Bannerman of their arrival, he returned some answer sufficient to convey an invitation to barter, but expressive of no exact desire for it; a day or two passed, and they sent to say that they would come to look at the goods he had; at the appointed time, the whole body came in procession, some carrying a little bit of rag tied up, and containing the gold; the goods were displayed, and after a time food was given to them, so far they were gainers; they made an offer, Mr Bannerman all this time was walking backwards and forwards on his verandah above, apparently indifferent to the whole proceeding, and refusing or acquiescing but by a simple monosyllable, he said nothing more; all day the country traders were crouching about the yard, nor left till sunset; this scene was repeated for days, the object of the African being to weary out the patience of the Englishman, an attempt utterly futile as it applied to Mr Bannerman; at length the respective parties agreed, the gold dust was weighed and tested, a very necessary precaution, the merchandise chosen, the traders fed, and by the evening they were on their journey to their own homes.[1]

During this period returning prosperity among the indigenous people led to an increase in the internal slave trade. Cruickshank observed that 'while the diffusion of wealth and the progress of knowledge are creating a spirit of industry, and exciting a desire for greater freedom among the native Fantees, a fresh tide of slavery is pouring into the country from another direction', and that 'several thousands were added to the population of the country under our protection every year'.[2] These slaves were imported in large numbers annually in the country through Asante from the north with their price varying from £6 to £8. They passed under the general name of 'Donko' and provided most of the labour for the country.[3] The significance of the importation of slaves into the Gold Coast at a time of rapid economic growth cannot be overrated. It would

---

1 H. Huntley, *Seven Years' Service on the Slave Coast of West Africa*, London, 1850, 2 vols., ii, pp. 81–82

2 Cruickshank, *Eighteen Years*, ii, p. 246   3 *Ibid.*, ii, p. 244

seem that such slaves were not only a source of labour, but a form of capital investment as well.

The beginning of the possibility of accumulating wealth among a wider group inevitably led to the third phase. It was noted that 'the certainty of protection, and the profitable nature of mercantile speculation at the time, allured numbers to try their fortune as trading adventurers', and consequently 'small capitalists invested what gold they had in goods, and either carried them into the interior, or sent them in charge of confidential agents to be sold'.[1]

The apparent success of those who engaged in the carrying trade to the interior changed the whole trading system. Merchants on the coast began to realise that the goods transported inland for sale were reducing the profits at their stores and factories on the coast. They were, therefore, forced to participate in the trade to the interior and employed agents to whom goods were sent.[2]

The carrying trade had a dramatic effect upon the people of the Gold Coast and even affected the landscape of the country:

> Instead of the dull, stagnant, lifeless appearance which the country presented some time before, the monotony of which was only varied occasionally by an act of gross outrage, or the sudden outbreak of an old hereditary feud, all was now cheerful bustle and activity. There was not a nook or corner of the land to which the enterprise of some sanguine trader had not led him. Every village had its festoons of Manchester cottons and China silks, hung up upon the walls of the houses, or round the trees in the marketplace, to attract the attention and excite the cupidity of the villagers.[3]

As the trade to the interior increased, most of the important towns on the route to Asante became extensive depots where all kinds of European goods were available for purchase. There were also many trade agents in Kumasi, the capital of Asante.[4] For example, when the Rev. T. B. Freeman visited Asante in 1839 he found a considerable Fante population just outside Fomena at Kwisa.[5] Freeman reported: 'I was delighted to find in Quissah several Fantees members of our society who had come hither for trading purposes.'

Since there was no beast of burden to carry the merchandise into the interior, thousands of people were employed to transport the goods inland.[6] The inland trade also became open to everyone, including slaves. Cruickshank tells of a Mossi slave at Cape Coast called Bissoo who made his fortune in the carrying trade. After the peace of 1831 opened the interior for trade, his master granted him freedom to go inland. Bissoo invested the little money he had in goods and obtained additional supplies on credit. He transported the merchandise into Wassa and exchanged it for gold and ivory. The slave became wealthy through his trade and it is related that 'all idea of servitude was swallowed up in his riches, which also supplied the means of overcoming the prejudices of the Cape Coast cabboceers, and of elevating him to an equal rank with them'.[7] The penetration of European goods into the interior and their general availability to the people made them necessities. As was reported:

1 *Ibid.*, ii, p. 32   2 *Ibid.*, ii, pp. 32–33   3 *Ibid.*, ii, p. 33   4 *Ibid.*

5 Metcalfe, *Maclean*, p. 132. Also see John Mensah Sarbah, *Fanti Customary Laws*, London, 1904 and *M.M.A.* MS dated 11 March 1839

6 Cruickshank, *Eighteen Years*, ii, p. 33   7 *Ibid.*, i, p. 244

Since the commencement of the carrying trade, they had become accustomed to many trifling luxuries within the reach of their scanty pay, to which they had formerly been strangers. These had now become absolutely necessary to them, and they were willing to turn their hands to any work, in order to obtain the means of procuring them.[1]

The nature of the trade became one of simple credit based on trust which became very widespread and led to the diffusion of property among all classes of people. The widespread credit necessarily meant that a large number of the people would default in the payment of their debt obligations. The result of the inability to pay one's debts resulted in pawning which often implicated innocent relatives. However, as it turned out, Maclean introduced a system of limited liability by which 'relations were relieved from all responsibility respecting debts incurred without their especial suretyship'. Despite the new system the old custom of pawning relatives continued and the English courts could act only when an application was made to them.[2] Yet, notwithstanding the influence of an established custom, in preventing the relief which was put within their reach being universally or even generally accepted, the knowledge that it might be had recourse to, had a very sensible effect in curtailing the extent of credit.[3] An examination of the prison records of this time also indicates that a large number of the prisoners at Cape Coast were debtors.[4]

The question of slaves also came to the attention of Maclean's court. When a slave initiated judicial proceedings an investigation was made into the nature of the master's claim over him. If the master's claim was valid and he could prove that money had been paid for him the slave was obliged to pay the price for his freedom. The amount paid was normally £8 or two ounces of gold which was the price of a slave.[5] Since most slaves were without the means to redeem themselves it was often arranged for them to work at the forts on half wages, the other half being retained or paid to their masters in consideration of their redemption from slavery.[6] Since slaves were both property and 'capital', the interference with slavery was undoubtedly a hindrance to economic development in a society where there were few choices for the investment of capital.

The limitation of credit, partly due to the operation of the British courts and the reduction of prices, and the end of price agreements imposed by a 'self-constituted Board of Trade' dealt the carrying trade a death-blow. This led to the emergence of a fourth phase of trade. With the end of the restriction upon trade, stores on the coast were able to make reductions in their prices and to induce inland traders to come to the coast in greater numbers than before to purchase goods, instead of buying them from petty traders or from depots in the interior. Inland traders came to prefer this mode of trading for obvious reasons:

The greater choice of merchandise in the stores of the merchants, the presents which the traders were in the habit of receiving, and which eventually became an established perquisite, their little consideration of the value of time,

1 *Ibid.*, ii, p. 40   2 *Ibid.*, ii, pp. 35–37   3 *Ibid.*, ii, p. 39

4 C.O. 96/6, 7: List of Prisoners, Extract of Cases Adjudicated upon in Cape Coast Castle

5 Cruickshank, *Eighteen Years*, ii, pp. 228–29

6 C.O. 96/8: Stanley to Maclean, 3 July 1845; *Ibid.*, Letter of Stanley, 20 June 1845

and their consequent indifference about the length of their journey, combined with more consideration for themselves, and greater fairness of dealing than guided the transactions of adventurers, far removed from any sufficient control, all conspired to place the trade entirely upon a new footing.[1]

An important consequence of the inland traders becoming their own carriers was to exclude employment from many people who had participated in the trade, and to force them to seek other means of living.

The palm oil trade

Since the people had become accustomed to certain luxuries, it was necessary for them to find a new means of procuring them. For most of the coastal people who did not have staple articles of export like gold and ivory a new branch of trade had to be found. Palm oil was the answer for some of the people and the manufacture of the product began to give employment to a large portion of the population. Palm oil which had been made in small quantities before the 1830s became an important export.[2]

It has been suggested that the production of palm oil would not have risen to the position it assumed if it had not been for a new circulating medium on the coast. Slaves for some time had been used as the staple of commerce and had 'held the most conspicuous place as a test of computation, and an article was ordinarily reckoned at the value of one, two or more slaves'. However, it was stated:

> But the immense variety of circumstances which depreciated their value or otherwise, made it of such a relative quality, that even the classification into prime, good, bad and indifferent, conveyed but a doubtful and indefinite idea of their true worth.[3]

Gold dust was a standard currency in the western region and Asante, but since its supply was limited it was an inadequate medium of circulation. To make up for this deficiency, various trade articles which passed from hand to hand at a market or an agreed price were also used. Such a medium of exchange was unsatisfactory because unless it was required for immediate consumption it was of little use to the receiver.

> As long as this state of things continued, and there was no ready and convertible price for labour of easy access, there was little inducement to work; but when labour could be very profitably employed in the manufacture of an article of great consumption, for which there was always a ready market, and which was paid in a commodity capable of great subdivision, and in constant use as the circulating medium of an extensive district of the country, motives for exertion were only limited by the extent of desire.[4]

The use of cowrie shells provided the needed medium of exchange:

1 Cruickshank, *Eighteen Years*, ii, pp. 39–40   2 *Ibid.*, ii, pp. 40–42

3 *Ibid.*, ii, p. 42   4 *Ibid.*, ii, p. 43

The introduction of the cowrie-shell and its application to this purpose supplied the desideratum necessary for the prosecution of the trade in palm oil, the supply of which is found to fluctuate according to the supply of the cowries. If these have been exhausted in the stores of the merchants, no oil is brought to the market unless in such small quantities as may be required for immediate consumption; and although the manufacture of oil may go on in the meantime, in the expectation of new importations of cowries, yet if these be long delayed, the activity of the labourer slackens and finally ceases; the object of his labour being to obtain what to him is tantamount to ready cash, which he can apply in any manner he thinks fit.[1]

By 1850 150 tons of cowries were annually being imported to the Gold Coast.[2] It is significant that the eastern region became the centre of the production of palm oil which was devoid of products like gold and kola for either the interior trade or the coastal trade. The oil was manufactured 20 to 40 miles in the interior and brought in earthen pots to the European settlements and there exchanged 'for such articles as they require for their trade in the Interior markets'.[3] The problem of transportation must have been a factor in limiting the area of production to places within the easy reach of the coast. The export of palm oil came to depend upon the availability of cowrie shells,[4] which were used as currency in the eastern region.[5] The concentration of the palm oil in the eastern district is significant and undeniably the cowrie shells that the people there secured for their oil were essential for their trade in the interior.

The area where cowries were in use was limited mainly to the region east of Anomabo; they were forbidden in Asante and in other areas where there was a strong prejudice against them. West of Anomabo cowries were little used and gold dust, silver and copper coins passed as currency. In places like Cape Coast the expenditure of the government allowed for the circulation of enough money for the exigencies of the people and induced them to work in order to obtain what had become necessities to them. But where there was no currency there was not sufficient inducement to labour.[6]

Missions and schools

The importance of missionary work and education in the process of change taking place on the Gold Coast at this time cannot be over-estimated.[7] Mission-

1 *Ibid.*, ii, pp. 43–44. The 'introduction' of cowrie shells used in this quotation is somewhat misleading because cowries had been in use on the Gold Coast long before the 1830s. It is probable that Cruickshank means the increasing use of cowries.

2 *Ibid.* A ton of cowries was equivalent to $350.00 around 1850

3 C.O. 267/93: Rowan Report

4 For a study of cowrie shells, see Marion Johnson, 'The Cowrie Currencies in West Africa', *J.A.H.* xi, Parts 1 and 2, 1970, pp. 17–49 and 331–53.

5 Cruickshank, *Eighteen Years*, ii, p. 43 and C.O. 96/18: Fitzpatrick to Grey, 10 March 1850

6 Cruickshank, *Eighteen Years*, ii, p. 44

7 See I. Tufuoh, 'Relations between Christian Mission, European Administrations, and Traders in the Gold Coast, 1828–1874', in C. G. Baeta, *Christianity in Tropical Africa*, London, 1965.

Governor George Maclean

aries had been on the Gold Coast since the time of the European discovery but the sporadic attempts made to foster African education had met with little success. The Dutch and the Danes had made half-hearted efforts to operate schools for mulattos and periodically some of these and other Africans had been sent to Europe to be educated. However, it was not until 1828 and 1835 when the Basel and Wesleyan missionaries began their effective work that education reached a high level of attainment.[1] By 1850 there were 21 schools on the Gold Coast with a total enrolment of 1,140 students of whom 901 were men and 239 women.[2]

Education during this period, to be sure, was imperfect and often consisted of memorising, reading, writing, arithmetic and some acquaintance with scripture.[3] Nonetheless, as was noted, 'It enabled young men to keep memoranda, copy papers and accounts, to superintend the discharging of cargo from vessels, oversee out-of-door work, and such simple employments.'[4] The same observer wrote:

> I believe a new era in the trade of the Gold Coast has commenced and that for years it will increase in an extraordinary manner. The increase is the result of the small measure of education which can be given here. Every year now more than 100 boys or young men from schools are turned out of the seminaries of Cape Coast, Anamboe and Accra. These are compelled to seek out a way of respectable living and as they generally turn their attention in the direction of trade, it has given a most extraordinary impetus to business here and is most essentially adding to the amount of exports from the country.[5]

Most people receiving education believed that their qualifications confined them to the service of the government and commerce and precluded them from ordinary labour; to them manual labour was fit only for slaves. A mulatto trader lamented this:

> All the young men leaving schools become traders as they see that all the Europeans are Merchants; I believe not one boy that can read or write has yet become a Canoeman or a planter of corn; the whole of these instructed young men are following one occupation, that of trading and hawking goods about the country . . . It is a very great pity that something has not been done to induce some to become Carpenters and Bricklayers.[6]

Education on the Gold Coast was not without other harmful effects upon the society:

> It fostered ideas of expense above their means, induced them to seek the gratification of their tastes, regardless of the consequences, enabled them to

1 Philip Foster, *Education and Social Change in Ghana*, London, 1965, pp. 48–51

2 C.O. 442/10, 1850. By 1860 there were 45 schools with an enrolment of 1,986.

3 For more information, see Foster, *Education*, pp. 52–58.

4 Cruickshank, *Eighteen Years*, ii, p. 60

5 C.O. 96/17: Cruickshank to Forster, 26 May 1849

6 *Ibid.*, C. H. Bartels to M. Forster, 28 Sept. 1849

minister their wants by the credulous simplicity of the ignorant, and ended by involving their relations in debt and bondage.[1]

In Cruickshank's view, it was no wonder that some Africans who observed the process of education sometimes remarked that 'the school was a very good thing for white men, but not for black'.[2]

Import and export trade

The level of trade and economic activities of this period of change can be seen in the scope of the internal and the external trade. The imports into Cape Coast alone in 1831 were estimated at £130,851 3s 11½d and had risen to £423,170 by 1840. Cape Coast exports also increased from £90,282 9s 6d in 1831 to £325,008 in 1840. In 1840 the imports of British Accra were judged to be a figure between £65,000 to £70,000 of which from £12,000 to £15,000 came from America. The exports to Europe were from £85,000 to £95,000 and to the United States £15,000 to £20,000.[3] Annomabo imports stood at £50,000 and exports at £60,000.[4] The trade figures for the two major ports Cape Coast and Accra from 1831–1840 can be broken down as follows:

CAPE COAST[5]

	Imports	Exports
1831	£130,851 3s 11½d	£90,282 9s 6d
1832	£188,067 7s	£181,104
1833	£151,439 12s 4d	£124,147 10s
1834	£181,262 5s 7d	£182,737
1835	£175,985 3s 9d	£171,705 10s 3d
1836	£243,023	£174,832 10s 3d
1837	£264,990	£122,703
1838	£159,405	£124,207 5s 7d
1839	£354,460	£194,576 19s 1d
1840	£423,170	£325,008

ACCRA[6]

	Imports	Exports
1831	No returns	No returns
1832	£23,716 5s**	£62,474**
1833	£61,607 10s	£73,613 5s
1834	£18,359 16s 9d**	£87,299 10s**
1835	£20,638**	£12,435**
1836	£24,986**	£52,311**
1837	£28,957 6s 5½d**	£5,065 12s 10½d*
1838	No returns	£66,450 10s*
1839	No returns	No returns
1840	£65,000 to £70,000	£85,000 to £95,000

* For a three-month period.   ** For a six-month period.

1 Cruickshank, *Eighteen Years*, ii, p. 67   2 *Ibid.*

3 *Parl. Papers* 1842, XII, Appendix   4 *Ibid.*   5 *Ibid.*, p. 43

6 See C.O. 267/117, 131, 136, 144

Furthermore, Manchester goods shipped to the Gold Coast were bartered to American vessels for rum and tobacco which they used to purchase palm oil on the Windward Coast and coffee at the islands of St Thomas and Principe.

The trade figures for the 1830s reveal that imports to Cape Coast far exceeded exports, and those to Accra were much less than exports. The preponderance of imports over exports at Cape Coast can be partially explained by the fact that the town acted as an entrepôt from where goods were shipped to other parts of the Gold Coast as well as areas east of the Gold Coast.[1] Some of the goods involved in this trade might even have found its way to some trader on the Gold Coast, because despite the report that by 1831 the slave trade had ceased to exist on the coast from Apollonia to Accra, it continued in the eastern part of the country, and as late as 1842 it was said that slaves were still being smuggled from time to time especially from the eastern region to the area beyond the Volta for sale.[2] Between 1831 and 1842 Curtin estimated that 0·5 per cent or 1,830 of the slaves exported from Africa by ships known to the British Foreign Office came from the Gold Coast. In 1844 during political disturbances in Akuapem some people from Labadi, Teshi and Accra kidnapped five young people from Akropong and sold them. While on their way to Vay on the Slave Coast to be exported, they were fortunately rescued by an attendant at Fort Princeston at Keta.[3] Edward Carstensen, the Danish Governor, related in 1845 that there were a number of slave-trade agents and commissioners who went around the country buying slaves for export. He said that slaves from the Gold Coast were taken to places on the Slave Coast like Vay, Adafo, Popo and Whydah.[4] Carstensen also mentioned that there were some agents at Accra who acted as correspondents of slave dealers in Vay and Popo.[5] Brodie Cruickshank and Governor Hill confirmed this practice of transporting slaves from the Gold Coast to places where 'British influence was less felt'.[6]

Goods imported to the Gold Coast also found their way often to slave dealers who plied their trade in the area eastwards of the Volta River. Gold Coast merchants admitted to this when they said that before the proclamation of December 1839 prohibiting trade with persons connected with the slave trade they had sold goods to Spanish, Brazilian and Portuguese vessels and other persons suspected of being implicated in that traffic. Even though trade with persons connected with the slave trade was forbidden it was not always easy to distinguish between those who were dealing in slaves and those who were not.[7] As a merchant on the coast put it:

> Some of the large English houses give orders to their captains and supercargoes not to traffic with men reputed to be slave dealers; but, if a purchaser comes along with money in his hand, and offers liberal prices, it requires a

1 See C.O. 96/87, Ussher to Kennedy, 14 Dec. 1970, on the discussion of bonded warehouses and reshipment of goods from the Gold Coast.

2 *Parl. Papers* 1842, Report of Select Committee in West Africa, XII, Appendix

3 *G.J.*, No. 82, 14 Jan. 1845   4 *Ibid.*   5 *Ibid.*

6 C.O. 96/23: Proclamation of Hill dated 27 Nov. 1851; C.O. 96/23: Cruickshank to Hill, 24 Nov. 1851

7 *Ibid.*, Evidence of J. G. Nicholls, Q.262 and F. Swanzy, Q.577 and A.755

tenderer conscience and sterner integrity than are usually met with, on the coast of Africa, to resist the temptation. The merchant at home, possibly, is supposed to know nothing of all this. It is quite an interesting moral question, however, how far either old or New England can be pronounced free from the guilt and odium of the slave-trade, while, with so little indirectness, they both share its profits and contribute essential aid to its prosecution.[1]

Both the respectable firms of F. and A. Swanzy and Forster and Smith were known to have traded with slave dealers on the Slave Coast.[2] There is no evidence that there was any success or attempt to keep British goods or to prevent slavers from using the British goods for carrying on the trade.[3] The preponderance of dollars and doubloons on the Gold Coast was one indication of commerce being carried on with persons involved in the slave trade. According to evidence at the Select Committee on West Africa, vessels from Havana sometimes brought nothing but dollars and doubloons to purchase goods for the slave trade.[4] Isolated instances of dollar exports from Cape Coast and Accra are indicated in the following table:

	Cape Coast	Accra
1833	$4,237	
1834	$2,230*	$3,600*
1835	$9,320	$4,300*
1836	$13,712*	$4,912*
1838		$2,200*
1840	$187,304	
1841	$42,000*	
1843	$166,700	

* A period of six months.

The demand to purchase goods on the coast for the prosecution of the slave trade evolved because of changes in the trade necessitated by the activities of British cruisers trying to stop the illegal traffic. Formerly, slave ships could sail down the coast picking up slaves at the various settlements as they went along until their cargo was complete. With the activities of the cruisers, slavers were forced to load to capacity at one point and to attempt to leave the coast in darkness. This state of affairs led to the establishment of what were called slave factories at scattered points along the coast, mostly at points east of the Volta. Briefly, slave factories were placed where there was a resident slave trader who secured slaves from the African interior for the external slave trade.[5]

1 H. Bridge, *Journal of an African Cruiser*, London, 1845, p. 51

2 C. W. Newbury, *The Western Slave Coast and Its Rulers*, p. 38

3 *Parl. Papers* 1842, Evidence of J. G. Nicholls, *loc. cit.*; Evidence of H. Broadhead, Q.2503 and Q.2498

4 *Ibid.*, Evidence of J. G. Nicholls, Q.265 and H. Dring, Q.2092

5 Lieutenant Forbes, R.N., *African Blockade*, London, 1849, p. 83; *Parl. Papers* 1842, Evidence of F. Swanzy, A.735

All the slave factories maintained baracoons where the slaves were kept until they were exported. These were sheds thatched with palm leaves, the walls between 4 and 6 feet high. Between the roof and the wall there was an opening about 4 feet for the circulation of air and at intervals of 2 feet ran a large neck-link in which each slave was padlocked. The floors were often planked to protect the slaves against skin diseases.[1]

With the exception of occasional cargoes of roll-tobacco and rum, dollars and doubloons were often sent for the purchase of slaves or goods for the slave market. It was mainly the resident slave trader who needed trade items to carry out his trade. The slave factor obtained goods and used them in bartering for slaves. And when the slave ships called, in most cases, they paid for their slaves with dollars and doubloons. Other slave dealers paid slave factors half in goods and half in money. The slave factor in turn used the money received to buy more goods to carry on the illegal traffic.[2] Sometimes the slave dealer secured the goods necessary for the slave trade indirectly through the indigenous people who would buy goods and then sell them to a slave trader for dollars.[3] Evidence at the hearing of the Select Committee of 1842 indicated that some London and Liverpool commercial houses shipped goods to the West Coast for Africa via Brazil and Cuba for the express purpose of being used for the pursuit of the slave trade.[4] As the slave trader T. Canot commented:

England, today with all her philanthropy, sends, under the cross of St George, to convenient magazines of lawful commerce on the coast, her Birmingham muskets, Manchester cottons, and Liverpool lead, all of which are righteously swapped at Sierra Leone, Accra, and on the Gold Coast for Spanish or Brazilian bills on London. Yet, what British merchant does not know the traffic on which those bills are founded, and for whose support his wares are purchases? France, with her bonnet rouge and fraternity, despatches her Rouen cottons, Marseilles brandies, flimsy taffetas, and indescribable variety of tinsel gewgaws. Philosophic Germany demands a slice for her looking-glass and beads: while multitudes of our own worthy traders who would hang a slaver as a pirate when caught, do not hesitate to supply him directly with tobacco, powder, cotton, Yankee rum, and New England notions, in order to bait the trap in which he may be caught. It is the temptation of these things, I repeat, that feeds the slave-making wars of Africa, and forms the human basis of those admirable bills of exchange.[5]

A significant change in the imports into the Gold Coast during this period was the gradual replacement of Indian cottons by British manufactures. As W. F. Hutchinson observed of the West African trade: ' Many of the favourite lines of goods were known by Indian names because they had originally been made in

1 Forbes, *African Blockade*, p. 83

2 *Parl. Papers* 1842, Evidence of F. Swanzy, Qs.622–624, 735–751 and Appendix, p. 77

3 *Ibid.*, Q.265, J. G. Nicholls and Q.237

4 *Ibid.*, Evidence of W. M. Hutton, Qs.3872–3881

5 Canot, *Twenty Years*, p. 105

India, but after 1840 they were mostly made in England where the cost of production was lower.'[1]

The decline of Indian cotton imports and their replacement by English ones had actually started about 1830 as the import figures indicate.[2] From approximately the 1820s until about 1850, the values of European exports to West Africa fell and at the same time quantities of these exports increased. Dr Newbury has given examples of the decline in prices.[3]

	1817	*1850*
Calicoes and prints, cost per yard	1s 2d	$3\frac{1}{2}d$
	1817	*1825*
Powder, per pound	$8\frac{1}{2}d$	5d
	1830	*1850*
Iron and steel, per ton	£8 0s 0d	£7 12s 0d

When the values of goods imported to the Gold Coast from 1827 to 1841 are compared with those of Sierra Leone and the area from the Volta to the Cape of Good Hope, those from the Gold Coast show a more steady growth, while the two other areas fluctuate erratically.[4]

The increase in African exports into Europe during the period under consideration was no doubt helped by the rise in prices of African produce and the removal of heavy duties that had often impeded the trade. Prices seem to have become stabilised by 1850 and after that date the prices of items like palm oil even began to decline.

In terms of exports from the Gold Coast during this period most of the exports from the Gold Coast made from Cape Coast and Accra were recorded, but often returns from other settlements were not included. Exports also came from a wider range and in many instances the export returns in the figures were simply of those ships that took their final departure from Cape Coast and Accra. Thus, the account of exports did not include the cargoes of vessels which might have taken their final departure from other parts of the coast.[5]

Exports from the Gold Coast in the 1830s (see table of exports on page 94) consisted of gold, ivory, palm oil, guinea grains, corn, pepper, coffee, barwood, camwood, gum copal, red or guinea wood, teakwood, rice, beeswax, hides and ginger. Of these items gold was the most important. For the five years leading up to June 1834 it was estimated that gold exports from Cape Coast averaged about

1 W. F. Hutchinson, 'The Gold Trade of the Gold Coast 1826 to 1890', *E.D.M.* xiii, No. 4, March, 1925, p. 8

2 See import figures in Appendix.

3 C. W. Newbury, 'Prices and Profitability in Early Nineteenth Century West African Trade', in Meillassoux, *Development of African Trade*, p. 94

4 For comparison see Appendix for trade figures for Sierra Leone and the area from the Volta to the Cape of Good Hope.

5 *Parl. Papers* 1842, Evidence of F. Swanzy, Qs.871–872 and Evidence of W. M. Hutton, Qs.3949–3952

18,226 ounces a year and those from all the settlements about 25,000 ounces.[1]
Recorded instances of gold exports were:[2]

Cape Coast			Accra		
1831	11,250 oz*	£45,000	1834	3,237 oz*	£12,948
1832	12,580 oz*	£50,320	1835	1,515 oz*	£6,060
1833	24,064 oz	£96,256	1836	9,083 oz*	£26,332
1834	11,889 oz*	£40,504	1837	1,039 oz*	£4,156
1835	26,985 oz	£126,000	1838	10,154 oz*	£40,616
1836	15,883 oz	£99,864			

* Period of six months.

Ivory exports up to 1841 fluctuated and ranged between 595 cwt and 1,065 cwt.
The bulk of ivory came from the area east of the Volta, but that from the Gold
Coast accounted on an average for a quarter to a third of the total British ivory
imports from West Africa. Palm oil was another staple whose exports steadily
increased during the period after 1831. Palm oil from the Gold Coast in 1831
was 16,750 cwt and in 1840 it was 46,778 cwt. Compared with the West African
totals of 163,468 cwt in 1831 and 315,458 cwt in 1840, the amount from the
Gold Coast was extremely small. Included in the exports from the Gold Coast
were large amounts of dollars.

The quantities of barwood, camwood, ebony, teak, ginger, gum and hides
from the Gold Coast varied and greatly fluctuated. Probably the most striking
thing about Gold Coast exports was the noticeable role agricultural produce
was beginning to play. What was perplexing about these seemingly respectable
exports from the Gold Coast was their irregularity which no doubt was related
to external demand and local conditions. Guinea grains formed a significant export and the bulk of this product from West Africa came from the Gold Coast
that from 1831–1841 ranged from 6,417 lb to 84,403 lb with the total volume
from West Africa between 7,911 lb and 124,539 lb. Coffee exports were also
noticeable, amounting to 12,265 lb in 1831, reaching a respectable total of
130,949 lb in 1837, but dying out altogether in 1841. Irregular but respectable
exports of corn were made. 1,500 bushels of corn were exported from Accra for
a six-month period in 1833 and 13,650 bushels in 1835 and 7,000 in 1837. Cape
Coast also shipped 35,000 bushels of corn in 1835. Some exports for certain
years were not recorded; there might also have been some overlapping with
some areas in West Africa in recording the exports from the Gold Coast; European market factors and possible increases in local consumption could partially
explain the fluctuations. The amount of agricultural produce leaving the Gold
Coast in a way indicated that there was a trend, albeit slow and gradual, towards
production for export.

The mode of the external trading at this time still consisted of both the floating trade and castle trade. In the floating trade which merchant vessels sailed
along the coast bartering European goods directly with the indigenous people.
In this method the merchants never considered a voyage unless they realised at
least 60 per cent profit on their original invoice.[3] The other mode of trade was

1 *Ibid.*   2 See C.O. 267/117, 131, 136, 144

3 *Parl. Papers* 1842, XI, Evidence of J. G. Nicholls, Q.162

RETURN OF EXPORTS 1827–1841[1]

	Barwood	Camwood	Coffee	Ebony	Guinea Grains	Gum Animi Zopal	Palm Oil	Pepper	Red or Guinea wood	Rice	Ginger	Teeth, elephant	Teak wood	Bees-wax	Hides, untanned
	tons	tons	lb	tons	lb	cwt	cwt	lb	tons	cwt	cwt	cwt	loads	cwt	cwt
1827		13	15,581	41	12,306	36	4,962	85				312		19	
1828			14,017	3	1,603	2	7,351	4		264		280		6	
1829					5,302	5	7,002	1,000				640			
1830		17			15,283	2	13,575	29,071	1			595	200		
1831	313		12,265	29	6,415	17	16,750	3,914		952		1,069	25	40	
1832	5	33		107	39,896	11	16,544	568				409		18	
1833	16	78	42,814	1	84,403	105	25,599	64	47	135		719		19	
1834	160	215	68,797	16	31,408	62	21,485	174	136			787		44	
1835	50	136	33,317	2	31,592	163	19,008	2,432				714	3	55	
1836	214	28	25,856	8	32,574	360	22,042	8,231	1	23		732	4	172	2
1837	82	220	130,949	58	6,241	2	21,986	5				451	3	16	
1838	335	84	64,696	70		9	35,673					615	34	12	
1839	208	75	2,994	3	16,635	7	40,332	5				609		16	
1840	276	70	58	53	13,351	34	46,778	6			1	938		77	
1841	170	175		10	6,482	81	42,745					851		72	

1 *Parl. Papers* 1842, XII, Appendix

that carried out by resident traders at the forts who maintained stores on the coast.[1] There were even indigenous people importing goods from England to the amount of £20,000 to £30,000 annually on their own credit.[2] Most resident merchants received goods on credit principally from about half a dozen merchant houses: Forster and Smith, F. and A. Swanzy, Hutton and Company, Sewell Ross and Company, Banner Brothers and Company and R. and W. King of Bristol.[3] A great number of merchants supplied by merchant houses on credit often became bankrupt.[4] Many of these same firms which maintained stores on the coast also operated in the floating trade.[5] At the time of merchant rule there was often a conflict between resident British merchants at the outforts and Africans who dealt with vessels engaging in the floating trade. The merchants who often acted as governors of those forts resented the competition, tending to foster a monopoly of trade, and were oppressive towards the indigenous traders.[6]

No trade was carried out at the forts and the resident merchants often had their stores and factories in the towns where the indigenous people came to buy what they needed.[7] While merchants on the coast kept their accounts in shillings and pence, those between them and the indigenous people were kept in ounces, ackies and takus.[8]

Crown authority and the role of merchants

By 1840 reports were reaching the Colonial Office that the British settlements on the Gold Coast were in the habit of trading with slave vessels. Slavers, it was alleged, called at the forts and purchased goods needed for the conduct of their slave trading activities. These reports reached England at a time when the anti-slave trade fervour was at a fever pitch. The specific case that brought about the storm of the relationship between English traders and slave traders was that of the Portuguese vessel *Duos Amigos* captured for contravening the abolition act in November 1838 and condemned by the Court of Mixed Commission court at Sierra Leone. It was found that this ship had traded at Cape Coast before being captured and as it was being equipped for the illegal trade while purchasing goods at the forts should have been seized by the authorities. Maclean did not deny that slave vessels did business at the British forts but felt that he did not have the obligation or power to stop them. Of course, this did not mollify the

1 *Ibid.*, Evidence of G. C. Redman, Qs.3320, 3340 and 3345

2 C.O. 96/18: Fitzpatrick to Earl Grey, 10 March 1850

3 C.O. 96/39: Letter to Labouchere, 29 Feb. 1856

4 *Parl. Papers* 1842, XI, Evidence of J. G. Nicholls, Q.176. See ch. 5 for a discussion on bankruptcies

5 C.O. 96/18: Fitzpatrick to Earl Grey, 10 March 1850

6 C.O. 96/2: Maclean to Stanley, 13 Sept. 1843; C.O. 96/3: Lucas, Gwyer and Lucas, Merchants of Bristol to Stanley, 6 March 1843; C.O. 96/3: Simon Samuel to Stanley, 20 Nov. 1843

7 C.O. 267/136: Letter of Maclean, 14 Oct. 1836

8 C.O. 96/11: Winnett's Report to accompany the Blue Books for 1846

Colonial Office which sent him a direct warning.[1] It was decided that the only way to prevent the recurrence of the evil of trading with slaves was for the Crown to resume control of the fort. Meanwhile an agreement was reached to send out a special commissioner to investigate and to make recommendations for the future administration of the settlements.

The choice as commissioner fell upon Dr Richard Madden who had been a judge of the Court of Mixed Commission in Cuba. The doctor, who was ill for most of the period he was on the Gold Coast, wrote a report on the settlements and gravely impeached individuals engaged in the trade on the Gold Coast. He said that he found British subjects on the Gold Coast buying, selling and holding slaves and that there was cooperation between British commerce and slave trade interests at the factories of notorious slave dealers on the West coast.[2] Some of Madden's important recommendations were that the Home Government should take the forts out of the hands of the merchant committee; the Governor and officers of the settlements should not be allowed to carry on trade; and measures should be taken to prosecute persons buying, selling or holding slaves on the Gold Coast and those in London.[3]

The bias of the Madden Report led to the selection of a Parliamentary Committee to look into the affairs of West Africa before his recommendations could be acted upon. The Select Committee of 1842 suggested that the Government of Gold Coast settlements should be resumed by the Crown; the forts abandoned in 1828 should be reoccupied; in order that better judicial authority be established, an assessor to the chiefs of the neighbouring territory should be appointed and the military force should be increased; and more effectual steps taken to reduce slavery and the slave trade. The committee also exonerated Maclean of the charges brought against him by Madden and praised him for his work in the settlement.[4]

Although the Colonial Office did not accept these recommendations of the Select Committee, it agreed to assume the government of the forts and to appoint a Judicial Assessor.[5] While President of the Council at Cape Coast Castle, Maclean's commercial connections with London Houses had been suspect. He was therefore not appointed Governor when the Crown resumed control of the settlement in 1843. That office went to Captain H. W. Hill whereas Maclean was appointed Judicial Assessor. Until Hill arrived in February 1844 Maclean continued to hold the top office. Exclusive of the charges for the military force that had been employed on the Gold Coast a grant of £4,000 was voted for the settlements of the forts.[6] Meanwhile in response to the recommendations of the Select Committee of 1842, the coastal chiefs were asked to state their acknowledgement of British jurisdiction, an acceptance which came to be known in Gold Coast history as the Bond of 1844.[7]

---

1 Metcalfe, *Maclean*, pp. 245–7   2 *Parl. Papers* 1842, XII, Appendix No. 3

3 C.O. 267/170: Madden's Report   4 *Parl. Papers* 1842, XI, pp. 4–7

5 C.O. 96/2: Hope to Stephen, 3 Dec. 1842; Metcalfe, *Documents*, pp. 187–8

6 C.O. 96/2: Stanley to Hill, 16 Dec. 1843; Metcalfe, *Documents*, pp. 192–4

7 C.O. 96/4: Declaration of the Fante Chiefs dated 6 March 1844; Metcalfe, *Documents*, p. 196

So the merchant rule of the Gold Coast, begun in 1828, came to an end. However, problems affecting economic matters followed. These involved the use of
West Indian troops on the Gold Coast, the conflict with advocates of merchant
rule, and the question of slavery which formed a vital part of the economic
structure of the country. Upon the resumption of Crown rule the local corps of
natives who had been used by Maclean to maintain peace, security and to open
routes were replaced by West Indian troops. Because of their ignorance of the
language and customs of the people, the new troops were incapable of fulfilling
the police role of the old garrison.[1] Indeed, there were frequent quarrels between the West Indian soldiers and the local people at places like Accra, Winneba and Kormantin. This reaction was understandable because:

> While the forts were garrisoned by the local corps, Natives of the Country,
> the Chiefs and people had the most entire faith in the intentions of the govern-
> ment, and considered the local authorities as aiding and assisting them in the
> good government of their country; but when they saw a force introduced who
> had no interests or feelings in common with them, ignorant of their customs
> and their language and composed of a despised race they regarded as in the
> light of invaders bent upon their total destruction.[2]

In 1844 Hill had suggested the creation of a Council of Merchants, subject to
the approval of the home government, empowered to make their own laws. Hill
believed that 'a government conducted by a Committee of Merchants would
unite the cooperation of the resident traders and give them some interest in the
advancement of the Government views'. But the home government had refused
to agree to this.[3] The problem of the control of the government on the coast was
to bedevil relationships between the Gold Coast mercantile community and the
local government. The merchants insisted on being a part of the local government, claiming that the secret of Maclean's success had been the Council of
Merchants innovated in 1828. They argued that the Governor was generally
unacquainted with matters relating to customs, laws and trade and that the least
mismanagement on his part would bring on a war. In the view of the merchants:

> Much of the prosperity, which the settlement enjoyed under the former sys-
> tem of Government may very justly be attributed to the assistance which the
> President received from his council. It was entirely composed of merchants
> whose pursuits brought them into habitual intercourse with the Natives, and
> who on that account, had the best opportunities of studying their character
> and providing for their efficient Government.[4]

They suggested that a council of government composed of six members be established. This council was to consist of the Governor, Judicial Assessor, and four

1 C.O. 96/4: Maclean to Stanley, 5 Feb. 1844

2 C.O. 96/12: Cruickshank to Forster, 6 Feb. 1847

3 C.O. 96/4: Hill to Stanley, 5 Aug. 1844

4 C.O. 96/12: Forster to Grey, 22 March 1847; Metcalfe, *Documents*, p. 203; C.O. 96/19:
  Letter to Winniett, 18 Dec. 1850

merchants residing within the settlement. It was suggested that a unanimous negative on the part of the council to any of the Governor's measures would have the effect of suspending such measures until the sanction of the home government had been attained for them.[1] Needless to say the Colonial Office did not accede to these proposals.

The question of slavery

During Madden's mission in 1841 the vital questions of slavery and pawning which also involved the vital economic problems of property, investments and security came up. At that time Sir John Jeremie, the Governor-in-Chief, issued a proclamation that by the Slave Trade Abolition Act and the Slave Emancipation Act it was unlawful for any person to hold slaves in any British territory.[2] When Madden had tried to enforce the proclamation, slaves who were told they were free asked him to provide for their subsistence saying, 'unless the Queen intended to give them something to eat, they would prefer their master who supplied their wants'.[3] Mulatto families, joined by merchants, protested against the proclamation. The merchants argued that:

> The country is at present in a state of profound tranquillity, and beginning in some measure to feel the benefits of civilisation, by means of the influence of the local government, the Christian efforts of the Wesleyan Missionary Society, and the extension of legitimate commerce; and that the rash and premature introduction of such an extensive revolution would inevitably destroy the British influence, ruin commerce, and plunge the country in the same state of anarchy and confusion from which it is only now gradually recovering.[4]

There was no problem enforcing the proclamation upon the European population. When the question arose of why the proclamation had been limited only to Europeans Maclean told the Colonial Office:

> I do not find my physical means backed by my moral power, insufficient. But I should say the very foundation of that power, were I to attempt the execution of a measure which would bear, upon the face of it, the appearance, at least, of the grossest tyranny and injustice – the depriving people, namely, without compensation, of property which they have inherited from their ancestors or acquired by their own industry.[5]

The question of pawn-slaves also came up soon after Governor Hill's arrival when he discovered that the Methodist missionaries employed pawns as labourers. The missionaries had to resort to slave and pawn labour with slaves normally hired as individuals and their wages paid to them. In the case of the

1 C.O. 96/12: Letter of Cruickshank, J. Bannerman and J. Coulston, 12 Feb. 1847

2 *Parl. Papers* 1842, XII, Appendix, p. 48

3 Cruickshank, *Eighteen Years*, ii, p. 236

4 *Parl. Papers* 1842, XII, Appendix, p. 49

5 C.O. 96/2: Maclean to Stanley, 13 Sept. 1843

pawns only a portion of their wage was paid to them, the remainder going to meet the debt for which they were held. Hill interpreted this as buying the pawn and tried to bring proceedings against the missionaries. When the case reached the General Secretary of the Wesleyan Missionary Society he agreed that the missionaries had acted wrongly and issued a warning to them.[1]

Governor Hill's intervention did not solve the question of slavery and domestic slavery. The problem which was tied to the economic system of the country was to come up again and again in the governing of the Gold Coast. Was domestic slavery recognised? Should runaway slaves be handed back to their masters? Were educated Africans and indigenous merchants to be allowed to hold slaves and pawns? Fluctuating British policy did not provide any answers to these questions until it abolished domestic slavery altogether in 1875.

Withdrawal of Denmark

While the British Crown was resuming control of the English settlements changes were taking place in the Danish sphere that would bring an end to the control of their West African establishments in 1850. The forts were sold when further efforts failed in the 1830s to make the settlements profitable.

The question of selling the Danish forts came to the fore again in the 1840s. This time Denmark was very anxious to rid herself of the settlements. In 1840, in order to reduce his government's budget, King Christian VIII resolved to sell both his East Indian territories and the Gold Coast forts. Besides the forestalling of the establishment of a third power in the Danish territories and humanitarian zeal, British merchants became interested in the territory because of the palm oil trade in the area. James Bannerman wrote to emphasise the commercial importance of the Danish territory:

> . . . within this tract is grown all the palm oil, ground nuts and Indian corn purchased at this place, moreover every article of live stock such as oxen, sheep, turkeys, ducks and fowls is reared within these territories, from whence we here, as well as the residents of Elmina, Cape Coast and Annamaboe, derive our supplies.[2]

According to Bannerman, if another power obtained the settlement, they would 'without question endeavour to monopolise the trade of Akim, Aquapim, Crobo, etc. by prohibiting those people from trading at the English settlements'.[3] Bannerman was not alone in his belief as others shared his view; even the Governor wrote to confirm this point:

> The plains of the River Volta which extend for many miles (say 50 miles) along the Danish Territories, are very rich, and abound in Palm Trees and fine tracts of land well adapted to the cultivation of corn, so much so, that nearly all the Palm oil and corn shipped from this part of the coast is supplied from the fertile country under the Danish flag . . . The only river which is ever likely to become of any commercial importance on this line of coast is the

---

1 Metcalfe, *Maclean*, pp. 311–13

2 C.O. 96/2: Letter of J. Bannerman dated 7 March 1843   3 *Ibid.*

Volta, now in the possession of the Danes; and this river, by British enterprise, might soon become an easy medium of communication with an extensive part of the interior.[1]

With commercial prospects and mercantile urging Great Britain purchased the Danish forts and took them over in 1850.

The import and export trade of the Gold Coast seems to have fallen somewhat after the Crown assumed control over the forts and, except for an export return of a six months' period in 1842 from Cape Coast amounting to £190,086 (which included 27,280 ounces of gold dust, 166,700 dollars, 716 tons of palm oil and 334 tons of ivory), there is a gap in the returns. Before Crown rule in 1840 when more complete trade data are available the total imports to Cape Coast had been estimated at £423,170, at between £65,500 to £70,000 to Accra. The exports from Cape Coast were valued at between £325,008 and £95,000. But the figures for all of the Gold Coast imports in 1846 (the first year trade figures are available) amounted to £55,305 and the exports £120,000. The apparent drop is evident from the comparative table below:

	Imports £	Exports £
1836	243,023	174,703
1837	264,990	122,703
1838	159,409	124,207
1839	254,460	194,576
1840	423,170	325,008[2]

	Imports £	Exports £
1846	55,305	120,000
1847	79,400	148,030
1848	82,950	167,174*
1849	110,600	167,174*
1850	88,656	200,707[3]

* This figure given in the Blue Books probably represents a mistake in one of the two years quoted.

It appears from the above figures that the most perceptible drop was in the table of imports. Although the exports dropped, they were not radically different from what they had been earlier. Taking into account the former practice of goods imported into the Gold Coast being re-exported or being sold to slave dealers for the prosecution of the slave trade and the overlapping or the inclusion of exports from other areas, some possible explanations emerge. First and foremost, as is evidenced by the low import figures from 1846 to 1850, the items imported seem to be just sufficient for the trade of the Gold Coast in view of its

1 C.O. 96/2: Winniett to Grey, 31 Dec. 1847; C.O. 96/2: Letter of Hutton and Nicholls dated 23 March 1843

2 *Parl. Papers* 1842, XII, Appendix

3 C.O. 100/2, 3, 4, 5, 6. Blue Books 1846–1850.

exports, and suggest that the former practice of goods in the country finding their way to slave dealers had ceased or diminished. Furthermore, if places like Cape Coast had acted as entrepôts, it is possible that the increase in the West African trade which multiplied the number of shore and river factories available as bulking centres precluded the importation of goods to the Gold Coast before being reshipped elsewhere.[1]

The external trade could be broken up to show the major imports and exports as follows:[2]

IMPORTS

	Manchester goods and manufactures £	Spirits and wines £	Hardware £	Gunpowder £	Tobacco £	Beads £	Total £
1846	19,650	6,740	8,790	1,780	5,345	8,660	55,305
1847	31,000	8,500	12,000	4,000	4,500	11,000	79,400
1848	34,750	10,300	13,050	4,000	4,650	9,000	82,950
1849	48,440	15,500	22,180	7,710	1,280	3,050	110,600
1850	41,763	7,142	4,733	8,256	4,599	5,060	88,656

EXPORTS

	Gold dust £	Palm oil £	Ivory £	Miscellaneous £	Total £
1846	90,000	12,500	16,800	1,500	120,800
1847	108,000	16,450	21,300	2,280	168,030
1848 and 1849*	127,980	20,506	16,380	2,308	167,174
1850	146,412	45,185	8,620	500	200,707

* The repetition of the figures for 1848 and 1849 must represent a mistake in the original records.

By 1850 it was evident that the Gold Coast was showing trade and economic progress which were the result of changes in the society. 'There is a vitality of change diffusing its innumerable currents through every class of society, and giving expansion to an entirely new class of ideas, affecting the moral, religious, social and domestic condition of the people,' wrote Cruickshank. He further observed that 'a taste for many of the European necessaries and luxuries of life, and a partial assimilation in the construction of their houses, in dress, in manners and in religion, are daily more observable. . ..'[3]

As a long-term resident on the coast he summed up the changes that had taken place thus:

The Gold Coast is progressing satisfactorily, and though apparently slowly, it is not so in reality, and if I could look back on my fifteen years in it and remark all the changes, I would be astonished, as I am from a partial recollection of it, at what has been done. This has been the result of non-interference, the absence of law-making and the presence of self-interest to take advantage of the available chances of improvement as they presented themselves.[4]

1 See also Newbury, 'Prices and Profitability in Early Nineteenth-Century Trade', p. 93ff.

2 C.O. 100/2, 3, 4, 5, 6. Blue Books 1846–1850

3 Cruickshank, *Eighteen Years*, ii, p. 231

4 C.O. 96/17: Cruickshank to Forster, 29 Sept. 1849

In 1850 when the administration of the Gold Coast was separated from that of Sierra Leone, trade and economic development were forging ahead. That these changes could take place was in great measure due to the transformation of the traditional society with institutional and ideological adjustments to the emerging commercial order.

CHAPTER FOUR

The age of African merchants, 1850–1863

Increased British presence and 'educated' Africans

The decision of Earl Grey, the British Secretary of State, to separate the administration of the Gold Coast from that of Sierra Leone in 1850 meant that the British were assuming a greater degree of potential presence in the country, thus entailing the need for a larger government staff and more expense.[1] Yet Great Britain was hindered by lack of money and authority to meet these increased responsibilities.[2]

Without sufficient funds, the British could not establish a regular system of order as they wished, and without the cooperation of the chiefs, they could not enforce their authority. Yet, the more the British interfered with the traditional rulers, the less effective the power of both became. The uncooperative attitude of the Dutch to the British need to raise funds for expenses and development brought about financial measures which resulted in the disillusionment of the British colonial government as well as a rising African merchant class and a group often referred to as 'educated Africans'. This has been defined as 'a group of Africans, mostly literate, who led life more or less outside the old tribal society, and often devoted themselves to trade'.[3]

Some 'educated Africans', often poorly educated, were the products of the government and mission schools of the period. Others like George Blankson who were referred to as 'educated' Africans were even illiterate. Many of these

---

1 Andrew Swanzy wrote that 'In consequence of the greatly increased expense attending this change, it became necessary to provide an increased revenue'. 'On Trade in Western Africa with and without British Protection', p. 479.

2 The liabilities of the British local government can be clearly seen by looking at a breakdown of its revenue and expenditure:

	1850	1851	1852	1853	1854	1855	1860
Revenue total in £s	4,884	5,550	5,147	13,249	10,211	9,830	7,948*
Expenditure total in £s	5,231	6,637	6,401	6,178	9,376	8,501	9,558

* This total includes £174 for conveyance of mails, £33 for postage and £1,356 for the category termed 'special'.

The sources for the information contained in the above table are from: C.O. 442/27 for revenue and expenditure of 1850–1854; C.O. 442/28 for revenue and expenditure of 1855 and C.O. 442/33 for revenue and expenditure of 1860.

3 Linnart Limberg, 'The Economy of the Fanti Confederation', *T.H.S.G.* xi, 1971, 1, p. 83

'educated' Africans secured positions as agents for missionaries or as government clerks, but in the increasingly differentiated occupational structure of the time they frequently sought employment connected with European trade.[1] Education was viewed by the Africans as an entrée to financial success. As one study of education during the period has revealed, 'Education meant one thing above all, the opportunity to enter more highly paid posts within the exchange sector of the economy.'[2] To be sure, the prospects for many individuals entering trade as merchants were limited, since the modern economy had not expanded sufficiently to absorb all who wished to enter trade. Cruickshank observed, 'the whole trade of the coast was very insignificant, and to so few, that there was but little room for employment from this source'.[3] These so-called 'educated' natives, concentrated mainly in the urban centres of Cape Coast and Accra, were often blamed for reactions or protests against the growth of British administration on the Gold Coast.

Urban centres of Cape Coast and Accra

The presence of the educated natives in Cape Coast and Accra and their desire to enter the modern exchange economy were in themselves manifestations of the changes taking place in these urban areas and part of the process of economic transformation in the country being worked by the growth of trade. Although precise details of the development of these two major urban centres during this time are lacking, nevertheless some observations can be made.

The importance of Cape Coast before 1807 was derived from the slave trade and consequently declined after abolition. With the revived and increased trade, especially during the era of Maclean, the town re-assumed status as a depot for import trade into the Gold Coast.[4] As a growing urban area, Cape Coast, by the middle of the nineteenth century, presented a marked contrast between the dwellings of the masses of the people of the town and the residences of the wealthier class. One traveller described Cape Coast thus:

> It consists for the most part of mud houses . . . Here and there may be seen a residence of better construction belonging to some chief or merchant.[5]

Another visitor to the town between 1847–1848 left a description:

> The town of Cape Coast extends inland immediately from the Castle. It presents an odd intermixture of native huts and houses, more or less of European style . . . That part of the town occupied by the poorer classes consists of houses terribly huddled together, composed of 'swish' . . . In parts of the town where European merchants or wealthy natives reside the houses are of superior kind, being composed of brick, flat-roofed, and well white-washed.[6]

1 Foster, *Education*, p. 64   2 *Ibid.*, p. 66

3 Cruickshank, *Eighteen Years*, ii, pp. 64–65

4 Swanzy, 'On Trade in West Africa with and without British Protection', p. 479

5 Allen, *The Gold Coast or, a Cruise in West African Waters*, p. 16

6 C. A. Gordon, *Life on the Gold Coast*, London, 1874, pp. 3–4

Both Cape Coast and Accra briefly experienced municipal governments in 1858 when Governor Benjamin Pine encouraged experiments in local corporations.[1] In Cape Coast a municipal council was elected composed of F. C. Grant, J. Smith, J. Tandoe, H. Barnes, T. Hughes, J. R. Thompson and R. Hutchinson. The municipal corporation was to establish a court with the jurisdiction to impose fines up to £50 and prison sentences not exceeding six months.[2] A proposed house rate by the corporation probably reflected the increasing differentiation in wealth and habitation. Houses were divided into seven classes and assessed rates.[3]

Cape Coast had been a prosperous centre of commerce before the abolition of the Atlantic slave trade and Asante invasion of 1807, as was Accra. Accra's prosperity was confirmed by Henry Meredith:

> Prior to the present war [Asante invasion of 1807] and to the abolition of the Slave-trade, a vast trade was carried on at Accra by many nations. Here might be seen a conflux of Ashantees, Akims, Aquapims, Fantees, Aquamboes, Crepees, and even a remote inland people who went under the appellation of Duncoes; a name given by the Fantees to men, whose country is not known, or who come a long way from the interior.[4]

Although trade at Accra was somewhat disrupted because of the Asante war commerce was flourishing more than in other parts of the coast. In 1811 Meredith noted that 'Accra is the only country on the Gold-coast, that has a free trade with the interior; and it is in general very much resorted to by the Ashantees'.[5] Accra's flourishing commerce was no doubt helped, as evidenced by the bulk of Gold Coast exports from the town especially after the 1830s, by its location near the rich palm oil district of the eastern region.

In addition to its choice site, Accra was supposed to be one of the most healthy areas along the Gold Coast.[6] One British navy officer confirmed this when he said, 'Accra is a settlement the most attractive of any on the coast, to the officers of the ships of war, employed in now vainly endeavouring to suppress the slave trade. . . .'[7]

Appropriate to its prominence as a commercial centre, Accra had a hotel:

> Accra boasts an hotel where a traveller can put up in comfort. There is neither sign nor name, nor any emblem which could lead a casual traveller to know it was an inn. Casual travellers, however, must be few indeed at Accra,

1 C.O. 96/43: Pine to Stanley, 7 March 1858; Kimble, *Political History*, pp. 185–6

2 Kimble, *Political History*, p. 185

3 C.O. 96/43: Bird to Lytton, 10 Aug. 1858. The following classes and rates were charged: 1st at £3 per annum; 2nd at £2 per annum; 3rd at £1 per annum; 4th at 10s per annum; 5th at 5s per annum; 6th at 3s per annum and 7th at 1s per annum.

4 Meredith, *Account of the Gold Coast*, pp. 217–18   5 *Ibid.*

6 George Alfred Henty, *The March to Coomassie*, London, 1874, p. 254

7 H. Huntley, *Seven Years' Service on the Slave Coast of Western Africa*, ii, p. 82

and the customers of the hotel must be principally the captains of ships trading there, or agents of mercantile houses stopping there for a week between the arrival of one steamer and the departure of the next.[1]

Besides the hotel there was a market house in the town by 1874, but the people preferred trading on the streets. G. A. Henty described the scene:

> The principal street of Accra is an amusing sight; some effort appears to be made to keep it clean, and the sales people sit upon little mats, or upon low stools which are used all over this country. They line both sides of the street, and expose for sale every sort of article prized by the natives, and the goods being contained in wooden trays everywhere in use here.[2]

In these growing urban[3] centres the appearance of a regular labour force by 1850 was inevitable.[4]

The rise of an African merchant class

Among the 'educated' Africans there had emerged by 1850 in the urban centres on the Gold Coast a class of indigenous merchants who were in no way inferior in education and culture to their local European counterparts.[5] Such a group in itself was nothing new; in earlier centuries there had been influential men of trade like Edward Barter, John Kabes and John Konney.[6] However, by the 1850s these African merchants were more numerous, more influential and wielded more power than their predecessors. At a time when British rule was becoming entrenched on the Gold Coast, they often used their ascendancy to encourage protests against British administrative acts and frequently used their position to further a policy of social and economic development:[7]

The power of the African merchants grew at the expense of that of the chiefs. This phenomenon marked very significant changes in the character of the economy. The traditional ruler's power was in some way associated with wealth

---

1 Henty, *March to Coomassie*, p. 255   2 *Ibid.*, p. 258

3 Despite their importance, Accra and Cape Coast were by no means the only urban centres. Winneba, Dixcove and Anomabo were also important towns with a fair amount of trade. The latter town which was the operation centre of leading merchants like George Blankson, Samuel Collins Brew and R. J. Ghartey was important.

4 C.O. 442/27–41. Between 1850 and 1872 the following wages for labour were quoted:

Description of labour	1850	1854	1860	1872*
Domestics per month	10s	15s	10s	£9–£20 per year (6d–1s 3d per day)
Predial per month	5s	10s	10s	£9 per year (6d to 9d per day)
Trades per month	£1 0s	£1 0s	15s	£18 to £25 per year (1s–1s 6d per day)
Trades – jobbing per day	–	–	1s	–

* By 1871 where labour was undertaken at a distance, an additional rate of 3d per day was granted for subsistence.

5 Forster, *Education*, pp. 68–69; Priestley, *West African Trade and Coast Society*, p. 143

6 See Daaku, *Trade and Politics*, pp. 96–114

7 Kimble, *Political History*, p. 168

but the riches of the chiefs were acquired through their status (presents, fines, tribute and in some cases through trading) and they dispersed wealth to others through feasts, presents and other customary activities on a non-economic basis.[1] Merchants, on the other hand, acquired their possessions through profits of trade and spent it in economic ways in the sense that they sought value for money. Although rising African merchants had some social obligations of economic and non-economic kind, it was true that there was a widening of the economic sphere in Gold Coast society which included a measure of individualisation, with greater difference of wealth between persons of similar traditional status and a growth of importance of personal achievement in economic activities.

In Gold Coast society in old times, status was either inherited or attained by the political skills of rhetorical eloquence, diplomatic ability or military prowess.[2] By the middle of the nineteenth century it was achieved through the creation of wealth by trade and production for market[3] by a group whose commercial and political interests frequently overlapped. Because of the significant economic role played by these men, the lives of the prominent ones should be delineated in some detail.

James Bannerman

James Bannerman,[4] son of a Scottish father and African mother, was educated in England[5] – an opportunity he, in turn, was to extend to his children.[6] He married one of the three daughters of the Asantehene after the capture of the former during the war with Asante in 1826.[7] In 1817 it was reported that he had long been a resident at Accra as a free trader and by 1819 that he was exporting corn from the Gold Coast.[8] His volume of trade increased to the extent that in 1828 it was asserted that

> Bannerman house at Accra consumed 1,100 puncheons of rum during the last 17 months. 34,000 oz of gold have been collected during the same period and in the last six months, 10 tons of ivory and £7,000 worth of palm oil have been sent to England.[9]

1 Bowdich, *Mission from Cape Coast Castle*, p. 295; J. E. Casely Hayford, *Gold Coast Native Institutions*, London, 1903, p. 96

2 Bowdich, *Mission from Cape Coast Castle*, p. 295

3 Cruickshank, *Eighteen Years*, ii, p. 41

4 Bannerman was prominent enough to be noticed by most travellers who visited Accra when he resided there. See C. W. Thomas, *Adventures and Observations on the West Coast of Africa and Its Islands*, London, 1864, p. 159; Peter Leonard, *Records of a Voyage to the Western Coast of Africa*, Edinburgh, 1833, p. 255; J. Holman, *Travels*, London, 1840, p. 235 and Bridge, *Journal of an African Cruiser*, pp. 140–1.

5 Bridge, *Journal*, p. 142

6 M. J. Sampson, *Gold Men of Affairs*, London, 1937, pp. 87–89

7 Bridge, *Journal*, p. 141

8 Despite the slump in the Gold Coast trade in the 1820s he was apparently doing good trade. C.O. 267/94: Denham to R. W. Hay, 1 Feb. 1828

9 *Ibid.*, 34,000 oz export is probably an exaggeration.

His commercial success was matched politically when he became the Civil Commandant at Christiansborg in 1850 and when Governor Winniett died that year the merchant community petitioned the Colonial Office to appoint Bannerman Governor because of his experience on the coast and his personal knowledge of the people.[1] Even though he was not offered the post, he acted as Lieutenant-Governor from December 1850 to September 1851, was appointed to the Gold Coast Legislative Council when it was established in 1850 and served on it until his retirement in 1856.[2]

George Kuntu Blankson

The son of Chief Kuntu of Egyah, a village two miles from Anomabo, George Kuntu Blankson[3] (1809–1898), although not educated abroad, would see fit to send his children to Europe to study.[4] Blankson was initially employed by a trader on the coast but later traded on his own account in Asante. It was probably because of his trading connection and knowledge of Asante that Governor Maclean sent him on a mission in 1834 that was to detain him in Asante for a period of eighteen months. His career also briefly embraced lay preaching for the Methodist Church and by 1843 he had become the manager of the Wesleyan Mission with six sub-agents under him. He soon left the mission to resume his trading activities to Asante.

In 1853 during an Asante threat, Acting-Governor Brodie Cruickshank sent him to negotiate with the Asantehene in order to re-open the trade routes. Perhaps as a consequence of this arrangement Brodie Cruickshank took him to the merchant house of Forster and Smith with whom he commenced business. In order to accommodate his increasing business he established factories at Small Cormantine, Assafo, Arkrah, Apam Mankwadi and Winneba.[5] Sampson has called him 'a commercial king and a patriot' and has written that Blankson 'was so prosperous in a business set up by himself as to be able to build a castle in his own town of Anomabu, wonderful to behold, and to support 100 slaves as servants of the palatial building'.[6]

From 1862–1873 he became a member of the Legislative Council until charges were brought against him of treason for an incident during the Asante War.[7] Three years later the Rev. T. B. Freeman influenced him to rejoin the church where he was to function as a lay preacher until his retirement.

Samuel Collins Brew

Facts surrounding the trading life of Samuel Collins Brew (c. 1810–1881),[8] son of Sam Kanto Brew, a mulatto slave trader who died in 1823, are few. Nonethe-

1 C.O. 96/19: Gold Coast merchants and principal natives to Secretary of State, 21 Dec. 1850; Kimble, *Political History*, p. 65

2 Kimble, *Political History*, pp. 405–6

3 See Sampson, *Gold Coast Men of Affairs*, pp. 101–8; Metcalfe, *Documents*, p. 245, n. 3

4 Sampson, *Gold Coast Men of Affairs*, pp. 107–8

5 *Ibid.*, p. 104   6 *Ibid.*, p. 101   7 *Ibid.*, p. 107

8 See Priestley, *West African Trade and Coast Society*, pp. 143–57

less a broad picture of his commercial activities can be reconstructed. The centre of his trading activities was at Anomabo. Samuel Brew concentrated mainly in the ivory and gold dust trade, with no interest in the palm oil business and in his commercial activities he dealt with the London merchant houses of Hutton and Sons and with Forster and Smith, from whom he received goods on credit. He sold his goods at Anomabo and other places on the coast, often placing his wives in charge of his stores. Extensive trading enabled him to be ranked among the substantial Gold Coast traders by the 1840s. Brew's business, however, declined and he experienced financial difficulties following the disruptions of trade in the wake of troubles with Asante in 1853 and 1863–1864. No doubt the system of extended credit established on the coast was also responsible for his pecuniary disaster and in 1867 Brew and other African traders became insolvent.[1] In addition to his trading activities, Brew served the British administration on a voluntary basis from 1857 until 1867, but took a salaried post from 1868 to 1879 after he became bankrupt, serving as a Justice of the Peace and later as Commandant of Anomabo, Saltpond and Winneba. Like Bannerman and Blankson, Brew sent his children, including Prince James Hutton Brew of Dunkwa, to be educated abroad.

Robert Johnson Ghartey

The future King Ghartey IV of Winneba, son of Gyateh Kumah III, Chief of Winneba,[2] Robert Johnson Ghartey (1820–1897) had an aversion towards fishing, the main occupation of the people of his hometown. Ghartey's interest in business was enhanced by the experience he gained learning coopery with a European firm on the coast. He then embarked upon a career at sea, but after his employer was murdered at sea, he returned to Appam to work again as a cooper for Stooves Brothers. The agent of Stooves Brothers became fond of Ghartey, encouraging him to study and to learn to read and speak English. For fourteen years he worked for Stooves Brothers after which he established his own business at Anomabo. On the death of the last surviving member of the company, he purchased the business which then consisted of thirteen factories.

According to Sampson, Ghartey was the first person to introduce palm-nut cracking on the Gold Coast, thus making palm kernel a staple export of the country. He was a pioneer of the timber industry and was reputed to have opened up the Ayensu River at his own expense, rendering it navigable for floating timber down from the hinterland to Winneba.[3] Furthermore Ghartey was a promoter of gold mining, and a moving personality of the Fante Confederation. However, in 1872, after the disintegration of the Fante Confederation and the death of his cousin, Chief Henry Acquah I, he was elected Chief of Winneba. In order to help improve the town of Winneba and to promote its rapid development, Ghartey invited the European firms of F. and A. Swanzy and the Basel Mission Trading Society to establish factories in the town.[4]

1 *Ibid.*   2 Sampson, *Gold Coast Men of Affairs*, pp. 112–28

3 Other pioneers of the timber industry included Messrs. C. Barns, Clinton and Carew who carried on their enterprise on the Ankobra River at Axim and the Pra River at Shama. Sampson, *Gold Coast Men of Affairs*, p. 118.

4 *Ibid.*, p. 119

James Robert Thompson

James Robert Thompson (1810–1886) was educated at the Government School at Cape Coast at an early age and shortly after leaving school was appointed agent on the Liberian coast for an English firm. He returned to Cape Coast in 1840 and three years later married the daughter of Joseph Smith. Between 1844–1846 he worked for the Wesleyan Missionary Society but left their service to enter trade in his own business at Cape Coast, thriving as a merchant there from 1849–1852. He was elected a chief (*Tufuhin*) of Cape Coast in 1853.[1] When, on the initiative of educated African merchants, a native court was set up in Cape Coast in 1853 to replace the courts held in the private homes of various chiefs, Thompson was appointed to preside over it.[2] When after one year Kofi Amissah, King of Cape Coast, attempted suicide by blowing himself up with gunpowder and consequently ended his political career, Thompson virtually became ruler of the town.[3] Thompson also took an active part in all the Asante wars and invasions up to 1874.[4]

Frank Cleland

Great-grandson of Kofi Akrashie, Manche of James Town, and son of Frank Cleland of Christiansborg, George Frank Cleland (1830–1887) was educated at the Accra Wesleyan School and upon completing his education there taught at the same school until his transfer to Prampram.[5] While at Prampram, Cleland abandoned teaching in favour of trading to become one of the leading merchants at Accra.[6] At the end of his commercial career he became a member of the Gold Coast Legislative Council.

Robert Hutchinson

Reputed to be worth £60,000 in 1855,[7] Robert Hutchinson (died 1863) was an agent of F. and A. Swanzy on the Gold Coast. In 1858, after the British expedition against the Krobos, a fine imposed on them was farmed out to him.[8] In the same year he was elected to the Municipal Council of Cape Coast and appointed mayor of the town.[9] Five years later during the Asante invasion, business interests led him to form the Gold Coast Rifle Volunteer Corps to help repel Asante aggression.[10]

Francis Chapman Grant

'A native gentleman, who is certainly not the inferior of any European on the Gold Coast in character, ability or mercantile position.'[11] Thus described by

1 Brown, *Gold Coast and Asanti Reader*, ii, pp. 154–5. It was because of his appointment as *Tufuhin* that he often styled himself as the Mayor of Cape Coast, although the first person to hold that title officially was R. Hutchinson in 1858.

2 Kimble, *Political History*, p. 196   3 *Ibid.*, pp. 196–7

4 Brown, *Gold Coast and Ashanti Reader*, ii, p. 155

5 Sampson, *Gold Coast Men of Affairs*, pp. 109–11   6 *Ibid.*, p. 110

7 Kimble, *Political History*, p. 5   8 *Ibid.*, p. 6   9 *Ibid.*, p. 186

10 *Ibid.*, p. 90   11 Sampson, *Gold Coast Men of Affairs*, p. 117

Governor Pope-Hennessy, Francis Chapman Grant (1823–1894), a leading Cape Coast merchant, was a member of royal lineage of Ekumfi State who received his education in Britain and the United States.[1] In 1872 he was reported to be equal to any European on the coast in commercial standing. Grant became interested in mining in the 1880s, first as a promoter and then as chairman of the Gold Coast Native Concession Purchasing Company, the first mining concession syndicate owned entirely by Africans.[2] Active also in politics, in 1858 he was elected to the Cape Coast Municipal Council[3] and in 1863, after Robert Hutchinson's death, he was appointed to the Legislative Council whose interests he served from 1863–1866 as well as 1869, 1871, 1873 and 1887.[4] Grant was also appointed treasurer of the Fante Confederation in 1872.[5]

John Sarbah

Father of the famous John Mensah Sarbah, John Sarbah (died 1892) was a leading Gold Coast merchant with stores at Anomabo, Saltpond, Elmina, Winneba, Dixcove and Axim,[6] with interests in the Gold Coast Native Concession Purchasing Company[7] and the rubber trade.[8]

Thomas Hughes

Merchant and pioneer in the modern mining industry, Thomas Hughes imported some heavy machinery to start mining activities in western Wassa. He struck a rich vein in 1861, but the chief forbade him to exploit it and destroyed his machinery.[9] Hughes became involved in politics when he was provisionally appointed the Collector-General of the poll tax in 1856[10] and two years later was elected to the Cape Coast Municipal Council.[11] Playing a leading role in the fight of King Aggrey of Cape Coast against the encroachment of the British government on the traditional authority in Cape Coast, he was appointed in 1866 to represent the king and people of the town of Cape Coast and to assist King Aggrey.[12] Despite the fact that Hughes had clashed with the British authorities on the coast while fulfilling these responsibilities, the British local government entrusted him with an intermediary role between them and the Fantes who had

1 Dumett, 'The Rubber Trade of the Gold Coast', p. 82

2 Kimble, *Political History*, p. 22; Dumett, 'Rubber Trade of the Gold Coast', p. 82

3 Kimble, *Political History*, p. 186   4 *Ibid.*, p. 407   5 *Ibid.*, p. 249

6 Dumett, 'Rubber Trade of the Gold Coast', pp. 82–83

7 Kimble, *Political History*, p. 22

8 Dumett, 'Rubber Trade of the Gold Coast', pp. 82–83

9 Kimble, *Political History*, p. 15; H. W. Debrunner, *A History of Christianity in Ghana*, Accra, 1967, p. 178

10 Kimble, *Political History*, p. 189   11 *Ibid.*, p. 186

12 *Ibid.*, p. 215; for details on the conflict between Aggrey and the British authorities at Cape Coast, see Kimble, *Political History*, pp. 192–221.

met in council at Mankessim during the formative years of the Fante Confederation.[1]

John Smith

Educated at the government school at Cape Coast where he had been a pupil of Rev. Philip Quaque[2] (chaplain of the Committee of Merchants[3]) Joseph Smith became a teacher and by 1838 a local preacher for the Wesleyan Mission. Later he became secretary and an accountant in the service of the local government. Appointed Justice of the Peace in 1851, he was Acting Colonial Secretary under Maclean[4] as well as Collector of Customs,[5] finally being appointed to the Cape Coast Municipal Council in 1858.[6] Smith was also a merchant during these years and from 1844 to 1859 was a commercial correspondent of Forster and Smith, whose trade practices contributed to his bankruptcy in 1861.[7]

Other merchants

Henry Barnes, a Cape Coast merchant, was another correspondent of Forster and Smith until he discovered that he was losing money in his transactions with the firm and initiated trading on his own account in 1850.[8] Besides his commercial activities he was elected to the Cape Coast Municipal Council in 1858.[9] Other successful merchants include J. C. Hansen, who was described as 'a very extensive and respectable coloured merchant' and was elected to the Accra Municipal Council in 1858,[10] and William Lutterodt, L. Hesse and J. E. Richter – all of Danish ancestry. In 1836 when the Danish Governor had occasion to fine the Krobos he farmed it out to Richter's father, H. Richter, who was to recoup his money in palm oil.

These African merchants (with the exception of a few pure Africans like Ghartey) were mostly of English or Danish descent. Yet, even as Afro-European descendants they had an unquestioned place in African society because of their African mothers. In a way, their position in Gold Coast society was unique because of their dual relationship with European and African society and many of them, for instance Frank Cleland of Accra, Samuel Brew of Anomabo and James Bannerman of Accra, were related to traditional authorities by birth or marriage. At a time when trade was largely based on credit, the individual standing and applications probably played a part in the credit-worthiness of the

1 *Ibid.*, p. 225

2 See F. L. Bartels, 'Philip Quaque, 1741–1816', *T.G.C.T.H.S.*, i, part v, 1955, pp. 155–77

3 Kimble, *Political History*, p. 63   4 *Parl. Papers* 1865, Evidence of Smith, 8452

5 C.O. 96/58: Petition of Joseph Smith, 12 April 1862; Kimble, *Political History*, p. 66

6 Kimble, *Political History*, p. 186

7 C.O. 96/58: the petition of Joseph Smith, 12 April 1862; *African Times*, 4 Nov. 1862 and 24 Oct. 1870

8 *Parl. Papers* 1865, Evidence Q's.5730–5826, *passim*

9 Kimble, *Political History*, p. 186   10 *Ibid.*, p. 185

person concerned. It is probable that Africans like R. J. Ghartey and Frank Cleland who adopted European names did so for trade purposes.

In 1873 when George Alfred Henty arrived on the Gold Coast to cover the Asante war for a London newspaper he observed that, 'It is curious that all the names which one meets with in Bowdich are those of the leading people fifty years later.'[1] Some of them, Joseph Smith and George Blankson, for example, were often associated with and worked for the Wesleyan Mission. At some stage of their business career they were frequently employed as the correspondents of the two main British Merchant Houses, Forster and Smith or F. and A. Swanzy,[2] so that it is difficult at times to distinguish their views from those of British traders. It is also noteworthy that a number of them, like Samuel Collins Brew and Joseph Smith, failed in business at one time or another.

In addition to the African merchants, there were wealthy African women who were wives of Europeans on the coast. H. Bridge, who visited the Gold Coast in 1844, reported that 'all the Europeans have native wives'.[3] According to Bridge, 'These women are entrusted with all the property of their husbands, and are sometimes left for months in sole charge, while the merchants visit England.'[4] Prominent among these African women were Mrs Kate Swanzy, wife of Andrew Swanzy, and Mrs Barnes, wife of Henry Barnes.[5]

In 1873 when the British experienced difficulty finding carriers to transport loads into the interior Mrs Swanzy, Mrs Barnes and other wealthy women of Cape Coast provided the necessary people. Mrs Swanzy alone sent eighty of her people, of whom Henty thought perhaps about half a dozen were her slaves and the rest were her clients. Henty explained this system:

> The Clients include freed men and women, and their children and descendants, together with a number of others who have, from some reason or other, chosen one or other of the great houses as their protectors. Thus the Swanzys have for fifty years been the leading merchants of the place, and the descendants of the domestic slaves whom they have held during that time would in themselves, amount to a large clientele. There, too, are the families of their work people, who would, in times of distress or illness, come to them for assistance, and who look up to them as protectors as well as employers. So the connection extends, and becomes hereditary. On the one side there is advice, kindness, gifts at Christmas, help in sickness; upon the other, a sort of feudal obedience, a reliance in trouble, and a readiness, upon occasions of this sort, to carry out the wish of the protector. It is, indeed, a good deal the same position which the other natives occupy towards their chiefs; except that in the cases of persons like Mrs Swanzy and Mrs Barnes, the actual assistance and kindness shown to their clients is greater than that which the chiefs can afford to dispose.[6]

1 Henty, *March to Coomassie*, p. 207

2 Merchants like Joseph Smith and Robert Hutchinson worked for these firms.

3 Bridge, *Journal*, p. 141   4 *Ibid.*, p. 142

5 According to Andrew Swanzy, in 1874 Mrs Barnes was the only African with sufficient capital to trade on her own account by ordering goods directly from England. See 'On Trade with Western Africa with and without British Protection', p. 479.

6 Henty, *March to Coomassie*, p. 207

This quasi-feudal role imposed on the merchant-class was hardly compatible with their evolution into a class of capitalist entrepreneurs. Such a role played by the African merchants seems to be of key importance which partly explains the decline of this class when called upon to stand up to serious competition from European firms who had no social obligations on the coast. The clientele of the merchants was but one indication of their growing position, and influence and of the declining power of the traditional rulers. In 1873, after the British experienced considerable difficulty securing troops from the chiefs and people to carry loads inland, a reporter observed:

> It was supposed that the policy of the last twenty years (a policy which has very properly been directed to breaking the authority of the Kings here, of reducing their importance, and of making the people look up to the Government as the only authority) could be cancelled at once. The petty Kings and Chiefs of Cape Coast were called upon to raise armies of fighting men; but the Kings and Chiefs had years ago been deprived of their power by the Government here, and reduced to nonentities. Their authority was gone, and the police had to be called in to enable them to take out their men to the field.[1]

The decline of traditional rulers

The local merchants were able to rise to their position of eminence because of their wealth and their state as a power filled a vacuum as the influence of traditional rulers and chiefs declined. Wealth is a positive resource to be wielded in the maintenance of power but the interdiction of the Atlantic slave trade ended a profitable source of income for chiefs on the Gold Coast. The waning of the power of chiefs in the country probably began in 1807. Before this date, large profits from trade had enabled the chiefs to buy the firearms necessary for defence and customary ceremonial purposes; to maintain a position consistent with their dignity and authority; and even to act as a distributor of wealth among their people. However, with the passing of the slave trade went an important source of wealth and with it power and authority.

Beginning in 1807, when Asante invaded the coastal states, the gradual inability of the rulers to satisfy their subjects' demands was becoming evident. A diminishing source of wealth for rulers with the consequent inability to purchase sufficient firearms meant that they could not defend themselves against Asante attacks. This responsibility was to fall upon the British.[2] Beginning with Asante confrontations with the coastal states in 1807, and subsequent clashes in 1811, 1814–1816, 1823–1826, 1863–1864 and 1873–1874, dispatches from the Gold Coast, although sometimes highly biased, were not far from the truth in asserting that if the British left the country Asante would overrun it.[3] At any rate without British aid the defence of the coastal states would have been difficult after 1807. As two merchants put it, 'the great bond of attraction which unites the people to us [British] is the value of our support against Ashanti'. The in-

1 *Ibid.*, p. 210

2 Kwame Arhin, 'Diffuse Authority among the Coastal Fanti', pp. 68–69

3 C.O. 96/19: J. Bannerman and Brodie Cruickshank to Winniett, 22 Aug. 1850; Metcalfe, *Documents*, pp. 219–20

ability to defend their states was one indication of the gradual diminution of the power of the Gold Coast chiefs.

Further evidence was the cessation of customary rents, gifts and salaries they had formerly been entitled to receive from European traders. From the start of European trade on the Gold Coast there had been the practice of paying customs, rent for the ground on which the fort stood and of giving presents to chiefs and men of influence and authority on the coast in order to promote trade.[1] As Meredith wrote in 1811:

It may be necessary to remark that we appear to claim no right of conquest in Africa, as far as it respects the natives: the company pay ground-rent and water-custom at most of their settlements. The people are regulated by their own laws and customs, and will not submit to ours. When they agree to any laws between the Whites and themselves, they generally break them, if they operate against the interests of the Blacks. The forts have been maintained for the purpose of trade only, and to enforce laws is attended with much difficulty, expense, and risk; consequently, it is prudent to avoid hostilities, if they can any way decently be avoided; and indeed it must be so, while our force in that country is so small.[2]

While the English clearly distinguished between ground rent and customary contributions, the Dutch did not. Dr Daaku has pointed out that in agreements between the Dutch and Africans on the payment of ground rent it was expected that at a certain time the Dutch should pay their rents in specific goods. It is therefore possible that in fulfilling their obligations, Europeans, at times, obscured their true significance by describing them as gifts or presents.[3] Whether or not gifts to chiefs were an integral part of the ground rent for forts, all residents were expected to contribute towards customary obligations. John Mensah Sarbah has written:

In addition to the ground rents paid to them, the headmen of the towns enforced the payment of sundry monthly allowances, including Christmas presents, chiefs' customs, water customs, Sunday and Wednesday liquor, and other contributions towards the expenses attending the observance of the yearly stool custom of the principal local ruler.[4]

Daaku further elaborates this point:

There were and still are festivals held annually at different times in many places, on which occasions every member of the community contributed towards the cost of the celebrations. The festivities comprised of dancing and merry-making, as well as the renewal of the bonds between the living and the

1 Sarbah, *Fanti National Constitution*, p. 89; Daaku, *Trade and Politics*; Davies, *Royal African Company*, p. 282

2 Meredith, *Account of the Gold Coast of Africa*, pp. 103–4

3 Daaku, *Trade and Politics*, p. 64

4 Sarbah, *Fanti National Constitution*, p. 89

dead. Theoretically the rulers were expected to entertain their visitors on a lavish scale. In actual practice, however, it was the people who bore the expenses, through the tributes and presents made to the chiefs. It was a common practice to ask the people to contribute specific items according to their geographical environment or their profession. The regular payments that the Europeans made during such periods, therefore, were nothing but their expected contribution made in accordance with customary law. All the resident Europeans were expected to fulfil such obligations.[1]

The practice of giving customary gifts became expensive and in 1780 the president and council at Cape Coast Castle attempted, without success, to abolish some of the contributions towards customary observance.[2]

In the last years of the rule of the Company of Merchants on the Gold Coast, the payments of presents and rents amounted to between £500 and £600[3] but these payments were not resumed when the Crown took over the settlements.[4] Although the payment of tribute was rejected the provision of the arms to African allies was continued on a small scale.

The Committee of Merchants resumed the customary payments, gifts and salaries when they began administering the settlements in 1828, but in 1836 George Maclean abolished it. Maclean said that the monthly allowances to chiefs amounted to securing their friendship or their services when required for war and that the coastal chiefs who received salaries were also required to render certain services such as defence and keeping certain roads cleared. Since George Maclean felt that the people had in no instance performed any of the services they were bound to perform, he discontinued the pay.[5] But if there is any truth in a memorandum King Joseph Aggrey of Cape Coast sent to London in 1836 to protest about the suspension of salaries to African chiefs, it would seem that the protest of African chiefs against Maclean's rule was a factor in discontinuing the salaries.[6]

Maclean could take such an action because with the declining influence of chiefs, he could afford to flout their authority. Furthermore, the ground rent paid for the forts which had reverted to Asante after 1807 was not paid to the coastal chiefs after her defeat in 1826.[7]

The Colonial Office later instructed the local government on the coast that the allowances in question were never given for any specific purposes and that they should be resumed. The British Government, however, added in reference to duties such as cleaning of streets and the like that:

1 Daaku, *Trade and Politics*, p. 64   2 Sarbah, *Fanti National Constitution*, p. 89

3 Newbury, *British Policy Towards West Africa*, p. 14. These payments are obviously much smaller than the customary payments European traders had made to African rulers at the height of the slave trade.

4 *Ibid.*

5 Metcalfe, *Maclean*, p. 149. The customary payments amounted to about £360 in coast money.

6 C.O. 96/15: Petition of Joe Aggrey to Governor Winniett, 30 Jan. 1849

7 C.O. 98/1A: Council Minutes, 8 Feb. 1836; Metcalfe, *Documents*, pp. 141–2

We think it highly necessary and conducive to the health and comfort of all classes, and cannot be too strictly enforced; we do therefore direct that, in the event of any refusal to comply with this requisition, the portion of the town showing the least neglect be mulcted for a time of a part of the whole of their allowances.[1]

The Danes followed the British example of abolishing payments to African rulers. At a meeting of the council at the Danish settlement at Accra, the members resolved that payment to African rulers was antiquated and that they ought to follow the practice of other Europeans in abolishing it. They argued that they settled numerous cases among the Africans in the castle at Christiansborg without any payments from the local people. The council said that the fact that cases were brought before local merchants rather than the chiefs showed that the traders had advantages over the traditional authorities and that the time had come for the Danes to restrict gifts to chiefs in the Danish establishments.[2] Consequently, all salaries to chiefs in the Danish settlements were suspended in 1844.[3]

While salaries and ground rents were disallowed, occasional presents to the chiefs were continued until the British Crown resumed control of the settlements. In 1847 resident merchants held a meeting at Cape Coast Castle and wondered how much longer the chiefs who were deprived not only of this source of employment, but also of the exercise of complete authority, would continue to submit to British authority. The merchants present at the meeting resolved:

That since the discontinuance of occasional presents to the Native Chiefs which during the Government of the President and Council had been so useful in securing the obedience and respect of the People, and the consequent general peace and prosperity of the Country, there had been a gradual and perceptible change in the feelings of the different Tribes to the British Government, not that their attachment and obedience were now more the result of necessity than the spontaneous feeling of the heart, and it was doubtful how much longer the chiefs, deprived as they were by the British Government of exercising uncontrolled authority over the people, would submit to the dictation of the British authorities; that it is therefore highly expedient to resume the practice of giving occasional presents to the Native Chiefs.[4]

The disappearance of salaries and the use of presents to buy the loyalty of indigenous chiefs were further overt signs of the waning influence of the coastal rulers.

The chiefs' influence had especially suffered under the extended jurisdiction of Maclean. 'The Supervision of the government tended to lessen the consequence

1 Sarbah, *Fanti National Constitution*, p. 90

2 *G.J.* No. 504, 22 Aug. 1843, Edward Carstensen to George Lutterodt

3 *G.J.* No. 553, 1844

4 C.O. 96/21: A meeting of the sessions held at Cape Coast Castle on Wednesday, 1 December 1847. Present were: Brodie Cruickshank, F. Swanzy, Thomas Hutton, Henry Smith and Andrew Swanzy and all European merchants.

of the chiefs,' wrote an observer.[1] One Governor who deplored this practice asserted: 'I may say here, once and for all, that I consider of late years, there has been too much interference with the authority of the native chiefs . . . This interference has been exerted by ignoring the native tribunals, and by allowing the chiefs to be summoned before our courts in comparatively trivial cases.'[2] The decline of their influence and the interference with their power did not go without protest. King Joseph Aggrey, whose prestige and power suffered at the hands of George Maclean, wrote:

> This President aforementioned ruled the people in the Town with vigour without consulting me. His sway was such that the Town's people daily complained of him. Your memorialist himself could not advise the said President Maclean. At length the Pynins [*sic*], Chiefs and other respectable members in the Town without the knowledge of your memorialist wrote a letter to the Colonial Office in England informing the then Secretary of State of the conduct of Captain Maclean. The letter was received and the President received a check to reign with ease and humanly. After the President had received his instructions your memorialist and Chiefs of the Town were assembled in the Hall of Cape Coast Castle and were shamefully treated, after which your memorialist's pay was stopped without a cause as a punishment.[3]

Another observer remarked upon the chiefs' protesting the infringement upon their authority by stating that

> . . . individual chiefs have, upon several occasions, attempted to assert their independence, and to resist the authority of the government; but although a partial and temporary success has sometimes attended their efforts, yet they have never been able to withstand its power for any length of time. The arms of rebellion have dropped one by one from their hands, without the intervention of force, and left them naked and defenceless, at the mercy of the government. Their own dependents, sensible to their increased privileges through the intervention of the Europeans, did not desire to see their chiefs independent of control, and were therefore lukewarm in their support.[4]

With their ever-decreasing political and economic power, it was unlikely that the chiefs could successfully reassert their former influence.

Whatever vestiges of the traditional ruler's economic power and political influence remained by the middle of the nineteenth century were eclipsed by the emerging indigenous merchants. Africanus Horton observed this change writing that Mankesim, the old capital of Fante, used to be a 'famous Fetish town for all the Fantees, and exercised considerable control over the Government of the country; but, through the Government aided by the educated inhabitants, it has now no influence'.[5]

1 Cruickshank, *Eighteen Years*, ii, p. 11

2 C.O. 96/41: Pine to Labouchere, 31 Aug. 1857

3 C.O. 96/15: Petition of Joe Aggrey to Governor Winniett, 30 Jan. 1840

4 Cruickshank, *Eighteen Years*, ii, p. 12

5 Horton, *West African Countries and Peoples*, p. 120

Basel Mission Factory

Basel Mission Carpentry Workshop

Trade, economic and social change

The rise of the African merchants was the result of many factors, chief among which were opportunities for entering trade enhanced by London merchant houses like Forster, Smith and Swanzy which sent quantities of goods to correspondents on the coast to be sold on commission and often available on easy credit. Another clearly discernible factor contributing to the prominence of the African merchants can almost be described as a revolution in the Gold Coast, and, indeed, the West African, trade – the arrival of steamships. The formation of the African Steamship Company in 1852 for trade in West Africa regularised and shortened the transportation between England and West Africa from 35 days to 21 days and less. More important, the steamships took the seasonal problems out of shipping. While all previous shipping to the coast had belonged to trading firms and carried goods to their agents and correspondents the steamship company was an innovation in the sense that it provided a freight service only for its customers. This resulted in an increase of trade of the variety of products dealt in, and in the tonnage of British shipping in West Africa which in 1854 totalled 57,000 and by 1874 stood at 504,000. In 1869, another steamship company, the British and African Steam Navigation Company, was also formed. Larger vessels, fewer crews and more voyages per year enabled the steamship companies to reduce freight charges.[1]

The impact of steamers on the Gold Coast was great with an increasing number of the people encouraged by the smaller firms in London to enter directly into the import and export trade. Such firms and their correspondents on the coast were able to compete effectively against the larger merchant houses which continued to send goods in their own ships on consignment to correspondents on the Gold Coast. So successful were the steamships that their operations elicited the jealousy of large merchant houses. Companies like Forster and Smith, and F. and A. Swanzy became alarmed at the increased direct trade with indigenous merchants and tried to interfere with the operations of the steamships which hit at the trade that had once been their monopoly.[2] The result was clear by 1857 when it was observed with slight exaggeration that 'the old class of large European merchants who greatly monopolised the trade have passed away and the amount of business done formerly by a few, is now in the hands of numerous small traders, chiefly natives'.[3] Despite the growing participation of the Africans in the trade a large part of it was still in the hands of Forster and Smith and F. and A. Swanzy.

With augmented trade and social change on the Gold Coast and growing influence of the power of a new class of merchants, this group came to dominate the affairs of the Gold Coast. Frequently in opposition to the British and sometimes vying for power with the traditional rulers, they often used their influence to protect and to foster their own interests. As Raymond Firth has observed:

> In a situation of economic growth, leaders are to a considerable extent self-recruiting or self-generating group. They also develop vested interests.

1 McPhee, *Economic Revolution in British West Africa*, p. 71; Brooks, *Yankee Traders, Old Coasters and African Middlemen*, pp. 126–7 and p. 269

2 C.O. 96/40: C. H. Gregory to the Secretary of State for the Colonies, 19 May 1856

3 C.O. 96/4: Freeman to Pine, 27 June 1857

Incentives to leadership may consist partly in substantial material benefits, but usually include, even more significantly, status attribution and the command of power.[1]

As leadership for economic growth depends, among other factors, upon the relationship of economic power and political power, it is to be expected that the indigenous merchants saw political power as a vital factor of their economic position. Such power was necessary for the promotion of an outlook and acceptance of new values needed to mobilise the resources of the traditional economy for progress. Thus, there is often a change in the structure of power and in economic growth with the old elite often being displaced.[2] The character of the chiefly and traditional institutions on the Gold Coast, however, were sufficiently flexible to accommodate a good deal of social change, so that a Ghartey or a Brew could rise through trade to chiefly office. Despite their wealth and influence the new class was often prepared to work with and through the chiefs.

Between 1850 and 1874, at a time when great social changes were taking place, this attempt by the merchants to obtain power and influence was reflected in all the major events in a critical period for the Gold Coast as the country was faced with many crises: the poll tax, the Krobo dispute, the Asante invasion, the Anlo war, the exchange of territories between the Dutch and the English and the Fante Confederation. The wars had a disrupting influence on trade and the other events brought to the fore the conflict inherent in the change of political and economic power. Economic factors often underlay these events and the so-called 'native merchants' or 'educated Africans' frequently used their influence to manipulate traditional rulers in furthering their causes. This is not to say that the chiefs and traditional rulers did not have any grievances of their own; the Poll Tax Ordinance failed to honour the stipends it had promised. The government was also pursuing a deliberate policy to reduce the chiefs' influence. As a traveller wrote:

> To ensure respect from the Ashantees and other African tribes here, their chiefs are not, it appears, to be shown much consideration. The policy here is to keep the chiefs at a distance; and to make them wait the white man's pleasure, until he has leisure to hear their 'palavaer'. In this way, and by the impartial distribution of justice to the natives living under English protection, the forts and the guns being in an efficient state, the troops well disciplined, has the English influence become so predominant.[3]

They also resented the recruitment of their slaves for the government's Gold Coast Corps. As Freeman observed:

> ... extreme dissatisfaction existed among the Chiefs and Headmen at the time of the raising of the Gold Coast Corps, when many of their domestic slaves enlisted as soldiers, and thus escaped from under their authority, with-

1 Raymond Firth, 'Leadership and Economic Growth', *I.S.S.J.* xvi, 2, 1964, p. 190

2 *Ibid.*, p. 199

3 James Edward Alexander, *Narrative of a Voyage of Observation among the Colonies of Western Africa*, London, 1837, pp. 155–6

out their approbation . . . and without any preparatory arrangement being made for their redemption.[1]

They complained, too, about

. . . the frequent long detention of the Heads of the people at the Police Court – Towns on the Coast, (especially at Cape Coast,) awaiting various judicial proceedings on matters of comparatively small moment; thereby putting them often to a heavy expense in supporting their numerous trains of domestic servants, without whom the etiquette and usages of the country would not allow them to travel.[2]

Merchants and political power

Although in 1849 a group of local merchants had written to Governor Winniett to say that the existing form of government they enjoyed under the Crown was the best and wished it to remain unaltered[3] it was not long before they began to oppose it. Some divergences of interest can be discerned within the trading clan. Even though many of the African merchants were indebted to, and more or less dependent on, the two principal European firms, Forster and Smith and F. and A. Swanzy, some indigenous merchants preferred a government not to be in the hands of the rival resident European merchants who had attempted to restrict their trading activities with ships engaged in the floating trade. Nonetheless the African merchants often acted in concert with European merchants in seeking to dominate the affairs of the Gold Coast and the merchants always held up the period of rule by the merchant committee as a period of unrivalled prosperity due to expert advice from the council of local merchants.[4]

In 1850 when a legislative council was established, the merchants agitated to dominate by constituting the majority of members and even though the merchant community had representatives in two of the five seats in the persons of James Bannerman and Brodie Cruickshank, they were not content.[5] This arrangement deliberately preserved an 'official majority' in the council. As a modern scholar has put it, 'the crux of the matter was that the merchants wanted not simply representation, but control of both Governor and Judicial Assessor'.[6] In the view of some merchants it was folly not to give the merchants a larger role in the government:

As long as the council is composed chiefly of executive officers resident in the castle, having few and faint sympathies with the people, and to whom the welfare of this country is, by the circumstances of their appointment, subordinate

1 C.O. 96/41: Freeman to Pine, 27 June 1857   2 *Ibid.*

3 C.O. 96/19: Memorial of Native Traders, in Winniett to Grey, 25 Aug. 1850. Also, C.O. 96/19: Bannerman to Cruickshank, 22 Aug. 1850; Metcalfe, *Documents*, pp. 219–20

4 C.O. 19/12: Forster to Grey, 22 March 1847; Metcalfe, *Documents*, p. 203; Bannerman, Cruickshank and Clouston to Forster, 2 Feb. 1847

5 *Ibid.* The other officials of the legislature included a Governor, Judicial Assessor and Collector of Customs.

6 Metcalfe, 'After Maclean', *T.H.G.C.T.* i, part v, 1955, p. 182

to their own direct pecuniary interests, who are utterly ignorant of the trade and nature of the country, who, looking upon their residence there merely as a stepping stone to a better appointment somewhere else and longing for the day when they shall finally quit the shores of Africa, feel little interest in its prosperity, and who do not possess that respect and confidence on the part of the inhabitants which long residence and continued intercourse with them confer – the co-operation of the merchants and people will not be obtained.[1]

Some of the European merchants like Swanzy and Cruickshank (who was for a long time the local representative of the firm Forster and Smith) were indeed long residents on the coast and were, generally, in closer touch with the people through trading, marriage and concubinage arrangements. They therefore urged the election of four more members by merchants and respectable inhabitants to the legislature because of their close association with the people.[2] It was argued that if the scheme to elect additional members failed and the council continued in its present form, an alternative arrangement unconnected with the government would be the formation of a separate chamber composed of chiefs, or representatives of the rulers where local affairs of the country could be debated. The proponents felt that such a council would bind the inhabitants together and bring an end to quarrels among them.[3] But the Secretary of State who was not 'prepared to place in the hands of a few merchants (whose interests, or at least what they believe to be such, are by no means necessarily identical with those of the population) the power of controlling the government' did not look with favour upon the scheme.[4] Although Grey did not want the structure of the legislature altered he suggested that 'a chamber of commerce should be created and that by requiring the drafts of laws to be made public before they are passed, this body would be enabled to advise upon them'.[5] This proposal did not satisfy the traders.

Their hope of securing a majority on the council failing, the leading spokesmen of the merchants proposed (probably not very seriously),[6] that an 'Assembly of Native Chiefs' should be established. The merchants maintained that there was no legally acknowledged medium of communication between the people and the government except through proclamations, orders to individual chiefs and the intervention of the police. They felt that there was no way to assess the sentiments of the country on necessary measures and these could not be carried out without the agreement of the people. Furthermore, they deemed

---

1 C.O. 96/21: H. Smith and F. Swanzy to Earl Grey, 16 Aug. 1850, Metcalfe, *Documents*, pp. 217–18

2 The merchants changed their minds about an elective council in 1851 because it was felt that while merchants of the highest respectability could vote, such native authorities could carry an election by their sheer numbers. Metcalfe, *Documents*, p. 221.

3 C.O. 96/21: H. Smith and F. Swanzy to Earl Grey, 16 Aug. 1859; Metcalfe, *Documents*, pp. 217–18

4 C.O. 96/21: Minute by Grey, 5 Nov. 1850

5 C.O. 96/19: Minute by Grey, 16 Nov. 1850

6 See Metcalfe, 'After Maclean', pp. 186–7, where he suggests that the idea was not a serious one and that the merchants were taken aback when Grey favoured the proposal.

it essential to have the assistance and cooperation of the indigenous authorities in implementing legislation affecting the inhabitants. They propounded:

> That as it would be perfectly impossible to govern the immense population of the Gold Coast without the instrumentality of the chiefs, it is an imperative duty, incumbent upon the Government, to endeavour to elevate the moral standard of native jurisdiction by such a general code of Regulations as may be found necessary to meet the exigencies of the country. That for this purpose, a legally constituted deliberative assembly, to be called 'The Assembly of Native Chiefs', be appointed to meet at Cape Coast Castle twice every year for the purpose of framing with the assistance of the Judicial Assessor and other magistrates such laws as shall, when sanctioned and confirmed by the Governor, become generally binding upon the natives of the country; and, that the members of this Assembly receive a small annual stipend from the Government.[1]

The 'Assembly of Native Chiefs' suggested by Bannerman and Cruickshank was somewhat similar to the alternate proposal of Smith and Swanzy in forming a council of Chiefs. While realising that Bannerman and Cruickshank occupied a somewhat ambiguous position by their very association with the local administration and their position as the spokesmen of the merchants, it is not unlikely that their suggestion, following closely upon that of their colleagues, was one pressure tactic of the Gold Coast merchants to force the Secretary of State to give them what they really wanted – a majority in the legislative council. This, in part, would explain why the spokesmen of the merchant community eschewed their own proposal when Hill took it up. The merchants objected to the Assembly on the unconvincing pretext that:

> As each king or chief moves attended by a very large and imposing body of followers fully armed, a general meeting, under such circumstances, would be the means of showing them their great physical power, as compared to ours, and therefore might defeat the object we should have in convening the assembly, and possibly be productive of the most serious consequence, should it have the effect of weakening the influence now possessed by the authorities here; added to which, each king or chief, according to custom, would expect a suitable present, and, the number being very great, the expenditure to satisfy all would necessarily be a larger outlay than your Lordship might be disposed to sanction.[2]

The suggestion of the 'Native Assembly' as expressed by the merchants was not devoid of clauses inserted for the benefit of the mercantile interest. The Assembly in the form proposed would have included the principal merchants who were all magistrates. These magistrates and the Judicial Assessor were to assist the Chiefs in framing 'such laws as shall, when sanctioned and confirmed by the Governor, become generally binding upon the natives of the country'. In essence, if the Governor accepted the suggested 'Native Assembly' in the form

1 C.O. 96/19: James Bannerman and Brodie Cruickshank to Winniett, 22 Aug. 1850; Metcalfe, *Documents*, pp. 219–20

2 *Ibid.*

it was proposed he would in effect create an alternative legislative body where the influence of the Mercantile Community could prevail. Grey approved the idea of a Native Assembly put forward for consideration:

> I entirely approve of the proposal to have a half yearly meeting of chiefs to make laws and regulations for the districts, and that these chiefs should be paid. I think the salaries should be sufficient for their maintenance in a respectable manner, according to the notions of the people as to the manner in which chiefs ought to live, and that, in return for these salaries, they should undertake the duty and responsibility of maintaining the laws and enforcing order in their respective districts.[1]

In order to provide for the salaries of the chiefs Grey suggested a small hut tax, as had been instituted in Natal in 1849, or a poll tax.[2]

The poll tax issue

It is significant that the initial merchant opposition to Grey's proposal was not to the poll tax, but rather to the council of chiefs.[3] The Assembly which was to be 'composed of his Excellency the Governor, his council, and the chiefs and headmen of the countries upon the Gold Coast'[4] did not include magistrates as had been suggested by Bannerman and Cruickshank. For the tax itself there was no serious opposition, as Hill affirmed: 'All the persons to whom I have spoken on the subject seem to think that it would be a desirable tax, and that no serious opposition will be offered to such a measure.'[5] Among those consulted on the proposed tax were George Blankson, Samuel Collins Brew, and other prominent African merchants.[6] Bannerman and Cruickshank had also agreed in principle to the tax saying that they did not anticipate any difficulty in raising a revenue from the poll tax.[7]

Such a need to raise revenue from the Gold Coast had been considered long before the Poll Tax Ordinance was passed in 1852. The parliamentary grant of £4,000 was, of course, insufficient for the increasing commitments of the government when it assumed control over the settlements in 1843. Although customs duties had been a potential source of revenue, the Dutch and Danish forts, dovetailing those of the British, made the imposition of tariffs difficult.[8] In order to raise a revenue Governor Winniett in 1847 had proposed levying a duty of threepence on each gallon of rum and gin.[9] The possibility of raising a

1 C.O. 96/19: Minute by Grey, 16 Nov. 1850; Metcalfe, *Documents*, p. 221

2 *Ibid.*

3 C.O. 96/22: Hill to Grey, 27 Oct. 1851; Metcalfe, *Documents*, p. 230

4 C.O. 96/25: Poll Tax Ordinance, 19 April 1852; Metcalfe, *Documents*, pp. 230–2

5 C.O. 96/22: Hill to Grey, 27 Oct. 1851; Metcalfe, *Documents*, p. 230

6 Priestley, *West African Coast Society*, p. 159

7 C.O. 96/19: Bannerman and Cruickshank to Winniett, 22 Aug. 1850

8 Kimble, *Political History*, p. 169

9 C.O. 96/11: Winniett to Grey, 20 May 1847

revenue in support of the settlements had been one of the arguments advanced for purchasing the Danish forts.[1] The Poll Tax Ordinance of 1852 was, therefore, part of a measure to raise needed revenue for increasing governmental expenses and commitments.

The story of the poll tax is well known and cannot be told here in great detail.[2] It was instituted on the Gold Coast after the meeting of chiefs of the central and western regions at Cape Coast in April, 1852, which was set up as a legislature and presided over by the Governor to enact laws, subject to his approval, 'as it shall see fit for the better government of these countries'. In addition this assembly agreed to pay an annual tax of one shilling sterling per head for every man, woman and child residing in the districts under British protection. The agreement stated:

> . . . that the revenue derived from this tax, after payment of the stipends of the chiefs, and other expenses attending its collection, be devoted to the public good in the education of the people, in the general improvement and extension of the judicial system, in affording greater facilities of internal communication, increased medical aid, in such other measures of improvement and utility as the state of the social progress may render necessary, and that the chiefs be informed of the mode of its application, and entitled to offer such suggestion on this point as they may consider necessary.[3]

In spite of the obstruction from what Hill called 'educated natives', the ordinance went into effect. Hill had complained to Earl Grey:

> The great difficulty that I found in my Government was the impossibility of getting at the chiefs to secure their support in carrying out any measures of utility; added to which certain educated natives, with no real pretension to any power, were in the practice of assuming an authority which did not belong to their position; by such means exercising an undue influence with the chiefs and headmen, and generally opposing, in an underhand manner, the efforts of the Governor. And I am quite aware, in my own case, they have done all in their power to induce the natives not to agree to the proposed poll tax.[4]

Frank Swanzy of the firm of F. and A. Swanzy was among those opposed to the introduction of the poll tax. Swanzy wrote to the Colonial Office: 'I cannot but think that such a tax is highly impolitic and will lead by and by to disputes and bad feeling.' Swanzy wanted to ascertain whether the money produced by the tax would be at the disposition of the Governor alone or whether the Legislative Council would have any control over it. He suggested that it would be more satisfactory to the people who paid the tax if they knew that their money was expended by persons who had long been resident among them and who would

1 Metcalfe, *Documents*, p. 217

2 The story is examined in length in Kimble, *Political History*, pp. 168–91; Reindorf, *History of the Gold Coast*, pp. 324–33

3 C.O. 96/25: Poll Tax 'Ordinance', 19 April 1852; Metcalfe, *Documents*, pp. 230–2

4 C.O. 96/25: Hill to Grey, 23 April 1852; Metcalfe, *Documents*, pp. 230–2

spend it in a manner most likely to be beneficial to their country. Better still, the funds should be placed at the disposition of the natives and European magistrates who were, of course, merchants.[1]

In August, 1852, after instituting the poll tax in the western region Hill also secured the agreement of the people of the eastern region to pay,[2] but not without some hesitation.[3] With the population paying one shilling sterling each, it was estimated that the tax would yield a revenue of £20,000 per annum. The influential merchant and the chief agent of Forster and Smith on the Gold Coast, Brodie Cruickshank, became the first Collector-General of the poll tax, a post he relinquished upon becoming Acting Governor in August, 1853. The collection of the tax proceeded quietly during its first year and totalled £7,567.[4]

By late 1853 resistance to the tax was beginning to appear and Acting Governor Cruickshank decided not to collect the tax between 1 August and 31 December 1853.[5] In January, 1854, when it was announced that the second instalment of the tax was due, the people between Accra and the Volta refused to pay and riots broke out in Accra. Another attempt to collect the taxes in the Accra area in August led to more riots which in turn led to the bombardment of Labadi, Teshi and Christiansborg with the resultant loss of life and property.[6] The income derived from the poll tax collection declined after the first year as evidenced by the figures below:[7]

Year	£
1853	7,567
1854	3,625
1855	3,990
1856	3,353
1857	3,192
1858	2,921
1859	2,351
1860	1,725
1861	1,552

Ostensibly, the reason given for the opposition to the Poll Tax Ordinance was its failure to fulfil its promise to pay the chiefs and devote part of the money collected to social improvements. Despite Governor Benjamin Pine's attempt in 1857–1858 to reform the poll tax collection and its disbursement the tax re-

1 C.O. 96/26: F. Swanzy to Parkington, 13 July 1852

2 C.O. 96/25: Hill to Parkington, 29 Aug. 1852

3 Reindorf, *History of the Gold Coast*, 2nd ed., p. 324

4 Kimble, *Political History*, p. 187. The original figure sent to the Colonial Office was £6,656 9s 11d

5 C.O. 96/40: Ord to Labouchere, 16 May 1856; Metcalfe, *Documents*, pp. 255–6

6 Kimble, *Political History*, p. 179; Reindorf, *History of the Gold Coast*, 2nd ed., pp. 323–33

7 Kimble, *Political History*, p. 187. As Kimble has pointed out there are slight discrepancies between this table and the annual statements sent to the Colonial Office.

ceipts decreased, with no attempts made to collect it after 1862.[1] Although the poll tax scheme failed, its mere implementation in the first instance did not help the chief's declining influence. The whole poll tax episode must have affected the chiefs' standing among their people since it was they who consented to the tax. In 1857 Benjamin Pine reported that it had lowered them in the eyes of the people, and 'in some places almost destroyed their power'.

> As they have a percentage of the proceeds of the tax, the people have regarded them as mere instruments of extortion. The consequence has been that in some places the power exercised by the chiefs has fallen into the hands of the dregs of the people.[2]

Pine lamented the declining power of the chiefs because he felt it was a serious evil to destroy their power until an efficient substitute could be provided. Yet, because of the rising influence of the African merchants, he realised that it was impossible to restore the power of the chiefs:

> At any rate, the restoration of the power of the chiefs in these towns was impossible. There are parts of the population over which they could never acquire control. There has grown up a large class of native merchants and traders, the greater part of whom are in advance of them in wealth and intelligence.[3]

Much of the disaffection with the poll tax and with British rule in general centred on the indigenous merchants at Cape Coast. It was not without justification that the Colonial Office blamed them for the troubles on the Gold Coast:

> Cape Coast Town has always been under the influence of half-caste traders, men of a certain amount of substance and intelligence, connected with the houses of three trading firms [Forster and Smith, F. and A. Swanzy and Messrs. King of Bristol] which carry on the commerce of this part of Africa with England; mercantile brokers which governed these forts, until Parliament in 1846 [sic] thought it proper that the Government should take the control out of their hands. There has been already a contest between the officers respecting the Government and this trading interest.[4]

More important for the purpose of this study are the economic implications and impact of the imposition of the tax. It is significant that an imposition of tax had been considered and furthermore that the tax was to be levied in currency and not in kind. This in itself is an indication of the state of growth towards a modern economy that the Gold Coast had reached by the middle of the nineteenth century.

In the western region where gold dust passed as currency the taxes were collected in gold dust and in the eastern region where cowries were the currency the tax was levied in cowrie shells. The mint value of gold dust was nearly £4 an ounce, but in 1843 an order in council established its value at £3 12s. Although merchants continued to buy gold at £4 an ounce, the local government

1 *Ibid.*, pp. 189–91   2 C.O. 96/41: Pine to Labouchere, 30 April 1857

3 *Ibid.*   4 C.O. 96/31: Minute by Merivall, 14 Feb. 1855

on the Gold Coast used the £3 12s value which was known as the sterling value. The 10% difference was supposed to cover transportation, insurance and other costs involved in sending the gold dust to Britain.[1] Since the poll tax was one shilling sterling it meant that the tax was really about 10% higher than it would have been on the basis of the current mercantile rate.

At the time of Poll Tax Ordinance in 1852, the value of cowries at Accra was 2,400 = 1 dollar or ackie of 5s, and 1 string of cowries = 1d. The Governor had been expecting to collect the tax in cowries, valued at about 3s 8d per head, which would have been approximately 4s currency, nearly 10% above its current value.[2] However, by 1850 the Gold Coast was about to experience a cowrie inflation. With what Brodie Cruickshank estimated to be 150 tons of cowrie imports a year, the value of the currency could not be expected to remain the same. The decline of cowries which was to affect the poll tax is given in the table below:[3]

Value of 2,000 cowries, reduced to shillings and pence, 1850–1895 in Accra

1850	4s 2d		1874	1s 3d
1853	2s 9d to 3s		1876	1s
1855	3s 4d variable		1881	1s
1857	–		1882	2s
1859	2s 6d		1889	–
1863	–		1895	1s
1870	2s 3d			

Although cowries had been worth 1d a string at the time the poll tax was being discussed, when the first year's receipts of 20,000 heads of cowries, 40 million shells, were accounted they were worth only 2s 9d a head instead of the expected 3s 8d a head. There was an unexpected fall in the exchange rate of cowries which led to a loss of £900.[4] Thus between the assessment and the intake of the first year's yield cowries lost about a quarter of their value.

Marion Johnson attributes this sudden inflation to the poll tax collection itself, and she further reasonably attributes much of the discontent in the eastern region to inflation:

At first sight, the collection of some 20,000 heads of cowries might be expected to have a deflationary effect; but in fact the effect was probably the opposite. Most of the cowries probably came from hoards (which might also help to explain the diminishing yield of the tax in subsequent years). Moreover, the government did not transport the cowries to the capital at Cape Coast, where they were not current, but exchanged them locally (hence the loss due to the fall in the exchange etc.). Thus some 20,000 heads of cowries were thrown suddenly on the exchange market – sufficient to account for a decline in the value of a currency which had recently undergone a large increase in quantity. An export of some 300 tons of cowries to the Gold Coast is recorded in 1853.

1 Johnson, 'Cowrie Currencies in West Africa', pp. 337–8

2 *Ibid.*, p. 338   3 *Ibid.*, p. 340   4 *Ibid.*, p. 338

The loss of confidence in the cowrie currency, and the consequent loss of value of savings, must have been at least aggravating causes in the serious political troubles which followed upon the introduction of the Poll Tax in the Accra area.[1]

That the discontent in the eastern region and the resistance to the poll tax were to a large measure due to the inflation of the cowrie currency cannot be denied. While the people in the Accra region, led by their chiefs, categorically refused to pay the tax[2] most people at Cape Coast based their resistance to the tax on the fact that the expenditure of the tax revenue had not fulfilled the promises of the poll tax ordinance.[3] While the poll tax failed to bring in the expected revenue, the need for funds to meet local government expenses on the Gold Coast remained as urgent as ever. Consequently, in 1855 the government raised the import duty from $\frac{1}{2}$% to 2% but despite complaints from merchants the duty remained.[4] The need to find some income for the administration of the settlements could not have been far from the minds of local government officials when a heavy fine was imposed on the Krobo in 1858 as the result of incidents following the attempt to collect the tax in Krobo. The Krobo fine, amounting to £8,125, supposedly to cover the cost of a punitive expedition against them was farmed out to Mr Robert Hutchinson, an African agent of F. and A. Swanzy. By this arrangement Hutchinson would pay the government in cash and recoup it in palm oil from the Krobos. He subsequently farmed out £3,000 of his contract to W. Edwards, an African agent of Forster and Smith, and £750 to William Addo, an independent African trader.[5] The dispute with Krobo and the means adopted to collect the fine led to a palm oil hold-up, the first of its kind on the Gold Coast,[6] which affected the palm oil trade on the Gold Coast in the late 1850s and the 1860s.[7]

The Krobo fine in oil has remarkable similarities with the Danish expedition against the Krobos in 1836 which equally resulted in a fine collected in palm oil by the Danish merchant, H. Richter, who received the farming of it.[8] Clearly

1 *Ibid.*   2 Reindorf, *History of the Gold Coast*, 2nd ed., p. 327

3 C.O. 96/34: Connor to Russell, 8 Sept. 1855; Thomas Hughes to Cockrane, 16 Aug. 1855; Kate Swanzy to Connor, 17 Aug. 1855; and J. Bartels to Cockrane, 27 Aug. 1855

4 C.O. 96/34: Conran to Russell, 2 July 1855

5 C.O. 96/44: Bird to Lytton, 9 Oct. 1858; the story of the Krobo fine and the oil boycott that followed is covered in detail in Freda Wolfson, 'A Price Agreement on the Gold Coast – the Krobo Oil Boycott, 1858–1866', *E.H.R.* vi, Series 2, 1, 1953–1954, pp. 68–77. G. E. Metcalfe is right in his assertion that Wolfson reads too much into the incident – more than the facts warrant. However, the outline of her story is basically correct. Straightforward reporting of the incident is Wolfson's own account in her thesis *British Relations with the Gold Coast, 1843–1886*, unpublished Ph.D. thesis, London University, 1959.

6 *Ibid.* The second hold-up was the effective cocoa hold-up of 1930–1931 which is treated in an article by Sam Rohdie, 'The Gold Coast Cocoa Hold-up of 1930–1931', *T.H.S.G.* ix, 1968, pp. 105–18.

7 See below and ch. 5.

8 See Nørregard, *Danish Settlements in West Africa*, p. 207; Metcalfe, *Maclean*, pp. 198–200. Neither Wolfson nor Kimble who have extensively covered the fine of 1858 and its consequence mentions the earlier episode in 1836 in connection with the similar event some eighteen years later. See also ch. 3.

one wonders why the Krobos bothered to push an activity which attracted trouble. That they continued the palm oil trade was indicative of their growing dependence upon the external trade. At the time of the earlier fine, George Maclean believed a Danish oil monopoly was the object of the campaign against the Krobo. While the local British government did not seek such a monopoly, their interest in the potentially rich palm oil district had been amply manifested in their purchase of that area from the Danes. However, the government's injudicious farming of the fine to the agent of the largest British mercantile firm on the Gold Coast meant that the firm would have been able to corner the palm oil market in the richest oil producing district in the country. The Krobo fine episode, like other events of the period of 1850–1862, should be viewed and placed in perspective by looking at the trading background.

The fluctuations in the trade (see p. 133), while bearing in mind normal vacillations in demand, may be explained partially by events on the Gold Coast. By late 1854 it was clear from Gold Coast correspondence that the Asante invasion of 1853–1854 and the unsettled state of the eastern region following the disturbances and bombardment of the area were beginning to affect trade, as was confirmed by the trade figures. In November, 1854, barely two months after the bombardment, some James Town merchants, including James Bannerman and J. E. Richter, wrote to Governor Hill to put down rebellion in the region as it was beginning to influence trade. They wrote:

> We, representing the mercantile interests of Accra, beg leave most respectfully to approach Your Excellency for the purpose of making known to you how severely we have suffered from the late disturbances. For several weeks past, trade has been entirely stopped in consequence of these troubles which are entirely and solely attributable to the violent spirit of Rebellion which has broken out in the Towns of Christiansborg, Tashee and Labaddy ... We earnestly entreat that this spirit of Rebellion which has so long been troubling the country, to the grievous detriment of commerce, civilisation and the general interests of the settlements, for business of all kind is entirely stopped.[1]

Some months later, these same groups of merchants who claimed 'a large pecuniary interest in the tranquillity and peace of the country' protested against attempts being made to collect the poll tax. They were convinced that it would 'be resisted by the people and much bloodshed and destruction of property ensue'.[2]

In Cape Coast merchants who feared a repetition of what had taken place in the eastern region called a meeting to protest against any force being used to collect the tax.[3] In September, 1855, when the spirit of resistance reached a peak the merchants were not without concern for their trade interests. Hutchinson, a leading Cape Coast merchant, deplored the government's 'ignoring of commercial interests and commercial men' in dealing with the tax question. The influence of the government was declining according to him because of 'the mercantile community not having been treated in a manner consistent with their

1 C.O. 96/31: John Marman, Charles Bannerman, Richter, etc. to Hill, 1 Nov. 1854

2 C.O. 96/33: James Town Merchants to Governor, 8 May 1855

3 C.O. 96/33: Cooper to Russell, 8 May 1855

position and the stake they have in the country and the rights of the people having been trampled upon'. He saw the state of the political and commercial affairs of the country verging on a crisis unless the government changed its policy and believed that it was

> impossible for those sustaining heavy commercial responsibilities in this country and otherwise interested in its social progress and prosperity to look quietly on and calmly survey the progress of a policy which threatens with the most destructive and fatal results.[1]

Another merchant, George Blankson, in his protest about the tax was emphatic about the role the merchants should play in the affairs of the Gold Coast. An important aid which he considered would greatly promote the welfare and prosperity and peace of the country was

> that if on all occasions the representatives of H.M. Government consulted on public matters with the respectable merchants both Natives and Europeans who I have no doubt would be very happy to advise for the peace and welfare of the country the state of affairs might wear a better aspect than at present.[2]

If the African merchants were concerned about the poll tax and the disturbances that followed, it was because they were interested in protecting their own trade concerns as well as in the welfare of their country. The merchants were not only concerned with the poll tax and the disturbances that followed in its wake, but also with the revenue duties which they felt drove trade away from the Gold Coast.

Import and export trade

The raising of the *ad valorem* duties on exports from $\frac{1}{2}\%$ to 2% in 1855 was resisted by the traders on the Gold Coast because they feared that it would drive trade away from the English settlements. Two African merchants protested:

> In 1829, an *ad valorem* duty of half per cent was levied upon Goods imported into the settlements, which has remained since; the local government, for the interest of trade, deeming it unsafe to increase it, because it would have a tendency to drive the trade from our own Market into that of our neighbours the Dutch, who being under no such restrictions could afford to sell cheaper to the Ashantees, with whom neither time nor distance is an object, so long as they can have access to a cheap market.[3]

It would seem that it was not simply the increased duty about which the merchants objected but the customs ordinance of which the duties formed a part. Andrew Swanzy showed his dissatisfaction with the measure when he described it:

1 C.O. *96/34*: R. Hutchinson to Sir William Molesworth, 10 Sept. 1855

2 C.O. *96/37*: G. Blankson to Russell, 15 May 1855

3 C.O. *96/34*: Henry Barnes and Joseph Smith to Connor, 30 Aug. 1855

The details of this customs ordinance clearly proved the utter absence of commercial knowledge in those who framed it. The value for duty on all imports was held to be the cost price at place of shipment, say for instance in England, with ten per cent added for freight charges, etc., and it was competent to the customs officers, when not satisfied with the value as declared by the importer, to pay him 10 per cent on the value declared and sell the goods on account of the Government; and whereas the freight in a large proportion of articles shipped to the coast exceeds 20 per cent on their value, and in some instances 100 per cent, it follows that the importer of such goods is liable to have them seized for deficiency in valuation, and to be paid very much less than their actual cost, and this although he strictly complied with the rules laid down.[1]

A further problem that concerned merchants about the customs ordinance was the question of using Cape Coast as a depot and being able to re-ship goods to settlements beyond British jurisdiction without paying duties. A merchant observed:

For years [1857–1866] merchants trading beyond the settlements, as well as within them, were prevented from landing goods in bond at the British ports, and were not even allowed to tranship goods from one vessel to another in British waters; this was, of course, done with the view of extorting the duties on goods intended for sale beyond the Protectorate. The consequence was that my firm, among others, were prevented from shipping such goods by steamers, and the utility of Cape Coast, as a depot, was destroyed.[2]

Although this rule was changed and merchants importing a certain amount of goods were allowed to enter them in bond, small traders were deprived of that privilege. Nevertheless, even when, in 1866, British ports on the Gold Coast were opened as a receptacle for bonded goods, the imports had to be re-shipped within a short period of time.[3] Although it is true that trade between 1855 and 1861 declined slightly after the customs duties were imposed in 1855 the trade returns indicate that they had by no means a disastrous effect upon commerce in the British ports.

During this period gold and ivory, the old staples of the country, continued to remain important, although ivory was showing a remarkable decline, as may be seen from the table below.

Given total exports from the Gold Coast 1850–1862 in £s:

1850	200,707	1857	124,394
1851	219,050	1858	154,136
1852	159,250	1859	118,563
1853	115,000	1860	110,457
1854	200,002	1861	145,819
1855	140,697	1862	102,086
1856	120,999		

1 A. Swanzy, 'On Trade in Western Africa with and without British Protection', p. 479

2 *Ibid.*   3 *Ibid.*

PRINCIPAL EXPORTS FROM THE GOLD COAST 1850–1862[1]

Year	Gold	Gold	Ivory	Ivory	Palm oil	Palm oil	Gum	Monkey skins	Guinea grains	Ground-nuts
	oz	£	tons	£	tons	£	£	£	£	£
1850	40,670	146,412	20	—	3,035	45,185	—	1,900	—	500
1851	46,000	175,600	13	—	1,464	39,500	1,900	—	—	—
1852	—	129,588	4	—	900	23,400	312	—	—	—
1853	10,000	36,000	142	—	1,750	70,000	3,000	—	—	—
1854	22,834	82,202	48	2,000	2,400	115,000	800	—	—	—
1855	—	33,104	—	1,000	—	80,000	1,721	—	700	2,068
1856	—	59,360	—	1,984	—	54,471	390	—	922	2,420
1857	—	68,913	—	1,538	—	50,402	1,250	—	174	38
1858	24,044	96,139	—	1,952	5,612	55,388	426	—	144	349
1859	20,427	73,544	—	2,941	1,125	38,346	991	—	35	—
1860	19,783	71,219	—	2,795	831	26,604	1,642	—	—	—
1861	24,772	84,358	—	1,032	—	52,398	2,342	—	—	—
1862	—	7,758	—	1,330	—	85,910	2,699	—	—	—

1 Blue Books 1850–1862 and C.O. 442/10–42; 1850–1862

To judge from the trade figures, 1850 and 1851 were about the peak years for the gold trade until after the 1880s. The average that gold export had achieved in the mid-1830s was maintained very well until it dropped perceptibly in 1862 when it registered a decline from £84,358 to £7,758. There was a fall in the gold exports from £129,588 to £36,000 in 1853 but this can be explained by the conflict with Asante, when the question of the independence of Assin precipitated an Asante invasion of the British Protectorate. Despite the fluctuations in trade and the gold exports it is evident that from 1850 to 1862 gold was the most constant and reliable item of export. Ivory, by contrast with gold, had fallen off very noticeably from the 1830s and 1840s. The apparent explanation is that the Gold Coast has never been a major exporter of ivory and that her sources of ivory were probably becoming exhausted.[1]

The place that ivory had held before 1830 as a staple export of the Gold Coast was taken by palm oil. The palm oil export on the Gold Coast remained steady during this period in spite of occasional fluctuations in response to natural, internal and external factors. The yield of the palm crop depended upon adequate rainfall; the palm oil industry itself relied upon peace and tranquillity in the areas of production, and the sale of the oil to a large degree was contingent upon external demand.

The figures of export for 1850 reflect a steady growth of palm oil export from the 1830s and 1840s. However, between 1850 and 1853 the exports dropped somewhat. It is probable that as the price of cowries which were valued at 4s 2d a head in 1850 stimulated the export of the crop, their apparent decline to 2s 9d – 3s in 1853 might have affected the production of the palm oil for 1851 and 1852. Palm oil exports rose to a new height in 1853, in the same year that gold exports reached an unusually low point in the wake of the Asante conflicts, and for the first time overtook gold as the leading staple export. The palm oil exports continued to increase in 1854 and dropped a little in 1855. The rise no doubt was in response to the recovery of the cowrie currency which had risen from 2s 9d a head to 3s in 1853 and 3s 4d by 1855, and the higher prices for oil stimulated by the Crimean War, 1854–1855, with the consequent cutting off of the tallow supply from Russia.[2]

In 1855 a British official on the Gold Coast expressed concern over the export of palm oil after the war with Russia was terminated:

> I should hope that the stimulus given to this trade by the War with Russia introducing as it necessarily must, a much extended occupation in production, will be followed by persons once so occupied continuing producers of the oil when the price shall have fallen – There may however be the contrary effect for a time that the producers having received a higher price will refuse a lower (one) and will not sell at all.[3]

In 1856 there was another drop in the palm oil trade but it was not until 1858 and 1860 that there were drastic declines which may be corroborated by the trade figures and other evidence. Speaking before the Parliamentary Committee of 1865, Andrew Swanzy testified that the Krobo fine of 1858 led to a decline in the oil trade in 1858 and 1860. Obviously Swanzy, who was speaking from

1 Daaku, *Trade and Politics*, p. 28

2 C.O. 96/31: Connor to Russell, 16 July 1855   3 *Ibid.*

memory, made a mistake in referring to 1858 as the beginning of the decline – the dates in question were 1859–1860.[1] The Governor of the settlements also reported in 1861 that

> In the Eastern districts a considerable Trade for many years has been carried on in Palm Oil, but during the past year it has suffered materially on account of the unfortunate disturbances that took place in 1858, which resulted in having recourse to military operations against the chiefs.[2]

Although the oil trade recovered in 1861 and further increased in 1862, attempts to collect the Krobo fine and disputes in the eastern region after 1863 were going to affect the export of the crop. The effect of the Krobo fine on the palm oil export of the Gold Coast does not imply that the Krobos were the only producers. Akuapem, the Winneba and Saltpond areas also exported some palm oil.[3]

Another palm product was the palm kernel. Until 1855 when the first export of palm kernels was made, they had been thrown away after extracting the palm oil from the pericarp because they were regarded as useless. Despite the exports of £11 of palm kernel in 1855 it was not until after 1868 that the trade began to flourish.

Gum copal, used in making varnish, also became important on the Gold Coast in the 1850s. Small quantities had probably been exported from the Gold Coast before the 1850s but not large enough to figure prominently in the export figures. By 1851, even though the exports were low, they were respectable. Price fluctuations, however, made the export of gum copal irregular, and furthermore, because of its poor quality, it could not compete with gum from other areas.[4]

An export trade also developed in monkey skins in the 1850s. First commenced by William Bruce of James Town, Accra, handsome profits were reaped from shipments of monkey skins to England. The skins sold very cheaply at first, but later their prices increased. In 1856, for example, twenty to twenty-five skins sold for 4s 6d, but three years later they were fetching one shilling a piece. Prices rose further in 1860, by which time the price of good skins was no less than 4s 6d each on the Gold Coast.[5]

The skins were obtained from black monkeys in the eastern region, especially in Akyem and Krobo where the monkeys were hunted during the rainy season between May and August. During the dry season they were difficult to kill because they stayed near the tops of lofty trees, but in the rainy season they descended and took cover under trees and bushes.[6] Andrew Swanzy has left a description of his part in this trade, written in 1874:

1 *Parl. Papers* 1865: Evidence of A. Swanzy, Q's.4682 and 4683

2 C.O. 96/52: Andrews to Newcastle, 13 June 1861

3 Dickson, *Historical Geography*, p. 144

4 Horton, *West African Countries and Peoples*, p. 133

5 *Ibid.*, pp. 132–3   6 *Ibid.*

Some 15 years ago I imported 600 or 700 black monkey skins, and sent them to Messrs. Bevington and Morris, to ascertain if they could be made useful; they remained in their hands for many months, and most of them were made into rugs, which I presented to various friends, but a few of the best were reserved and made into muffs, which at first met with no sale, but after a time became fashionable, and finally the price for each good skin rose as high as 12s 6d; they have since fallen, and now vary from 3s 6d to 1s 6d each.[1]

Other products featured in the economy which were intermittently exported were guinea grains, groundnuts, and rubber.[2] Although not consistently recorded, coffee assumed some importance as an export product in the 1860s.[3]

There are no recorded figures for rubber, but its export was definitely becoming important as evidenced by Horton's report that rubber 'was in great request and remunerative'. It was obtained from Indian rubber and gutta-percha trees, and before becoming an export commodity it was used to repair earthenware pots. The export of rubber was begun by the commercial firm of the Bremen missionaries. Although the trade in rubber was profitable, Horton expressed alarm at the extravagant and destructive methods used to collect it. He said that they cut down the tree, burned one end, and allowed the gum to exude from the other, thereby destroying the tree.[4] Such destructive methods ruined the rubber trade at the time of its peak prosperity during the last two decades of the nineteenth century.

A close look at the imports into the Gold Coast reveal that all the consumer goods and most items on the list represented ephemeral luxury consumption. They consisted primarily of Manchester goods, spirits and wine, beads, hardware, provision, earthenware, tobacco and haberdashery.[5] The regular imports of these items indicated the extent to which foreign goods were playing a role in the local economy and how the people were beginning to depend upon them. The importance of Manchester goods on Gold Coast trade can be seen from the volume of import to the Gold Coast.

About sixty per cent[6] of our shipments to the Coast consist of cotton manufactures, chiefly of Manchester make, but including some few fabrics from Switzerland and Belgium, of finer colour and quality; and you will observe how singularly the names still used in the trade remind us of the time when India supplied a large proportion of our cotton manufacture samples. I believe I may say that my firm clothes the inhabitants of a district as large as England, but, of course, that district is thinly populated and the people more thinly clad; indeed, in most parts, the children of both sexes, up to the age of seven

1 A. Swanzy, 'On Trade in Western Africa with and without British Protection', p. 483

2 C.O. 442/10–42, 1850–1876; Blue Books 1855–1859

3 Dickson, *Historical Geography*, p. 157

4 Horton, *West African Countries and Peoples*, p. 135

5 See Table on p. 137 and Appendix.

6 From the trade figures available, this estimate of cotton manufactures is an exaggeration.

or eight, dispense with any covering than that of a slight coating of tallow to prevent their skins from cracking in the sun.[1]

The import figures of Manchester goods which ranged from £14,000 to £74,000 a year, show a very irregular and slow increase and indeed no increase at all for some years, and seem to point to the conclusion that commercial pro-

PRINCIPAL IMPORTS INTO THE GOLD COAST

Given total imports into the Gold Coast[2]

Year	Manchester goods in £	Beads £	Spirits and wines in £s	Year	£
1850	40,960	5,060	7,142	1850	88,656
1851	28,360	5,325	15,060	1851	84,880
1852	14,000	4,880	17,000	1852	71,635
1853	16,000	3,220	16,580	1853	60,000
1854	38,000	6,600	21,200	1854	107,200
1855	68,187	4,033	11,330	1855	149,587
1856	30,837	6,179	37,491	1856	105,634
1857	36,838	2,083	13,011	1857	118,270
1858	42,050	2,563	29,924	1858	122,457
1859	43,060	2,910	23,704	1859	114,596
1860	35,089	1,497	3,156	1860	112,454
1861	74,628	1,006	39,991	1861	162,971
1862	68,000	–	40,773	1862	145,100

gress was very slow and hard-won in this whole period. The import of beads which had always been a regular feature of Gold Coast trade was also maintained. Writing in 1874, again Andrew Swanzy emphasised the importance of the bead trade:

All the women of West Africa wear girdles round the waist, generally consisting of two or three strings of beads, in fact a row of beads constitutes the first approach to dress on the part of the female children; moreover, beads are much sought after as ornaments for the wrists and neck, and therefore we ship to the coast great quantities of beads.[3]

The importance of the import trade in spirits and wines can be seen from the trade figures. After Manchester goods, spirits and wines formed the second largest import to the Gold Coast. In relation to the total imports of goods to the Gold Coast, spirit imports were unusually large and caused protests from some quarters. A participant in the Gold Coast trade observed:

1 A. Swanzy, 'On Trade in Western Africa with and without British Protection', p. 482

2 C.O. 442/10–42; Blue Books 1850–1862. The figures of total imports given in the official records are at best very rough estimates because the itemised individual imports between 1850 and 1856 exceed the official totals.

3 A. Swanzy, 'On Trade in Western Africa with and without British Protection', p. 482

A large number of sincere and sensible men have protested against the trade
in spirits with uncivilised people, some of them considering that trade not
merely objectionable, but criminal. But after all the consumption of alcoholic
liquids by the natives of Western Africa is not by any means large in proportion to their numbers. With the exception of a little palm wine . . . The few
cases of drunkenness which I witnessed on the Coast arose from excessive in-
dulgence in palm wine, and indeed, the quantity of spirit taken at one time is
very small.[1]

Andrew Swanzy commented upon other articles of import into the Gold
Coast when he noted:

Cutlery and hardware form a considerable item in our trade, and include
knives of every shape and size, machetes or cutlasses, brass pans, pewter
basins, etc. Common earthenware helps, when needful, to fill our ships; and,
as a proof of advancement in the comfort of the natives, I may say we ship
large quantities of chairs and occasionally other articles of furniture.[2]

This need for a fully loaded ship may partially explain the varying quantities
of these items.

The progress of trade during this period was slow and any gains made by
African merchants were hard-won. By the end of 1862, however, serious conflicts were about to break out on the Gold Coast which would adversely affect
commercial operations for almost a decade. This and the prevailing system of
credit would bring the age of the African merchants to a temporary halt.

1 *Ibid.*, p. 483   2 *Ibid.*

CHAPTER FIVE

Trade and problems of economic development, 1863–1874

There had been no spectacular growth in the import and export figures of the Gold Coast between 1850 and 1862, but the trade returns had been more or less steady. During this time palm oil had joined gold dust and replaced ivory as the major staple export of the country. But whatever prosperity the country had known up to 1862 was brought to an end by the Asante invasion of 1863–1864 which had been provoked partly by the refusal of Governor Richard Pine to deliver to the Asantehene two fugitives. Not only did the invasion affect trade but Governor Pine's mismanaged campaign was to cause much recrimination.

The effect on trade of the Asante invasion is amply demonstrated by the perceptible drop in the trade figures in 1863. In 1862 the total imports into the Gold Coast had been £145,100 and the exports from the country had been £102,086, but in 1863 the imports and exports stood at £76,955 and £53,764, respectively. Horton reported after the Asante invasion that 'trade was stopped, and several of the merchants became bankrupt, and others in a state next to it'.[1] Among the merchants who became bankrupt was Samuel Collins Brew.[2]

The Krobo fine and trade

The plight of Gold Coast merchants and the condition of trade were further worsened by tactics adopted by the contractors of the Krobo fine. By 1861 the people of Krobo had paid only a fraction of the fine imposed upon them, and attempts to use soldiers to extract oil from them by force on their way to the coastal market led them to send oil to ports east of the Volta. The Governor wrote in 1862 that 'the people will not now bring oil down to the coast on account of its being seized, but take it to Kpong, a place on the banks of the Volta, where they find a ready market and some 50 miles away from our nearest military stations'.[3] As the seizures began to influence trade in the eastern region, the merchants in that area appealed to the Governor:

> Since the arrangement entered in the latter end of 1858 between the government and certain gentlemen who contracted to pay for the Krobboes . . . (the fine imposed upon them) . . . The legitimate palm oil trade has been seriously

1 Horton, *Letters*, p. 74

2 Priestley, *West African Trade and Coast Society*, pp. 143–57

3 C.O. 96/57: Governor to Duke of Newcastle, 13 Feb. 1862

impaired, the Krobboes for the last two years having held the monopoly of that article of commerce and consequently maintained their own prices. Oil being at this time 100% dearer than it was in 1858 the sale of merchandise in general and beads in particular is materially lessened, £1,800 worth of the latter article which was in stock at Accra at the breaking out of the Krobo disturbances having now become dead stock.[1]

Since the disturbances were disrupting trade the people involved in the palm oil trade wanted the government to do something about the fine. Consequently, in 1863, the Governor came to new terms with the contractors who agreed to forgo all their claims to Krobo oil and the Krobos were asked to pay £7,750 in cowrie shells. They promptly paid half of it and promised to pay the rest. When the remainder of the fine was not forthcoming two of the contractors, the agents of F. and A. Swanzy and Forster and Smith used private troops to seize oil from Krobo and stopped goods going up to Krobo country. This action again interfered with trade and predictably merchants, traders and chiefs at Accra called attention to the ruinous state of trade in the eastern region:

> The trade from Croboe and its neighbourhood is now entirely stopped by a system of seizure of all oil coming to the coast from that district which has been established by Mr Cuthbert who is acting in Pong for the contractors of the fine . . . In some instances actual seizures of oil have been made in Shai district, the inhabitants of which have no connection with the Croboe fine and to the further ruin of trade the men under orders of Mr Cuthbert have stationed themselves in bodies of from 8–12 in various localities favourable for the interception of traders returning from Accra and Pram Pram to Pong, Crepee, etc. and forcibly seizing and appropriating to themselves certain portions of the goods. The trade of the Volta districts prior to the so-called blockade being established was enormous. That passing to Addah having come principally from Pong and other places in its neighbourhood now under the blockade system, no business can now be transacted there unless that system which we may almost say has been reduced to the level of native 'panyar-ring' is abolished.[2]

The local British Government on the Gold Coast was finally pressed in 1865 to terminate the agreement that had led to the boycott by paying the two large contractors £3,500 in a final settlement. Although the dispute was brought to a conclusion in 1865, it had evoked a crisis that was going to affect the commercial life of the eastern region for a few years at least. The attempt of F. and A. Swanzy and Forster and Smith to corner the palm oil market met with the resentment of other merchants, but the disorganisation of trade resulting from the attempt to collect the fine, as is evidenced by the quotation above, aroused the indignation not only of the merchants, but also of the residents and chiefs of the eastern region. For the Krobo people themselves, the effective long boycott and hold-up of palm oil showed that economically they were quite sophisticated and

1 C.O. 96/59: Merchants, Agents and Traders of Accra to Governor, 1 May 1863

2 C.O. 96/68: Petition from Accra Merchants, Traders, Residents and Chiefs in Conran to Doorly, 2 Oct. 1865

at the same time not dependent on European trade, which they were prepared to forgo for years on end if need be.

Trade and the lower Volta

The diversion of Krobo palm oil trade from the Accra-Prampram area to the Volta basin had begun at a time when the people of this latter area were disengaging themselves from the slave trade to interest themselves in the palm oil trade. The people of the lower Volta had long-established trade links with the interior,[1] and eighteenth-century accounts give a vivid impression of economic activities in the region. The Adas, who looked down on agricultural activities, leaving such occupations to their neighbours, engaged in salt mining and fishing and sold the products to the people inland.[2] Salt from Ada reached Asante.[3] According to Lind, a Dane who sailed up the river, Dodi was an important salt market from which salt reached Kwahu, Asante and the far interior.[4] This information agrees with that supplied by Colonel Starerrenbury, a Dutchman who went on a mission up the Volta in 1817. By the middle of the nineteenth century the trade in salt up the Volta River was still important.[5]

The Volta basin was notorious for the slave trade as well as for salt. Despite abolition the trade was carried on with vigour until the 1860s, with most of the important towns of the area like Atoko, Keta, Blekusu and Adina on the coast serving as slave markets.[6]

Of the slave dealers of the area, two stand out. Goncalves Baeta and Cesar Cequira Geraldo de Lima belonged to the long line of Brazilians who had established slave bases on the coast during the first half of the nineteenth century.[7] In March, 1850, when Governor Winniett visited the Danish possessions he met Baeta at Atoko; at that time the slave trader expressed a desire to carry legal trade in the form of palm oil under the British flag.[8] It is possible that in addition to his slave trading activities Baeta carried on some commerce in palm oil after 1850.

Geraldo de Lima established himself as a slave dealer in his own right after serving an apprenticeship with Goncalves Baeta.[9] De Lima built a factory at Vodza from where he shipped his slaves until his death in 1862. Upon de Lima's death his business was taken over by Adzoviehlo Atiogbe who had been his servant from the early 1850s. Atiogbe assumed his master's name in order to facilitate his business dealings in slaves, but by 1864 he had given up the slave trade to engage in the palm oil trading.[10] Once in the palm oil trade he began to corner

---

1 G. M. Grove and A. M. Johansen, 'The Historical Geography of the Volta Delta, Ghana, during the Period of Danish Influence', *I.F.A.N.*, xxx, Series B, No. 4, pp. 1373–1421, 1968

2 *Ibid.*, p. 1385 3 *Ibid.*, p. 1386 4 *G.J.* 264, p. 1829

5 Johnson, 'Migrants' Progress', p. 22

6 Amenumey, 'Geraldo de Lima: a Reappraisal', p. 66 7 *Ibid.*, p. 65

8 C.O. 96/18: Winniett to Grey, 30 March 1850

9 Amenumey, 'Geraldo de Lima: a Reappraisal', pp. 65–66

10 *Ibid.*, p. 67. Compare with Ross, 'Domingo Martinez'.

a sizable amount of it and carried on a flourishing trade in cotton goods, fire-arms and liquor in Kpong, the palm oil emporium, and in other towns along the Volta. De Lima's commercial activities successfully diverted much produce from the Accra and Prampram areas to Mafi on the Volta and to Anlo ports.[1] It was very likely that the reports reaching the Colonial Office and the African Aid Society in 1863 that there was a large-scale traffic in slaves from Asante in the Volta area[2] and that Asante was carrying on a vigorous trade at Ada and Keta exchanging slaves for gunpowder[3] were calculated to get the British Government to blockade these ports in order to limit de Lima's trading activities.

It was the scope of de Lima's trading activities and his competition for oil with traders west of the Volta, who were losing their grip on the oil trade after the Krobo fine, that led to disputes which resulted in the Anlo war. As a modern scholar of Anlo history has written:

> A trade competition between Lima and the European merchants based at Accra and westwards was superimposed on the inveterate Anlo-Ada commercial rivalry. Anlo had lately taken to acting as middlemen for the palm-oil trade. A fierce competition developed between Anlo on the one hand and Ada and Accra on the other. This rivalry was accentuated by the Krobo fine of 1858 and the tactics adopted by the Krobos in 1859–1864 to beat it.[4]

The growing importance of trade and commercial competition in the Volta basin was attested to by the number of commercial firms and agents who had established themselves at the end of the Volta basin at Adafo. These firms and agents were H. L. Rottman and Company;[5] W. P. Gunnell; John Clayton; W. G. Bruce, E. W. Bruce and M. Victor Sons of Bremen.[6] Besides these firms there were other commercial agents like the Basel Mission and unnamed individual traders who had established agencies at Kpong and penetrated Krepi country.[7]

Because of this trade rivalry a small misunderstanding between de Lima and an Ada debtor escalated into a war in 1865–1866 on which merchants west of the Volta staked their last hope for the rediversion of trade. They solicited the help of the government not only to settle the dispute between Ada and Anlo (supposedly being fomented by de Lima) but they also revealed their real motives for imploring government aid by asking it to destroy all the coastal towns of Anlo.[8]

1 C.O. 96/70: Conran to Cardwell, 10 March 1866; Amenumey, 'De Lima', p. 67; D. E. K. Amenumey, *The Ewe People and the Coming of European Rule, 1850–1914*, unpublished M.A. thesis, London University, 1964.

2 C.O. 96/63: Alfred Churchill to Newcastle, 20 April 1803

3 *African Times*, 23 Jan. 1864, 'O', p. 80

4 Amenumey, 'Geraldo de Lima: a Reappraisal', p. 69

5 This is undoubtedly H. L. Rottman representing the Basel Mission Trading Company.

6 C.O. 96/67: Julino Ungar to F. W. Richards, 14 May 1865

7 *African Times*, 22 August 1868, p. 22, in a letter to the Editor signed 'An Old Accra'.

8 Amenumey, 'Geraldo de Lima: a Reappraisal', p. 69; C.O. 96/71: Conran to Cardwell, 10 April 1866; C.O. 96/67: Richards to Jones, 17 May 1865

Obviously the Anlo war was a commercial quarrel in which merchants on the Gold Coast sought to involve the local government. The Governor-in-Chief of the West African settlements realised this when he wrote in 1866:

> These quarrels are generally caused by the jealousy of Traders who will go into the interior to 'get behind' each other. In places where we have no British Government as at Whydah and the Bonny, produce is brought down by the natives to the shipping port, and if plundered on the way, the loss is to the natives, but at the Gold Coast, Gambia, and even here [Sierra Leone] the merchants going to the interior expect British protection in carrying their property through a hostile country.[1]

Conran, too, noted that those who brought about the disturbances on the Gold Coast were indigenous traders in their own right or representatives of European merchants' houses.

> The native traders employed by the large merchants in distant and out of the way parts cause this kind of invasion on the part of those who differ and dispute points of trade with them [which] . . . ends in the suspensions of commerce altogether when the government at last is expected to open it again, a rule that has been followed on this coast for many years back, which has led many petty traders to think that wherever they may establish a grog shop there also should be a detachment of soldiers to protect them.[2]

The Anlo war seriously affected the palm oil trade in the eastern region, but even more important is the fact that it hastened the end of the developing trade in cotton in the Volta district. On 23 March 1867 a Gold Coast correspondent reported to the *African Times*:

> Our trade here is ruined on account of the existing Awoolah war. The enemy is assuming the offensive, and has lately killed a great many of our allies who were on their way down with the produce. This place and the interior are like what Lagos and Abeokuta were some time ago; produce shut up in the interior, and many of the merchants here becoming insolvent in consequence of this. The Government is silent now upon the subject. I have machinery alone to the amount of £500 lying now idle, besides a great quantity of cotton, shut up in Krepee.[3]

A ruined cotton merchant from James Town, Accra, wrote to the *African Times* in 1868 describing the situation in the cotton growing district and imploring that something be done about the conflict that had brought about the state of affairs:

> Can you not help us? For God's sake ring [*sic*] our troubles and most just grievances into the ears of the British Government. Here we are still, starving and bankrupt, because the Gold Coast authorities don't know how, or do

1 C.O. 96/71: Blackall to Cardwell, 20 June 1866

2 C.O. 96/71: Conran to Cardwell, 10 April 1866

3 *African Times*, 23 March 1867, 'J.C.', p. 104

not choose, to insist on that paltry little tribe of River robbers on the Volta, the Aquamoos, letting our carriers and cotton come down out of Krepee. You, Mr. Editor, ought, indeed, to fight for us in this cruel wrong; you urged enough upon us a few years ago . . . and have sent up plenty of cotton gins – and the people have entered heartily into the cultivation of cotton, and there is lots of it up there, for now 2 or 3 years *shut up* from us, because the Government does not choose to allow us to put down the Aguamoos, nor to insist on their leaving off to plunder and murder and kidnap our people if they attempt to bring down our cotton. The only people for whom this state of things answers is the Basel and Bremen commercial missionaries, who have mercantile agents at Quittah and Jellee Coffee, Awoonah places on the sea-coast on the other side of the Volta. The Aguamoos are the allies of the Awoonahs, and so the mission mercantile agents there get down their cotton to ship to Hamburg and Bremen, while we are not allowed to get ours to ship to Liverpool. At Awoonah they pay no duties to the British Government . . . we're overwhelmed with duties, and what not, and put under the restriction of all sorts of laws, and can't get down an ounce of cotton to take advantage of the now good prices at Liverpool, and so we are *ruined – ruined*. For God's sake get help of some sort for us.[1]

The decline of trade that followed the Asante invasion of 1863–1864, the attempt to collect the Krobo fine and the Anlo War (1865–1866) are best told by the trade returns:[2]

Year	Imports £	Exports £
1862	145,900	102,086
1863	76,955	53,764
1864	No returns	No returns
1865	No returns	No returns
1866	No returns	No returns
1867	206,920	160,291
1868	140,226	148,909
1869	213,491	281,913
1870	253,397	378,239
1871	250,671	295,207
1872	260,101	285,821
1873	225,525	330,624
1874	No returns	No returns

The return of imports and exports clearly shows the drop in trade after the Asante conflict began in 1863. No trade returns are available for the years 1864, 1865 and 1866, which were years of conflict and undoubtedly a period of decline and setbacks for trading activities. It was not until 1867 after the Anlo War had ended that trade began to recover. The pattern of trade in these years is clearly

1 *African Times*, 23 July 1868, 'The Ruined Accra Traders', p. 8

2 C.O. 442/10–42, 1850–1872; C.O. 100/6 following; *Parl. Papers* 1865, Appendix

reflected in the returns of gold exports from the Gold Coast as seen in the figures below:

GOLD EXPORTS[1]

Year	Gold, in oz.	£
1862		7,728
1863		27,009
1864		No returns
1865		No returns
1866		No returns
1867	26,784	81,791
1868	2,132*	73,495
1869	36,791	132,448
1870	36,604	131,776
1871	17,882	64,376
1872	15,456	55,644
1873		
1874	No returns	No returns

* This figure is obviously a mistake and probably should read 20,132 oz.

In the case of gold the drop had taken place in 1862 in consequence of the dispute which led to the 1863 Asante invasion. The fall in gold which came mainly from Asante can be partially explained by the fact that at the beginning of the dispute, an embargo was placed on the sale of firearms and ammunition.[2]

The export of palm oil, the other major staple of the Gold Coast, was also affected by the conflict, as seen in the figures below.[3]

PALM OIL EXPORT

Year	Tons	£
1862	–	85,910
1863	–	22,659
1864	–	–
1865	–	–
1866	–	–
1867	56	1,018
1868	2,663	57,953
1869	3,165	101,189
1870	5,161	185,710
1871	7,739	278,642
1872	–	–
1873	–	–
1874	–	–

1 Blue Books 1850–1872 and C.O. 442/10–42, 1850–1876

2 Hutchinson, 'Gold Trade on the Gold Coast 1826 to 1890', pp. 8–10

3 Compiled from C.O. 442/10–42; C.O. 110/6 following; Blue Books for 1850–1876; *Parl. Papers* 1865, p. 371, Appendix No. 1

The palm oil exports fell in 1863. While the export of gold seems to have recovered by 1867, the former exports were only just beginning to recover at that date. The palm oil trade on the Gold Coast was seemingly threatened after the discovery of petroleum in Pennsylvania in 1859. Other sources of competition to palm oil were oils and fats from India and tallow from Australia which began to supplement those from Russia in the 1860s.[1] Yet another threat to the palm oil export was the decline in its price from the middle of the nineteenth century.[2]

Despite the decline in prices the African producer did not have to sustain all the losses of low prices because transportation charges had also decreased.

Palm kernel had first been exported in 1855 and had become important in 1868 from which time the following sizable exports were recorded:[3]

Year	£
1868	7,354
1869	38,881
1870	22,035
1871	7,452
1872	5,874

The palm kernel oil came to be used in the manufacture of margarine, with the bulk of the product from West Africa going to Germany until World War I.[4]

Exports of ivory, declining since the 1850s, decreased still further with very irregular exports between 1862 and 1874. The isolated instances of recorded exports were:[5]

Year	£
1862	1,330
1863	1,547
1871	327
1872	439

1 McPhee, *Economic Revolution*, pp. 30–33

2 *Ibid.*, p. 33. The average quinquennial prices of palm oil per ton in Britain were:

Years	£
1856–1860	43·6
1861–1865	37·2
1866–1870	38·4
1871–1875	34·2
1876–1880	33·0
1881–1885	31·0
1886–1890	20·4
1891–1895	23·6
1896–1900	21·0

3 C.O. 442/10–42; C.O. 100/6 following; Blue Books for 1850–1876; *Parl. Papers* 1865, p. 371, Appendix No. 1

4 *Ibid.*; McPhee, *Economic Revolution*, pp. 34–35

5 C.O. 442/10–42; C.O. 100/6 following; Blue Books for 1850–1876; *Parl. Papers* 1865, p. 371, Appendix No. 1

The export of gum copal, whose first export was a successful experiment in the 1850s of the Accra trader William Addo, continued but with marked fluctuations. Gum was mostly collected in Akuapem, Akyem and Wassaw.

Gum Exports[1]

Year	£
1862	2,699
1863	850
1864	No returns
1865	No returns
1866	No returns
1867	588
1868	513
1869	642
1870	2,450
1871	4,548
1872	No returns
1873	No returns
1874	No returns

The export of monkey skins, after a rise to importance in the 1850s, also depended on its demand overseas.[2] Except for exports totalling £1,528 in 1871 and £3,221 in 1872, it was not of much commercial importance during this period.[3]

Other goods of this period which were reported from time to time were variable and in the main seem to have relied upon the demand for the produce and the initiative of African merchants who had become keenly aware of new commercial opportunities. Some products intermittently exported were guinea grains, groundnuts and rubber, as the following recorded instances show:[4]

Guinea grains		Groundnuts	
Year	£	Year	£
1862	No returns	1862–1870	No returns
1863	No returns	1871	2,750
1864	No returns	1872	495
1865	No returns	1873	No returns
1866	No returns	1874	No returns
1867	1,527		
1868	4,295		
1869	164		
1870	3,029		
1871	2,166		
1872	10,303		
1873	No returns		
1874	No returns		

1 *Ibid.*

2 See A. Swanzy, 'On Trade in Western Africa with and without British Protection'

3 C.O. 442/10–42; Blue Books 1850–1872

4 C.O. 442/10–42, 1850–1876 and C.O. 100/6 following

Trade and brokerage fees

The hostilities that broke out in 1863, leading to a general decline of trade, resulted in the suspension of the brokerage fee in that year. A fee of about 3% of items traded had been paid to the coastal brokers. In return for this sum the brokers had offered the traders accommodation and guaranteed their honesty and good conduct in dealing with the merchants. After 1868 when trade with the interior began to revive, the coastal people began to make claims for the brokerage fee. Although the old custom was revived on the coast, Cape Coast merchants refused to comply with it, and this obstinacy led to serious trouble on 25 October 1872. On that day nearly all the able-bodied men in Cape Coast came out to picket and 'placed themselves opposite the merchants' stores, and molested the people who were attempting to pass in and out for trading purposes and even ventured so far as to take goods from the people who ventured outside'.[1] The following day the *gong-gong* went round to the effect that no one should purchase goods from the stores of Swanzys or Forster and Smith, the two largest European trading houses on the Gold Coast; no canoemen were to work for the merchants until the question of the brokerage fee had been settled and that penalties would be inflicted on those doing so. This boycott of the European shops, probably the first of its nature, was so effective that the chief agents of F. and A. Swanzy and Forster threatened to sue J. R. Thompson, who had been responsible for organising it. Under this threat Thompson had the gong-gong beaten again to the effect that the people were now free to purchase from the stores that had been boycotted.[2] The attempt of the European merchants to carry on their trade in absolute independence of indigenous custom and the wishes of the people resulted in ill feeling between them and the Africans. As late as 1874 attempts were still being made to settle the brokerage question.[3]

The suspension and the abrogation of the brokerage fee was an inevitable result of changes in the system of trading which had been going on with trade and economic change on the Gold Coast even before 1868. Instead of traders exchanging produce for European goods they were beginning to exchange for cash and by this method bought their desired goods at any store they pleased without the intervention of their host. Thus cash was taking the place of what might be called barter. According to W. F. Hutchinson, by the end of the Asante War of 1873–1874, because of the large quantity of coined money which it brought into the country, the old barter trade was replaced by cash trade.[4] The question of brokerage fees was only one of many problems that vexed traders.

Competition for the interior trade

Another problem that was to bother African traders at this time was the competition from European traders who were beginning to penetrate the interior trade instead of staying on the coast and waiting for Africans to come to them. Such competition came from the Basel Mission Trading Company, now the Union Trading Company of Ghana (UTC), which had been officially founded

1 C.O. 96/94: William Cleaver to Pope-Hennessy, 4 Nov. 1872　　　2 *Ibid.*

3 C.O. 96/66: Pope-Hennessy to Kimberley, 8 Feb. 1874

4 Hutchinson, 'The Gold Trade of the Gold Coast, 1826–1890', p. 10

in 1859.[1] When the missionaries first came to the Gold Coast they had no intention of engaging in trade, but they found out later that it was difficult for missionaries to obtain the necessities of their life with many of these items obtainable only from Europe. To meet this need the missionaries seriously started to have dealings in trade in 1854. They found that the task of securing supplies consumed considerable amounts of time and felt it necessary to establish a trading company. In 1854 H. L. Rottmann arrived at Christiansborg to open a shop. Three years later the mission invested 60,000 francs in the shop. Rottman was urged to find good customers, to train African helpers, not to be too profit-minded, but to aim to make the shop 'an oasis in the desert of paganism'.[2]

By 1858 some Basel missionaries on the Gold Coast were becoming uneasy about investing mission money in trade; they felt such an investment was a risk and that a special fund should be set up specifically for commercial purposes. When a gift of 70,000 francs was donated in the same year to the trade company the bookkeeping for the mission and the trade was separated. The mission strictly supervised the trading activities and in January, 1859, the authorities at Basel converted it into a trading company under the charge of a committee of three.[3] This trading union was:

to be subject to the Basel Mission Committee at Basel; to supply all mission stations; to provide raw material for mission workshops at low prices; to introduce pagans to Christian industry and trade and to improve them morally; to raise funds for the running of the mission house; to help the mission to be financially independent or to prepare the way to such a status and to ensure that the trading should not disturb the peace and harmony of mission work.[4]

Rottman, in charge of the mission's commercial activities, also wanted to keep sale prices low. In order to accomplish this he had to order in large quantities and, in this way, the shop grew. By 1860, local traders were coming to order goods from the Basel Mission Trading Company and paying for them in African produce.[5] This business brought great profit which became a substantial support of the mission work. It has even been asserted that the work of the Basel Mission could not have expanded as fast as it did if it had not been for the financial support it received from the Trading Company.[6]

The Basel Trading Company, unlike other European trading establishments of the time, penetrated the interior and established factories in direct competition with indigenous merchants and middlemen. It is indicative of their deep concern with trade that the Africans were quick to protest against the activities and competition of the Trading Company in the interior:

. . . they are doing no material good in point of trade, but harm. Since they established themselves here as *merchants* they have been imitators and not

---

1 For the complete history of this organisation, see Von Gustaf Adolf Wanner, *Basler Handelsgesellschaft 1859–1959*, Basel, 1959. This definitive history was published on the centenary of the company for private circulation and was not available for sale.

2 *Ibid.*, pp. 27–30; Reindorf, *History of the Gold Coast*, 2nd ed., pp. 220–1

3 Wanner, *Basler Handelsgesellschaft*, pp. 30–32

4 *Ibid.*, pp. 70–72   5 *Ibid.*, pp. 51–52   6 *Ibid.*, p. 78

innovators; they have not conferred any boon on the public by introducing any industrial development of fresh resources here. They have not lent their energy by adding to the natural wealth of this country. There is not now one educated native buying palm oil in this place. With their large means they undersell everyone here, and by that means have wrested the trade from our hands. We go to Kpong, they follow us there; we go to Addah, they come there; we go to the far interior (Krepee), they come there. B was in Krepee in '60, '61, '62, '63, buying cotton for their benefit; they were not satisfied till they went there and established factories in opposition to him. With them 'Live and let live' is not the motto. They get their goods first hand from Germany and go far to the interior. Of course they will not take lead in anything; they go for all the profit without any intermedium, for they want all the profit for themselves. Even the latest (palm-nut kernel) trade they have taken from our hands. We must not live at all.[1]

This complaint in a letter to the *African Times* was simply signed 'An Old Accra'.[2] Although his strictures about the Basel Mission harming trade were unjustified, the fear and resentment of the protest were real. Another letter simply signed 'African' also complained:

... You must always bear in mind, as I know you do, that none of these people, the German missionaries and their commercial managers, have any permanent interests in these countries. They have the interest of the people at heart no doubt, in a religious point of view; but beyond that they would sell or dispose of the country in any way that seems best to suit their present interest.[3]

Similar complaints were to be lodged against European firms as they penetrated the interior in larger numbers at the beginning of the twentieth century.

Problems of credit and bankruptcy

There were clear and visible signs of commercial and economic change on the Gold Coast by the 1850s but there were problems that often inhibited the economic progress and development of the country, one of which was the question of credit – a feature of the African trade from at least the seventeenth century. Before the nineteenth century both Africans and Europeans had offered credit terms. Africans frequently offered the European trader staple exports on credit when the goods he wanted were not immediately on hand. The European trader likewise offered the African trader goods on credit to be paid for with the produce of the country when it was available. This practice often involved great risk as there were occasions when both sides defaulted on payment.[4]

1 *African Times*, 22 Aug. 1868, letter signed 'An Old Accra', p. 22

2 This 'Old Accra' was probably one of the African merchants at Accra who was beginning to feel the effects of competition from a European organisation with substantial capital.

3 *African Times*, 23 March 1868, letter signed 'African', p. 129

4 Daaku, *Trade and Politics*, pp. 41–42

The system of credit after abolition was altered by economic change. Trade conducted by chartered companies and government officially declined, or ceased, following the interdiction to the slave trade. Consequently, much of the trade of the coast came to depend upon individual and independent traders who largely relied on credit to pursue their commercial activities. These merchants received their trade goods in consignment from merchant houses in Europe, from super cargoes engaged in the floating trade, and later from the steamers, on credit. The systems of credit became especially prevalent when trade from the Gold Coast and West Africa began to increase.[1] Matthew Forster testified to this:

> I am sorry to say that the system of credit has been of late years, in consequence of the great competition in the trade, introduced at the Gambia, and on the Gold Coast, and, in fact I believe, on all parts of the coast. It is a most objectionable and unfortunate system, and has been attended with very bad effects; it is one of the causes of the heavy losses that have been lately sustained in carrying on the trade.[2]

Limited currency and the absence of banks no doubt exacerbated the problem of coastal credit, but European opposition to Africans securing credit during this period should be seen in the context of growing inter-group competition. This can be confirmed by Andrew Swanzy when he wrote in 1874:

> Gradually a number of partially educated natives were admitted to the same advantages as the resident English traders, and received their supplies direct from the London firms. These men, instead of exchanging all their goods for produce, built houses, bought slaves, and surrounded themselves with a large retinue of servants, expended a great deal of the means entrusted to them in extravagance; and many of them, unable to estimate the cost of their goods, *drove the European merchants from the trade by ruinous competition.*[3]

There is an apparent contradiction in Swanzy's statements. If African merchants spent so much on houses and slaves it was not going to be easy to undercut European merchants. But that there was a rivalry between African and European merchants could not be denied.

The fact that African merchants who received goods on credit so early started investing in slaves, houses and property when the surplus could have been re-invested in business is more a commentary on the trading practices rather than on the character of the Africans involved. Furthermore, it also reflected the social values of the people, which were not those of a developed capitalistic society.

Trade on the Gold Coast involved great risks in view of conflicts that often interrupted commercial activities and the constant fluctuations in trade. Yet for the African trader ordering goods on his own account there was no insurance against possible loss. Thus, investment in houses and slaves provided a form of

1 *Parl. Papers* 1842: Q.3346, Evidence of G. C. Redman

2 *Ibid.*, Q.10705, Evidence of M. Forster

3 A. Swanzy, 'On Trade in Western Africa with and without British Protection', p. 479, my italics.

security and a necessity for carrying on his trade. A case in point is the house of James Bannerman, used not only as a residence but also as a trading and storage place for goods. In view of the difficulty of obtaining paid labourers in those days slaves were also needed to perform a variety of duties such as canoemen, potters and workers around shops and establishments. Again, in view of their increasing social and economic importance, African merchants had to maintain a standard of living consistent with their status. Andrew Swanzy observed that:

> The uneducated trader, while pursuing his business, remained content with his native fare and native fashion, whereas the newly-created gentleman must needs vie with, and even excel, the white man in his personal and household expenditure, in order to assert and maintain his acquired position.[1]

The complaints of European traders that:

> Native Traders receiving supplies of Goods on credit do occasionally invest a portion of these goods in the purchase of slaves brought from the interior; that the slaves so purchased are employed as Labourers and Domestics about their Master's Establishment; that in case of insolvency while the other property of the Native Traders is available to his creditors, the portion of his property escapes confiscation.[2]

were very true, but as will be seen the causes of the Africans' insolvency were created by the European trading firms advancing goods on credit to the Africans. In order to reap the maximum possible out of bankrupt Africans traders and merchants connected with the trade on the Gold Coast proposed that the slaves of such debtors should become serviceable to the estate and work out their freedom, but nothing came of the proposal.[3]

In 1858 a bankruptcy law was passed on the Gold Coast, which, like the similar British bankruptcy act of the period, not only made the debtor's assets available to his creditors, but also included a short jail sentence. British merchants associated with the Gold Coast trade felt that the act was very lenient and unsuitable for conditions on the Gold Coast. Andrew Swanzy complained:

> Prior to preparing the Bankruptcy Act the system worked well enough, but since it has been in operation, fully one half of the Native Traders (finding they could with its assistance get rid of their liabilities) have passed through the Court, several of them having been convicted of fraudulently concealing the property of their creditors and there is little doubt that the majority of the Bankruptcies have been attended with fraud and concealment of property, which from the nature of Trade carried on are easy to commit but difficult to detect, for in as much as Books or Accounts are rarely or very badly kept, it is almost impossible to discover the numerous small debts due to the Bankrupt

1 A. Swanzy, 'Civilisation and Progress on the Gold Coast of Africa, as Affected by European Conduct with the Native Inhabitants', *J.S.A.* xxiii, 1875, p. 420

2 C.O. 96/21: Statement of Brodie Cruickshank, Francis Swanzy, Thomas Hutton, Henry Smith and Andrew Swanzy, all European merchants concerned with the Gold Coast trade, 1 Dec. 1847

3 *Ibid.*

or to trace the goods sent into the interior for sale in his behalf . . . Property on the Gold Coast is generally invested in Houses and Slaves, and the first thing the Trader does in receiving credit is to build or purchase a house and a number of slaves, when bankruptcy ensues the Bankrupt's family claim the house as family property and relative after relative is brought forward to prove that is the case and in the slaves the court can not possibly deal with them as available assets, and they remain practically the property of the Bankrupt.[1]

According to Swanzy, 'Of the native traders, who before conducted themselves well and paid their accounts, and were held to be respectable, more than two-thirds have since gone through the court, certainly one-half of them.'[2] He felt that as the traders there did not keep any books and their customs were so different from those of Europeans, British bankruptcy laws were not the remedy for insolvent debtors.[3] Some merchants like Matthew Forster advocated using the rules of equity and 'native' laws as they were expedient, as George Maclean had done in his day. He wrote:

Mr Maclean applied the rules of equity more than the rules of English law in cases where the natives were concerned, and he adopted the native law where he found it equitable and just; and native law, though rude and simple, is not ill-adapted to their condition, and a Bankruptcy Court has been established at Cape Coast which is doing great mischief.[4]

In spite of these protestations European firms continued to grant Africans credit. As Matthew Forster observed: 'It may be said, don't trust them, [the African merchants] but that is to say that no business was done.' It would seem that the more unreliable African creditors became, the higher would be the prices charged by European firms. That credit was continued is perhaps an indication of the fact that even with the bankruptcies European merchant houses were still reaping profits from African merchants.

Probably the most celebrated case of the credit system and bankruptcy was that of Joseph Smith of Cape Coast. For a period of thirty years Smith was in the service of the local government as a schoolmaster, secretary, accountant, assistant warehousekeeper, collector of customs and magistrate and from 1844 to 1859 he was a commercial correspondent of Forster and Smith. During this period the total business Joseph Smith carried with Forster and Smith amounted to £138,723 2s 9d. In addition to this he paid £32,000 in freight, interest and sundry charges. While the firm of Forster and Smith was making enormous profits from Smith's trade, they were unscrupulously cheating him by adding from 25 to 50%, and sometimes more, to the cost of the goods they supplied him.[5] This was, of course, an old practice. As early as 1836 it had been reported

---

1 C.O. 96/66: 6 Nov. 1864, Swanzy to Secretary of State

2 *Parl. Papers* 1865, Q.4673, Evidence of A. Swanzy

3 Quoted in A. Swanzy, 'On Trade in Western Africa with and without British Protection', p. 480.

4 *Ibid.*   5 C.O. 96/58: Petition of Joseph Smith, 12 April 1862

that trade goods were sold to Europeans on the coast at cost price, to mulattos at a higher price and to blacks at a still higher price.[1]

By 1856 Smith was heavily indebted to Forster and Smith and to rid himself of this obligation, he went to Badagry to trade, hoping that he would realise enough profits there to pay his debts. While at Badagry he had the opportunity to compare his invoice with that of the European traders and discovered that his invoices were 25%–75% higher. Smith remonstrated with Forster and Smith who indirectly admitted overcharging him on certain kinds of goods, but did not offer to make any reduction in the £18,000 he owed the firm. In order to salvage something from his trade Smith decided to use the name of a friend to get his palm oil sold in England, but when the oil arrived there, Forster and Smith confiscated it. The firm then sent agents to the Gold Coast to collect the £18,000 due them. When the matter reached the courts, it was conceded that Smith had been cheated. In this case Smith should not have owed anything, as the amount for which he had been deceived (£28,000) exceeded what he owed. But as Forster and Smith pleaded the statute of limitation the debt was reduced by only £2,000. The court ordered Smith to pay the remaining £16,000 in three months and as he was without the means to pay, he declared himself bankrupt in 1861.[2]

Significantly Joseph Smith's case was the first time the statute of limitation had been invoked on the Gold Coast and understandably this underlined the conflict in determining the kind of laws that were to be employed in governing commercial relationships on the Gold Coast. This situation was further emphasised by the intervention of the family of Joseph Smith. The relatives argued that it was a family house and that all of them had contributed towards its cost. They said that as a family house was the common and hereditary property of the family, it was not liable to be taken or sold for the debt of any one member of the family, referring to Brodie Cruickshank's *Eighteen Years on the Gold Coast* to support their contention. They regarded the seizure of Smith's house as an act of panyarring or the unlawful seizure of the property of the third parties.[3] Although some African merchants might have hidden the goods of their creditors and purposely declared themselves bankrupt, Joseph Smith's case was an exception. He went bankrupt, as did many others, because he was cheated and he over-extended himself with credit. The Governor of the Gold Coast settlements reported that he had the best reason to believe that Joseph Smith was 'utterly without means before his death'.[4]

The fraudulent practice of debtors to cheat their creditors was proverbially

---

1 *G.J.* No. 727, 1826; Nørregard, *Danish Settlements in West Africa*, p. 196

2 C.O. 96/58: The petition of Joseph Smith, 12 April 1862; *African Times*, 'A Relative', 24 Oct. 1870, p. 41

3 C.O. 96/66: Joseph Smith, for Nelly Thompson on behalf of themselves and other relatives to Edward Cardwell, 8 June 1864. They referred to a passage in Cruickshank, *Eighteen Years*, i, p. 316, which supported the contention: '. . . it was customary to regard the possessions of a house as a common family fund, in which all the members of the family, while they remained such, had a share; at the same time, that the head or representative of the family had the direction and disposal of it – such a species of possession, in fact, as passes in Africa under the name of "family property".'

4 C.O. 96/87: Kennedy to Kimberley, 11 Jan. 1871

called 'whitewashing' on the Gold Coast. In 1870 Governor Kennedy commented on 'whitewashing':

> This evil is of daily occurrence here. A debtor will tell you go on with your suit; you will not get a farthing. I will declare myself insolvent. You get indignant. After one or two years in which time the insolvent has made away with all his property and fictitious transfers, etc., he files a schedule alleging that he has no books or papers, no property whatever. It is not worth a creditor's while to offer any opposition and in a few weeks you will see him opening a shop full of merchandise, walking about the streets dressed like a gentleman triumphantly in defiance of his defrauded creditors.[1]

The chief magistrate of the settlements himself noted the abuse in the credit system and the bankruptcy law:

> I think it probable that adjudication of Bankruptcy has frequently been granted abusively; I mean when given to debtors on their own Petition without sufficient examination or regard to the circumstances under which the debts have been contracted. This facility may have given rise to an idea amongst some of the natives that they can get rid of liabilities by means of the Bankruptcy courts whenever they choose to take the necessary steps.[2]

While some African creditors might have defrauded the creditors by going through the Bankruptcy courts, there is ample reason to believe that many African merchants went bankrupt because of the credit and trading practices of the time.

Lack of uniform currency

Another major problem of the economic development of the Gold Coast at this time was the want of a uniform money or proper currency for commercial purposes. It is true that gold dust passed as currency on the Gold Coast but because of the practical problem of weighing, it was not always convenient in commercial transactions.[3] Cowries also passed as currency but their bulk did not always make them a convenient medium of exchange.[4] Commodity currency and barter also had limitations because unless the customer wanted the particular product being offered there was not the incentive to produce for exchange. The assortment of European coins circulating on the Gold Coast was diverse and too few to meet the needs of the commercial operations of the country. Among these were the Spanish dollar and the French five-franc piece.[5]

The first British coins were sent to the Gold Coast in 1818, but they were

1 C.O. 96/85: Kennedy to Kimberley, 8 Oct. 1870

2 C.O. 96/87: Letter of D. P. Chalmers, 30 Dec. 1870   3 See ch. 1.

4 For a full discussion of cowries, see Marion Johnson's two articles, 'The Cowrie Currencies in West Africa', pp. 17–49 and 331–53

5 Albert Adomako, 'The History of Currency and Banking in some West African Countries', E.B.G. vii, 4, 1963, p. 8

not really money. They consisted of silver tokens valued at 1s 6d and 3s which were coined under the direction of the African Company as rewards to children for going to school. In 1822 dollars were also introduced to pay the salaries of troops and to cover other expenses, and three years later British silver coins were introduced.[1] But in addition to this limited use of money, salaries of merchants and other officers were paid in goods as had been the case before the nineteenth century.[2] This money was not used in commercial transactions.[3] The payment of soldiers in money was discontinued immediately after the British government transferred the administration of the forts to the committee of merchants.[4]

In 1846 Governor Winniett noted that the coins in circulation on the Gold Coast were British gold, silver and copper coins, Spanish and South American doubloons, dollars and half dollars and a few five-franc pieces.[5]

By 1865 the lack of a common and convenient currency was keenly felt and there was growing an intense dislike for cowries by commercial interests. A Basel missionary, the Rev. E. Schrenk, suggested that in order to further trade the government should forbid the import of cowrie shells and devalue them so that the indigenous people would be forced to accept English or other foreign money.[6]

There was also a complaint in the *African Times* in 1867 which affirmed the adverse effects of the use of cowries and the extent to which the scarcity of coins affected trade:

It is deplorable to relate the heavy loss which the petty traders and almost every person here suffer by the use of these cowrie shells, and more so by the dislike of them of the principal merchants here, who, if cash is not brought to buy their goods, charge an extra percentage on them, to meet the fluctuations in their price or any deficiency that may occur . . . in counting, while in many cases they refuse them altogether; and in that case, if you have no cash at all, you are obliged to keep your cowries and go without your goods till you convert them. Formerly the dollar, 4s 6d value sold here for only 1 head 12 strings and a-half or 2,500 cowries . . . and now to the enormous price of 2 heads and a-half, this being the present exchange; and still dollars are scarce. Nobody on this Coast is unaware that it was this scarcity of coins here which made the palm oil become so dear and goods dearer. For instance, a trader buys goods from a merchant or supercargo on credit, and he sets him some short time to pay him. These goods he would sell well to his advantage but, alas! in cowries, which would not be taken by his creditor. He would then try to convert them either into cash or palm oil; the former being very scarce could not be obtained without a great loss of time and trouble; so, for fear of breaking his engagement with his creditor, he would try for the palm oil, which, too

1 *Parl. Papers* 1842: Q.1491, Evidence of Sewell and Q.1484, Evidence of Sewell

2 *Ibid.*, Q.1493, Evidence of Sewell   3 *Ibid.*, Q.1487, Evidence of Sewell

4 *Ibid.*, Q's1505–1514, Evidence of Sewell

5 C.O. 96/11: Report of Winniett to accompany Blue Books for 1846

6 Elias Schrenk, ' Was Soll aus der Goldküste werden?' *M.M.* 1865, reprinted in *M.M.* 1958, 38

through scarcity, could not be obtained without paying an enormous price, or putting more dashes on it, thus sacrificing all the accumulated profits he had obtained, and even perhaps involving him in debt beside; thus instead of gain, he has loss. This discourages many here from engaging in any trade at all.[1]

The need for proper currency could not be over-emphasised.

In 1869 it was reported that there was an unprecedented demand for British coins which had begun in 1865. Between 1866 and 1869 about £80,000 worth of British silver coins were imported into Salt Pond alone to buy palm oil. Many of these were taken into the interior and used as ornaments instead of currency. The people preferred coins bearing the effigy of Queen Victoria and refused those minted before her reign on the grounds that the monarchs whose subscriptions they bore were dead and so the coins were valueless. They also preferred new shiny coins and invariably rejected those that were even slightly worn. As British silver gained popularity, Africans 'who formerly used to purchase the smallest articles with Gold dust steadily refuse to accept it in the market or to give produce for it'.[2] By 1870 the use of cowries had also declined even in the eastern districts where they had formerly been very popular. Despite the increased use of silver coins by 1870, the time for better regulation of currency to aid economic activities was yet to come.[3] An Act to regulate currency was passed in 1880 – the 'Demonetisation Ordinance' – which restricted currency to the following:

(i) All gold and British sterling.
(ii) Spanish and South American doubloons at £3 4s.
American double eagles at £4 2s, American eagles at £2 1s, French 20 franc pieces at 15s 0d, and gold dust and nuggets at £1 2s per ounce.

Transportation

Economic development on the Gold Coast was also hampered by poor transportation. Much of the external trade on the Gold Coast came from the interior and invariably its accessibility vitally affected commercial life. It is significant that the palm oil trade was concentrated in areas close to the coast and in the Volta region where river communications were available. In 1887, for example, the Basel missionaries reported that bad transportation and a forty-five hour long trip from Kwahu prevented the people of that region from bringing their goods to the coast for sale.[4] While items like gold and ivory which fetched high prices could be carried from the far interior and sold for good profits on the coast, others like palm oil could not.

In the 1850s and 1860s the Basel missionaries worked on the first properly constructed road on the Gold Coast from Christiansborg through Aburi and

1 *African Times*, 'A Native', 23 Feb. 1876, p. 97

2 C.O. 96/74: Ussher to Blackall, 4 May 1869

3 Chalmers, *History of Currency in the British Colonies*, pp. 212–13

4 *B.M.A.*, Schmitt, 'Land Und Volk Okuawu', 23 Sept. 1886 in Heidenbote, 1887, p. 2

Akropong to Odumase that was to connect their stations. Two hours from Odumasi was the Volta basin.[1]

In 1861 an appeal from the *African Times* for funds to help with the construction of this road brought generous contributions. Messrs. Forster and Smith and Messrs. Swanzy and Company contributed £20 and £10 10*s*, respectively.[2] In 1865 when the Basel missionary Elias Schrenk visited Britain he also sought financial aid. He said that once their road was opened and frequented by carts, drawn by cattle, the Africans would perceive the importance of roads and would be encouraged to make others in various parts of the country. Shrenk estimated that approximately £500 were needed to complete the project, but if the British local government on the Gold Coast could persuade the chiefs in the eastern region to help, it would scarcely amount to half of the projected cost.[3]

The importance of roads for the economic development of Ghana figured prominently in 'What Will Become of the Gold Coast?', a pamphlet written by Schrenk in 1865. He said that roads were not only important for furthering commerce on the Gold Coast, but for maintaining peace as well. After reviewing goods exported from the interior, he pointed out the difficulty involved in transporting them to the coast. He expressed surprise that the British Government had not been sensible enough to build roads to exploit the resources of the country and dismissed the Government's claim that there was no money in the treasury for roads by pointing out that there had always been funds for the Asante wars.[4]

The cause of road building on the Gold Coast was championed by the *African Times* throughout the period under discussion. The *Times* was particularly interested in the opening of a road between the coast and the Asante frontier. The paper wrote in 1864:

> We must beg of our friends that they will not tire of our returning again and again to this theme of roads – roads – roads in Africa. It forces itself upon us at every step of our progress. And we are compelled to be persistent . . . Our statements of the large economy that would result from a road expenditure between the sea coast and the Ashantee frontier can no longer be termed visionary even by the wildest redtapist.[5]

Again in 1865, it commented about the Gold Coast:

> She of herself can never utilise or develop. Open roads – bring all the people into peaceful contact with one another, relieve them from being beasts of burden, and make them agriculturalists, and miners, under proper direction, and with the assistance of capital – or give them good examples.[6]

---

1 C.O. 96/45: Bird to Lytton, 17 May 1859; Wanner, *Basler Handels Gesellschaft*, p. 227

2 *African Times*, 22 Nov. 1862, p. 59

3 C.O. 96/69: Schrenk to Cardwell, 22 June 1865

4 Schrenk, 'Was Soll aus der Goldküste werden?', 1865, reprinted in *Mission Magazine* 1958, pp. 29–40

5 *African Times*, 23 July 1864, p. 9   6 *Ibid.*, 23 Feb. 1865

These efforts of the *African Times* evoked little response from the British Government. British local authorities on the Gold Coast, for example, felt that the suggestion to construct roads to the Asante was premature. They felt that without peace a road to the Pra River on the frontiers of Asante 'could not safely be undertaken and that possibly even the Assins might object to it in a strategic point of view, as affording an easy entrance into their territory'.[1] The first reasonably good track to Asante was constructed by British engineers for Wolseley's advance from Cape Coast in 1873–1874. When the British defeated Asante in 1874, transportation to the interior was still a problem, but the conquest marked the opening of avenues of communication with the inland states.

Institutional problems and economic development

Although not incompatible with economic growth, certain indigenous social institutions can impede economic growth. As two economic scholars have observed:

> Certain social institutions which are appropriate to a subsistence or near-subsistence economy may impede economic growth by reducing the rewards of individuals who take advantage of the opportunities presented by wider markets and the improved availability of co-operant resources.[2]

The extended family is an example of this hindrance. A specific example of this kind of relationship is the claim staked by the extended family of Joseph Smith on his house when he went bankrupt. Smith's relatives were not only interested in saving the house from the bankruptcy court, they also had a vested interest in it. As has been noted, while the extended family or the joint family may have many advantages at one level of economic achievement, it may later limit economic progress and development.[3]

Institutional arrangements like the communal ownership of land also restricted effective modern economic development. It has been affirmed that 'communal rights prevent the energetic or able individual members of the group from acquiring more land at the expense of the indolent or unproductive'.[4]

More important in affecting modern economic development was the prevalence of domestic slavery which before its abolition was an important feature of Gold Coast society and right up to 1874 was to form an integral part of the internal trade. As late as 1871 the Asante were reported to be bringing slaves aged between eight and twenty into the settlements under the British to sell them at £10 to £12 each.[5] Although slaves were a form of capital as well as an investment they could not be easily converted into cash for investment in the emerging modern trade. At the same time, interference in the institution deprived their owners of valuable property. One of the early attempts at freeing slaves on the Gold Coast was made by George Maclean. He made a beginning in the 1830s by manumitting slaves who had been badly treated by their masters and allowed some pawns to work off the debts for which they were held.

1 C.O. 96/85: Ussher to Kennedy, 11 Oct. 1870

2 Bauer and Yamey, *Economics of Under-Developed Countries*, p. 64

3 *Ibid.*   4 *Ibid.*, p. 52   5 C.O. 96/89: Salmon to Kennedy, 3 Nov. 1871

The abolition in 1863 by the Basel missionaries of domestic slavery among their congregations was one of the major attempts to interfere with the institution. The mission's struggle to free the slaves had begun in 1860. In that year the missionary George Widermann, then stationed at Akropong and head of the mission on the Gold Coast, wanted all Christians in that district to give up slavery in six years. This question was discussed at two conferences at Aburi and Akropong in 1860. At the conference at Akropong in November, 1860, they talked about freeing all the slaves of their converts in seven years, following the Laws of Moses. The director of the Basel Mission in Switzerland at the time, Joseph Josenhaus, supported this idea, but Zimmermann, the translator of the Ga Bible – who turned out to be the best expert the mission had on African affairs – opposed it.[1] Zimmermann argued that there was no hardship involved in domestic slavery on the Gold Coast and that the relationship between slave and master was akin to that of a father and a son. He pointed out that domestic slavery as a system of labour was better than that of Europe and that the slave was protected for life by his master. Zimmermann wanted the mission to consider the financial and the social implications involved in liberating the slaves. Widermann thought that Zimmermann was not sensible in his reasoning and that because he had a black wife (Jamaican) his views were coloured and could not be impartial. He felt that it would do Zimmermann good to return to Europe. For his views, Widermann sent him to the minor station of Krobo Odumasi. Another missionary, Locher, who contended that African domestic slavery was based on the Bible and that the Apostle Paul did not regard it as sin, was sent from Christiansborg to Abokobi for his views.[2]

Josenhaus, who insisted on freeing the slaves, argued that slavery was the centre of African darkness. He thought of raising money to pay for the liberation of slaves, but decided the Christians should not be compensated. The liberation efforts were helped by the African Evangelists, David Asante, Benjamin Tete and Wilhelm Oforika, who painted a dark picture of the institution and said that African Christians would be willing to relinquish their slaves.[3]

After the Basel missionaries had firmly committed themselves to abolishing domestic slavery they found out which of the church members were slave holders and asked them how much they had paid for their slaves and whether they would be willing to free them. Some said that they could never do that, others said that they would but not straightaway. The procedure the missionaries adopted was manumission, declaring the slave a debtor for the sum which his master had paid for him. The slave then worked to pay off the debt. Some masters gave their slaves a piece of land to cultivate when they were not engaged in working to redeem themselves, so that by the time they were free, they had some property of their own.[4]

At the time of liberating the slaves, there were about 956 Christians in the churches of the Basel Mission,[5] most of them in Akuapem in the towns of Akropong and Aburi and their out-stations. The other Christian bodies of the mission

1 Herman Klemm, *Elias Schrenk: der Weg eines Evangelisten*, Wuppertal, 1961, pp. 73–74

2 *Ibid.*, p. 76   3 *Ibid.*, pp. 76–79

4 *Parl. Papers* 1865, A's.3334–3335, Evidence of Elias Schrenk

5 *Ibid.*, Q.3334, Evidence of Schrenk

were at Christiansborg, Abokobi and Krobo Odumasi. As most of these former slaves were strangers they were therefore not entitled to land in the communities where they had been liberated. The presence of these people in the primarily agricultural region of Akuapem could not have been insignificant for the future of agriculture in that area. In the gold mining areas, for example, two thirds of the gold dug had often gone to the land owner and it is unlikely that strangers who farmed land belonging to others had a right to all the produce reaped from the land. What is being suggested here is that a characteristic labour practice in the cocoa industry evolved from earlier practices, *abusa*,[1] which means the proceeds are divided into three parts with the labourer receiving two thirds and the employing farmer receiving a third. The practice of *abusa* had certainly been applied in the Asante kola industry long before cocoa came to Asante.[2] The system was also employed in the rubber industry during the last two decades of the nineteenth century.[3] Thus it is possible that following the customary practice, the freed slaves in Akuapem worked and shared the produce from their farms through a system similar to that of *abusa*. It is true that domestic slavery was abolished in the British territories on the Gold Coast twelve years later in 1875, but the lead was given by the Christians of the Basel Mission congregation with provisions made for the slaves to enable them to pursue a life for themselves.

The major point to be made in connection with the freeing of slaves on the Gold Coast and subsequent labour arrangements for the manumitted chattel is that there was land to spare. Free and spare land often means a high land–labour ratio. At a primitive stage of agricultural development this may not generate a surplus above subsistence, and an incentive to enslavement; but at a more advanced stage, the higher land–labour ratio means that there is an excess of potential output above subsistence. With this excess, enslavement becomes a worthwhile proposition. So in order for landowners to obtain income from their land, it becomes necessary to restrict the mobility of their labour force. This restriction can take the form of preventing the labourers from acquiring their own land and confining their movements in a way that would benefit the landowners.[4]

In a sense, domestic slaves were a form of riches, an asset or capital for their owners. In addition to slaves, wealth on the Gold Coast during this period consisted of gold and beads which were secure forms of investment.[5] As wealth was often invested in these hoarded items there was an absence of capital to develop and to transform the economy of the country. While these forms of wealth have been used in traditional society as tribute, pawns and security for credit, they were not easily or readily translated into capital investments in a modern economy.

Realising the need for capital for Gold Coast and West African development, the *African Times* in 1868 called public attention to the problem in an article entitled 'Native Capitalists' which asserted that for the development of resources and for general progress what was needed was capital. Where capital did not exist it had to be created or imported. In some British colonies the economic development was stimulated by capital from Britain and from immigrants who occupied the lands and improved them with resources from imperial expenditure,

1 See Hill, *Gold Coast Cocoa-Farmer*, pp. 8–24

2 *Ibid.*   3 *Ibid.*, p. 10

4 Stanley L. Engerman, 'Some Considerations Relating to Property Rights in Man', *J.E.H.* xxxii, No. 1, 1973, pp. 56–57

5 *Parl. Papers* 1816, pp. 161, 197 and 201

or money lent from England. But because of the nature of the British West African settlements they did not attract such investments:

> From this it follows that if West Africa is to progress, it must be chiefly, if not entirely, by means of her own resources. In other words, there must be a creation of *native capitalists*. And the time has arrived at which this creation ought to take place. But it never can take place while the realised surplus product of industry goes out of the country. That realised surplus, which, in the infancy of trade and resources, went almost inevitably into the hands of the British merchant and trader, and has thus been lost to the country, must now be kept at home, for it is on the keeping it *at home* in the hands of natives that a rapid progress in Africa absolutely depends.[1]

Much of the early profits had gone to British merchants and traders since before the rise of a large African merchant class most of the traders on the coast had been European. As the bulk of the profits from trade went into Europe, the *African Times* suggested that means had to be found to keep as much of it as possible in the hands of African traders and producers. The paper suggested a way of accomplishing it:

> It must be done partly by them and partly for them. They must exercise prudence, self-restraint and self-denial, as well as industry and intelligence; and they must be aided in England by zeal and faithfulness, and the most strict and scrupulous honesty in every dealing with them. On this side they ought to have every advantage which the British markets can offer, paying on a fair and open and recognised charge for the services rendered to them; and they on their side, must restrain themselves within the limits which what they themselves possess will allow.[2]

The *African Times* pledged itself to help in the creation of the 'Native Capitalists', who could use some of their wealth for the construction of public works. The paper felt:

> It is time that the great body of native traders on the Coast, the indispensable medium of barter for European goods against native produce, should become something more than mere slaves of European capital, working for scanty profit or a mere subsistence, and not unfrequently to be overloaded with fictitious debt; it is time, we say, that this great body of native traders should begin to appropriate to themselves, for themselves and their country, the great profits of that trade, instead of a mere pittance from it. We call upon every one of them to say with firm resolve 'I will become a native capitalist;' and we are convinced that if they will do their part of prudence and self-denial and energy, while availing themselves of the advantages we have prevailed upon ourselves to offer them in our *commercial agency*, they will soon become the capitalists they may have resolved that they will become.[3]

Indeed with all the bankruptcies and failures in business there was need to complain about trade practices. The constant overcharging which often led to loss of

1 *African Times*, 23 May 1868, p. 130   2 *Ibid.*   3 *Ibid.*, italics added

only scanty profits surely made the African merchants in the words of Fitzgerald 'mere slaves of European capital'. In spite of the apparent concern of Fitzgerald and the *African Times*, they were not disinterested observers. They had also been interested in the African trade and felt that their 'commercial agency' could offer the African merchants better terms which would enable them to attain their goal of becoming 'Native Capitalists'. The 'commercial agency' of the *African Times* seems to have been established in 1870. At least from that date a regular advertisement appeared in the paper concerning it:

African agency

For Transacting Business in England for Natives and Other Traders on the West Coast of Africa

In consequence of wishes expressed from all parts of the West Coast, Mr. Fitzgerald has made arrangements for selling produce consigned to him by ships to London or Liverpool; and purchasing and shipping goods ordered against the proceeds of consignments or other effective remittances only, from either of the above ports, on a system by which the greatest possible advantage of the markets will be secured to the AFRICAN TRADER, who will not be charged one penny beyond what is actually paid, except only the commission openly debited in account.[1]

The problem of creating 'Native Capitalists' went beyond fair trading practices and Africans being able to keep the bulk of the trade profits at home. Clearly, institutions like banks and other forms of services needed by a growing modern economy were called for.

According to Andrew Swanzy, the only African who had enough capital in 1874 to trade on her own account was Mrs Henry Barnes of Cape Coast.[2] By this time merchant houses like F. and A. Swanzy had established their own stores on the coast instead of sending goods to African agents on credit;[3] the Basel Mission Trading Company had also become entrenched in the country[4] and Forster and Smith had ceased to operate on the Gold Coast. Consequently, the lack of capital on the part of the African merchants to trade on their own accounts[5] or their elimination from the commercial scene reflected the economic plight of African merchants and their support of a political organisation like the Fante Confederation was no idle speculation.

1 *African Times*, 24 Jan. 1870

2 A. Swanzy, 'On Trade in Western Africa with and without British Protection', p. 479

3 *Parl. Papers* 1865   4 *African Times*, 22 Aug. 1868, p. 22

5 Richard Brew, son of the merchant Samuel Collins Brew and a grandson of Sam Kanto Brew, was a good example of the new inferior role being played by African merchants around the 1860s and 1870s. Instead of becoming a merchant in his own right Richard Brew became a factor and commission agent of a European firm. Priestley, *West African Trade* and *Coast Society*, p. 151.

CHAPTER SIX

Economic change, conflict and African politics

Among the developments discernible on the Gold Coast by 1860 were the declining power, influence and wealth of chiefs; the increasing presence and power of Great Britain on the coast; the constant threat of Asante and the presence and the decline of the fortunes of African merchants.

Prelude to conflict

Following the abolition of the slave trade and the decline of state-oriented trade, chiefs lost an important source of wealth. The Asante invasion of 1807 and other subsequent incursions into the coast showed the inability of the coastal chiefs to defend themselves and this burden subsequently fell upon Europeans. Wars and disturbances were detrimental to trade in the country and defending and keeping peace between Asante and her southern neighbours became indispensable for prosperous trade. The responsibility of Europeans on the coast grew from defence to dispensation of justice to the point where Europeans felt free to suspend the salaries and rents they had paid African rulers in recognition of their sovereignty over the country. This increasing responsibility of Europeans came at a time when an African merchant class was rising and enjoying the benefits that the European presence and the peace they maintained offered. However, by the 1860s, the decline of the influence of the chiefs, the inability of Britain to meet its defence commitment, the talk of European retrenchment, the continuous threat of Asante, a period of trade recession and the declining fortunes of African merchants would lead to a challenge of British authority and efforts towards the economic and political development of the country. Although some of the political protests and the conflicts have been dealt with in other works,[1] what is emphasised in this brief chapter is how these events were interwoven with the trade and economic change of the time.

Much of the open rebellion and challenge to British authority came in the 1860s, but there had been signs of restlessness as early as the 1830s when George Maclean began to increase British jurisdiction of the Gold Coast. British jurisdiction went beyond the question of justice because removing cases from indigenous courts meant that African chiefs were losing fines they had been used to collecting from their clients. In 1865, for example, although the conflict between the British and King John Aggrey was that of authority, the

---

1 See Kimble, *Political History* and F. Agbodeka, *African Politics and British Policy in the Gold Coast, 1868–1900*, London, 1971

questions raised by Aggrey's court and British judicial authority were in a sense not unrelated to making an income from the judicial process. Conran, the British administrator, wrote to Aggrey:

> Yourself and every other Chief residing on the Seaboard Coast must be aware that where Her Majesty's Courts of Law are held open daily for the administration of Justice, there can be no other admitted by the Government. Whilst for the settlement of Land disputes, and other minor offences, and petty debts arising between Natives, there is no objection to their adjustment in your Court provided that the sentences awarded are not of a cruel nature or repugnant to British Law, and even these cases must be regarded as subject to an appeal to Her Majesty's Courts.[1]

British control of the judicial process deprived African rulers of an income from this source. As a British Governor observed, 'Day by day, the Kings and chiefs become more enlightened, and several have said to me, with great truth, "The Government takes all the money and we never taste any".'[2] Furthermore, the British courts did not recognise slavery and pawns and their interference with slaves often entailed financial losses to their owners since slaves represented capital. In 1858 Governor Pine had reported that 'the subject is perpetually brought to my notice by chiefs and others demanding back their slaves or payment for them'.[3] The increasing discontent with British presence was becoming obvious. As Thomas B. Freeman wrote, 'There is a great declension in the amount of confidence reported by the Native Chiefs and Headmen of the various tribes and peoples of their country in the Local Government under which they live.'[4] But disenchantment with the British Government was not confined to the chiefs alone but also to the African merchants. And as was observed, 'The general good intelligence which formerly existed between the Government and the mercantile community has also greatly declined'.[5]

As early as 1855 the discontent with British rule was taking a racialist tone. For example, a petition signed from Cape Coast protested against 'misrepresentations' made against the Gold Coast settlements by 'officials here who, because we are Blacks, fancy that we must be kept down, our mouths must be shut, our rights and liberties must be invaded with impunity and in short, not be permitted to think for ourselves'.[6] Moreover, as some chiefs were later to complain, 'the Gold Coast is not without educated Natives fit for government appointments or employments as well as Foreigners of their own colour'. The chiefs, therefore hoped that 'preference may be given to Natives, so that Natives may have the opportunity of gaining experience in public duties, and of further bettering their impoverished condition'.[7] The conflicts that broke out in the

1 C.O. 96/74: Conran to Aggrey, 6 Dec. 1866

2 C.O. 96/89: Kennedy to Kimberley, 8 Nov. 1871

3 C.O. 96/43: Pine to Labouchere, 2 Jan. 1858

4 C.O. 96/41: Freeman to Pine, 2 June 1857   5 *Ibid.*

6 C.O. 96/33: J. R. Thompson and Chiefs to Grey, 5 Jan. 1855

7 C.O. 96/94: Memorial of the Chiefs and Captains or Heads of Cape Coast to J. Pope-Hennessy in Dispatch from Hennessy to Kimberley, 29 Oct. 1872

1860s, which were not without economic basis, brought chiefs and African merchants together in a common course of action.

The war of 1863: Question of defence and trade

The Asante invasion of 1863 probably helped to bring to the fore much of the economic and defensive problems. This invasion was one of many in the nineteenth century. But if the need for peace and security and the need for defence had been lost upon chiefs and African merchants during previous Asante invasions, the question of the need to protect themselves and to maintain tranquillity for the sake of trade was forcibly brought home in 1863. The disastrous campaign against Asante shook the confidence of the people in the British Government. Africanus Horton described the aftermath of the Asante campaign when he wrote: 'Confusion now reigned in the whole of the Protectorate; the prestige of the ruling power suffered fearfully.'[1] The events of the 1863 invasion are well known and the details need not be reiterated here. However, the war was an important prelude to subsequent events in the 1860s – events which were the products of economic change.

The inability of Britain to protect its allies in 1863 was a failure of her responsibility to defend the coastal states. The words of Governor William Pine following the event are significant for later activities and the behaviour of chiefs and African merchants.

Pine wrote:

> I will not now enter into a discussion as to the past history of the relation between the King of Ashantee and the people of this Coast to whom protection (in return for corresponding concession) has been guaranteed by the British crown – it is sufficient for our own purposes to recognize this fact, that we have at this moment, through the conduct of our defensive policy failed – in that guarantee; for the Territories consigned to our Military guardianship have been invaded – their population in various instances driven from their homes and the produce of their industry pillaged – and this has been accomplished hitherto without almost any risk to the Invaders for no adequate check or punishment at our hands has followed the perpetration of these crimes.[2]

By 1864 it was clear that Britain was relinquishing the role that it had assumed of defending the territories on the Gold Coast. In August 1864 the people were told that they were to be left the responsibility of protecting themselves except for the possibility of being supplied with munitions of war.[3]

As the British authorities instructed Governor Pine:

> The duty of defending the extensive territory in the Protectorate can only be satisfactorily discharged if the chiefs to whom it belongs are united and they are not united, and will not take upon themselves the principal part of the exertions necessary, it will not be possible to defend them without exposing the Queen's Forces to the risks of a deadly climate, and to the hazard of being

---

1 Horton, *Letters*, p. 74   2 C.O. 96/64: Memorandum of Richard Pine, 1864

3 C.O. *96/65*: Pine to Cardwell, 5 August 1864

virtually defeated by the disastrous consequences of that climate, before they have been able to bring the native enemy to the issue of arms.[1]

By 1864 it had become clear that in the future chiefs and merchants would have to be self-reliant in defending themselves. If the late Asante war had brought the question of defending the country to the fore, the rumours and misunderstanding that followed the Select Committee of 1865 Report made the problem of defence urgent. Among its recommendations the committee had resolved:

> That all further extension of territory or assumption of Government, or new treaties offering any protection to native tribes, would be inexpedient; and that the object of our policy should be to encourage in the natives the exercise of those qualities which may render it possible for us more and more to transfer to them the administration of all the Governments, with a view to our ultimate withdrawal from all, except, probably, Sierra Leone.[2]

This policy of encouraging chiefs to depend upon themselves rather than on British support was new and unexpected. The *African Times* accepted it at face value and admonished the people of the Gold Coast to unite for their own defence, but it was to transpire that the British Government had no intention, in that short term at least, of accepting this drastic interpretation of the committee's recommendations. The effort of the Gold Coast people to unite for their defence and self-government was made in 1868. In that year the African merchants and the traditional rulers came together in a united action, for the common purpose of their defence, in the Fante Confederation.

The Fante Confederation

Admittedly the Fante Confederation came into existence following the exchange of forts between the British and the Dutch in 1868, but it came after almost two decades of discontent and conflict with the local government.[3] The reasons behind the Dutch and British exchange of forts were largely economic and it was the persistent need to raise a revenue from the British settlements that resulted in the transfers in 1868. The exchange of forts, ostensibly to 'facilitate trade and civilisation' was done without consultation of the people who were to be transferred to a different power under the arrangement.[4]

The reaction of the districts under British protection was predictable. The Dutch government on the Gold Coast had been an ally of Asante. Since Fante and other states under British protection had for years been the implacable enemy of the Asante, their transfer seemed in effect like handing them over to their enemies.[5] The Council of the Fante which came into existence after the

---

1 C.O. 96/64: Cardwell to Pine, 23 June 1864   2 See *Parl. Papers*, 1865.

3 See Kimble, *Political History*, pp. 220–63; Agbodeka, *African Politics and British Policy in the Gold Coast, 1868–1900*, pp. 15–33; F. Agbodeka, 'The Fanti Confederacy, 1865–1869', *T.H.S.G.* vii, 1965, pp. 82–123 and Limberg, 'The Economy of the Fanti Confederation', pp. 83–103

4 On the exchange of territory see Coombs, *The Gold Coast, Britain and the Netherlands 1850–1874*

5 Horton, *Letters*, pp. 24–28

promulgation of the treaty of exchange had the aim to 'advance the interest of the whole of the Fantee nation' and 'to combine for offence and defence in time of war'.[1] The attempts made to put the organisation on to a permanent footing showed that the Fante Confederation was more than an *ad hoc* association to protest an action of foreign governments and to defend themselves against Asante. Furthermore, the economic nature of the constitution that came out of the confederation reflected the concern and interest of the so-called educated Africans whose influence seems to have overshadowed that of the chiefs in the organisation.

Although every educated person on the Gold Coast was in sympathy with the objectives of the Fante Confederation,[2] it is significant that most of the leaders of the movement and allegedly disreputable advisers of the Fante Chiefs (except Ghartey and Blankson) were not the richer African merchants but, rather, ambitious literate clerks and employees who had failed to make good. Administrator H. T. Ussher's severe characterisation of the 'ostensible movers' of the Fante Confederation, probably mirror the economic, not to mention the political, discontent of these people. W. E. Davidson, a hotel keeper at Cape Coast, was 'considered a disreputable character especially in trading matters'. Ussher claimed that Davidson, abetted by others, had attempted to extort a large sum of money from a French nobleman. J. F. Amissah was 'a Bankrupt, now a clerk'. S. Ferguson was 'a trader of notoriously bad character and violent in his language towards British Government'. J. H. Brew was 'a pleader in the Courts, generally of bad repute, and is supposed on good grounds to have had incestuous intercourse with his sister, by whom he had a child'. R. J. Ghartey allegedly 'offered a compromise with his creditors, which he appears to carry out and is not otherwise of bad repute'. Joseph Hayford supposedly was 'gravely implicated in a robbery at Anammaboe from an American captain' and was also 'afterwards dismissed from the service of the commissariat for misconduct and embezzlement'.[3] George Blankson, Junior, was described as 'an habitual drunkard, dismissed from Clerk of Courts for dishonest practice'. J. M. Insiadoo, was the 'most respectable of the foregoing but eccentric and violent'. W. C. Fynn was 'formerly clerk of courts at Accra and Cape Coast dismissed for dishonesty and extortion – a very bad character'. Joseph Dawson was 'dismissed from the Wesleyan Society for evil practices'. Kwesi Edoo, King of Mankessim, was 'a great drunkard, violent and ignorant fanatic'. Anfoo Otoo, King of Abora, was characterised as 'the best of all, powerful and intelligent chief – ambitious and violent, but honest – is strongly disposed against the Government'.[4]

The serious imputations on the character of the leaders of the Confederation were unjust and unfair. Pope-Hennessy, to whom the allegations were sent, did not pay much attention to the grave statement.[5] However, it is significant that except for the two Kings of Mankessim and Abora, the leaders were 'educated natives' who had some vested interest in the economy. The interest of this edu-

1 *Ibid.*, p. 29   2 C.O. 96/94: Pope-Hennessy to Kimberley, 29 Oct. 1872

3 This can hardly be true since Hayford had recently been accepted as a candidate for the Methodist Ministry. F. L. Bartels, *The Roots of Ghana Methodism*, Cambridge, 1965, pp. 87–88.

4 C.O. 96/94: Ussher to Pope-Hennessy, 5 April 1872

5 C.O. 96/94: Pope-Hennessy to Kimberley, 29 Oct. 1872

cated group was amply reflected in the goals of the confederation as they appeared in the 1872 constitution of the organisation. This constitution, ratified by thirty-one kings and chiefs, was undoubtedly biased in favour of the 'educated' people. It was not without justification that W. W. Claridge wrote that 'the whole constitution seems to have been framed by a few educated and semi-educated men, primarily no doubt for the good of their country, but secondarily for the benefit of themselves'.[1]

Some of the aims were outlined in article eight of the constitution and emphasise the economic nature and aspirations of the organisation.

That it be the object of the Confederation:
i   To promote friendly intercourse between all the kings and chiefs of Fanti, and to unite them for offensive and defensive purposes against their common enemy.
ii   To direct the labours of the Confederation towards the improvement of the country at large.
iii   To make good and substantial roads throughout all the interior districts included in the Confederation.
iv   To erect school-houses and establish schools for the education of all children within the Confederation, and to obtain the service of efficient schoolmasters.
v   To promote agricultural and industrial pursuits, and to endeavour to introduce such new plants as may hereafter become sources of profitable commerce to the country.
vi   To develop and facilitate the working of the mineral and other resources of the country.[2]

These objectives strike a very modern note, and show foresight, keen sensitivity and awareness of the political and economic needs of the country on the part of the framers of the document. The first clause which called for friendship among the Fante and unity for offensive and defensive purposes was no doubt in response to British policy following the Parliamentary Commission of 1865 of encouraging the chiefs to depend upon themselves rather than British support. Clauses ii and iii called for improvement of the country and the construction of roads in the interior. In the confederation these roads would have immensely helped with the communication problem that often inhibited economic development. Clause iv dealt with the problem of social improvement. More important perhaps for this study clauses v and vi called for the promotion of agricultural and industrial pursuits and the development and facilitation of gold mining. These economic pursuits were close to the hearts of the educated group as their efforts in the rubber and gold mining activities of the 1880s were to prove.[3]

Perhaps one of the more germane aspects of the Fante Confederation for this study was its trade policy of levying road taxes. The bulk of these taxes seem

1 W. W. Claridge, *A History of the Gold Coast and Ashanti*, London, 1918, 2 vols., ii, p. 619

2 C.O. 96/94: Brew to Pope-Hennessy, 16 April 1872. Horton's influence on this and the Constitution as a whole is carefully analysed in Kimble, *Political History*, pp. 243–6.

3 On the rubber trade, see Dumett, 'Rubber Trade in the Nineteenth Century of the Gold Coast and Asante: African Innovation and Responsiveness'.

to have been collected between December 1868 and April 1869 and in the autumn of 1871. A duty of one shilling was levied on each load of merchandise passing through Fante territory. Much of the collection of these duties came from areas where the Fante Confederation's authority was strongest in the Mankessim and Abora districts. The duties levied in these two areas between December and April amounted to £67 in December, £50 in January, £46 in February, £38 in March and £38 in April.[1] The idea of levying taxes was opposed by both the government and traders like F. C. Grant and it was finally brought to an end in late 1871.[2] It is significant that African chiefs who had lost their stipends from Europeans on the coast would give taxation power to an organisation like the Fante Confederation in order to get a salary or a share from the trade taxes.

Governor Kennedy understood the plight of the African chiefs when he wrote:

> It must be remembered that, the slave trade at an end, the chiefs and kings in the interior have no means of living or supporting their . . . dignity save by contributions, either voluntary or forced, from their own people and traders passing through their country. *Nothing can be more destructive of trade than this levying of toll.*[3]

Governor Kennedy proposed paying the chiefs a stipend in order to keep the roads 'open and free'.

The Accra Confederation

The founding in Accra of a short-lived organisation, similar to that of the Fante Confederation, can be linked to economic grievance. As the educated people in the Accra region reasoned:

> Circumstances which have sprung up since the unsettled state of the country have compelled the educated natives, in conjunction with the kings on the sea-coast – viz., of James Town, Old Dutch Accra and Christiansborg – to form a close political combination, whose first object is to bring a speedy termination to the wars and disturbances which have nearly ruined Accra.[4]

Their concern was clear; Accra was ruined because trade was at a standstill due to conflict in the eastern region. The immediate occasion of their alarm was the failure of the Accra Chiefs even to attempt to fulfil their undertaking to Administrator Simpson to furnish an army of 2,000 men to go to the relief of Krepi attacked by Asante and Akwamu.[5] To deal with the conflict they formed an Association in August, 1869. The committee that the Association formed was

---

1 Other forms of revenue would include court revenue and some subscriptions. The method of dispensing the road tax was that one part went to the King and two parts to the Confederation.

2 Limberg, 'The Economy of the Fanti Confederation', pp. 86–97

3 C.O. 96/89: Kennedy to Kimberley, 8 Nov. 1871. Italics added by the author.

4 Horton, *Letters*, pp. 29–30   5 *Ibid.*, p. 37

composed of W. Lutterodt (president), George Cleland, J. E. Richter, W. Addo, James Bannerman and L. Hope. Except for the last named, all were leading merchants. There seem to have been about 60 educated people at Accra connected with the association, but the fact that a collection at this time for ammunition among them raised only £300 does not suggest many of them were well-off in 1869. The declining fortunes of Accra merchants and their losing grip on trade was illustrated by families with trading traditions leaving trade and seeking other occupations. Admittedly, the widening of occupations was a feature of the developing modern economy but seemingly it was circumstances that were driving these people out of commerce.

In the Accra area, especially around Christiansborg, Danish descendants who had inherited considerable wealth from their ancestors who had been merchants began to lose their mercantile position following the poll tax disturbances, the conflicts in the 1860s and competition from the Basel Mission Trading Company. After this period they began to seek employment with the Basel Mission as trading agents, teachers, evangelists and ministers. The case of the venerable Ghanaian historian C. C. Reindorf illustrates this change. He left school and went into trade, but later returned to complete his education. It is not clear why he returned to school but one would surmise that he probably failed in commerce. Even after finishing school and becoming a Catechist he retired temporarily to establish a coffee plantation near Aburi in Akuapem.[1]

Other Danish descendants with a tradition of trading in their families who turned to the Basel Mission as agents were Karl Quist, Thomas Svaniker, Samuel Holm, Christian Wrisberg, Frederick Palm, Jeremia Engmann and Paul Fleischer.[2] Outside the sphere of the Basel Mission, not much is heard of the Danish descendants between 1874 and the end of the nineteenth century as traders and prominent people; but their influence was to be felt again in local government and other walks of life in the twentieth century.

Asante and coastal trade

The rise and fall of the Fante Confederation were interwoven with the trade politics of the period. These events also affected the economic life of Asante. To be sure, there had been no formal peace treaty to end the war with Asante in 1863. In consequence of this conflict trade on the coast had virtually been closed to Asante.[3] In 1865 the Lieutenant-Governor testified to this:

> . . . it affords me an opportunity of mentioning that there can be no doubt as to the great sufferings the Ashantees have undergone during the last $2\frac{1}{2}$ years consequent on their being blockaded within their own territory, all communication without long line or sea coast have been shut out from them, depriving

1 Debrunner, *History of Christianity*, p. 162; see also the biography in *Gold Coast and Asante* by C. C. Reindorf.

2 Debrunner, *History of Christianity*, p. 162

3 Asante trade with the coast for most of this period was done through the intermediary tribes, especially the Assins and Akyem. See C.O. 96/77: Simpson to Kennedy, 5 Dec. 1868; C.O. 96/81: Simpson to Kennedy, 7 August 1869; C.O. 96/68: King Atta of Akim to Conran, 28 Oct. 1865.

171

them therefore of the means of obtaining those supplies such as arms, ammunition, cotton goods and salt being articles of trade, to them indispensable, as the little they may have received from the flanks of the Protectorate (East and West) can hardly be considered sufficient to be of any advantage to them.[1]

Whether or not the supplies from the flanks of the Protectorate were sufficient for Asante needs or not, it was relevant for later developments that trade east of the Volta had become important to her.

It was probably not without significance that during the conflict of 1863 and for the first time since the interdiction of the slave trade Asante was supposedly bringing slaves down the Volta for sale on the slave coast. The African Aid Society reported in 1863 that they had received information that there was a large traffic in slaves from Asante in the Volta region. The slaves were sent to Popo and Ahguay to slave merchants and shipped to Cuba.[2] The *African Times* also reported that the Asante were carrying on a vigorous trade at Ada and Keta exchanging slaves for gunpowder.[3]

The commercial avenues of the Volta region were becoming essential to Asante at a time when merchants from the coast were penetrating the Volta region because of the palm oil trade, the cotton trade in Krepi and the possibilities of the Volta developing into a major communication route into the interior. In fact it was the very conflict of trade interests in this region that had precipitated the Anlo War of 1865–1866. Thus, while restricted in her commercial dealings in the area West of the Volta, Asante could not have been unaware that her trade East of the Volta could also be circumscribed with the encroachment of British and other merchants East of the Volta.[4]

It is true that an Asante army had been in Akwamu in the 1850s and that the invasion and the war of 1869 were in response to Akwamu's request to regain suzerainty over her Krepi subjects who had rebelled. But it was in the trade interests of Asante east of the Volta to crush the Krepi enemies of her Akwamu and Anlo allies.[5] Even before the campaign east of the Volta began, European factories at Keta were called upon to pay a tribute of 100 dollars each for permission to continue their trade and for protection when the Asante took possession of the area.[6] The importance of the war of 1869 east of the Volta could not have been lost upon those with trade interests in the area. The clash of interests between the British, the Coastal States and Asante during this period was largely the inevitable result of trade and economic change.

1 C.O. 96/68: Conran to Cardwell, 8 Sept. 1865

2 C.O. 96/63: Alfred Churchill to Newcastle, 20 April 1863

3 *African Times*, 23 Jan. 1864

4 By 1865 there were six factories at Adafo, the Island at the mouth of the Volta: 1) H. L. Rottman and Company, Agents of Mr C. H. Mayer, 2) W. P. Gunnell, 3) John Clayton, 4) W. G. Bruce, 5) E. W. Bruce and 6) Bremen Factory: Julino Ungar, Agent for M. Victor Sons at Bremen.

5 For Asante activities East of the Volta see M. Johnson, 'Ashanti East of the Volta', pp. 33–59

6 C.O. 96/83: Commander Dowell on the *Rattlesnake* to the Secretary of the Administrator, 30 March 1869

The events of the decade of the 1860s were often affected by trade and vested interests and their consequences not infrequently influenced the commercial life of the country. African merchants who were losing an economic position especially in the 1860s found an outlet for their discontent in organisations to govern and to develop their country. Although the mining activities that followed the Asante war and the booming rubber trade[1] in the 1880s and 1890s enabled them to recover from their economic plight, the tendency towards large-scale enterprise and the growth of a European commercial oligopoly and the exclusion of African traders resulted in further discontent. It was probably no coincidence that the evolution of the Gold Coast Aborigines' Rights Protection Society came at a time when both chiefs and African merchants faced another threat and chiefs faced the possible loss of revenue from land. European firms were once more squeezing the African merchant out of big commercial operations, relegating to them the position of petty traders and agents to large European firms.

1 See Dumett, 'Rubber Trade of the Gold Coast and Asante in the Nineteenth Century: African Innovation and Responsiveness'

CHAPTER SEVEN

On the threshold of a modern economy

The British annexation of the Gold Coast in 1874 following the defeat of Asante and the removal of the seat of government from Cape Coast to Accra in 1877 may be said to have marked the beginning of a new era for the economic development of the Gold Coast. By this time a skeleton of modern government was operating over a wide area of the country; there were more government departments that needed permanent buildings and services; material civilisation was much in evidence, and the slow progress towards a modern economy continued. In fact, it was during the period following the formal establishment of British rule that the country entered what has often been called the 'economic revolution'[1] in the 1890s. The study of economic development between 1874 and the years of economic revolution is beyond the scope of this study; but before any conclusions are drawn from the earlier period some of the important developments up to the last decade of the nineteenth century need to be mentioned briefly.

The conflict of 1873–1874 had a tremendous impact on the Asante and the defeat suffered in war in part brought about the beginnings of the disintegration of the kingdom.[2] After the war, Asante faced not only internal conflict within the kingdom, but also dynastic problems as well.[3] The internal revolts affected trade, as Freeman noted:

> . . . Ashanti in the days of its power was one of the most important commercial centres in West Africa. It was the focus of a most extensive traffic with the Muslem nations of the far north and east. From Timbuktu and Jenne, from the land of the Tawareks, from Sokotu, Kano, Kachina and other cities, from Bornu by Lake Chad, even from the shores of the Mediterranean the caravans wended their way to the great negro Kingdom where the precious guru or kola could be purchased. With these great African nations Kumasi was brought into communication by means of two caravan roads; one leading from the east from Bornu and Hausa and passing through Borugu and Yendi (the

---

1 See McPhee, *Economic Revolution in British West Africa* and Szereszewski, *Structural Changes in the Economy of Ghana 1891–1911*

2 For the conflict within Asante after the war of 1873–1874, see Kimble, *Political History*, pp. 274–9; R. E. Dumett, 'British Official Attitudes', pp. 152–3 and W. Tordoff, *Ashanti under the Prempehs, 1888–1935*, Oxford, 1965

3 Kimble, *Political History*, pp. 274–5; see also Tordoff, *Ashanti under the Prempehs, 1888–1935*

ON THE THRESHOLD OF A MODERN ECONOMY

capital of Dagomba) to Salaga and Kantampo; the other from Timbuktu passing through Massina, Sofara, Jelasu, Kong and Bontuku to Kantampo. There appears to have been a second Timbuktu road which, starting from Kabara, the port of Timbuktu, passed through Banya-garra, Mandoli, and Wurga-duku (the capital of Moshi or Mosi), and joined the eastern road at Yendi; while at Sokoto or Kachina the same road was joined by the great caravan road from Tripoli.[1]

The disorganisation of Asante which followed the defeat of 1874 brought about a great decline in the volume of this trade.

An event of great significance following the 1873–1874 war which affected the economic life of the country was the abolition of slave dealing and the emancipation of slaves in the Gold Coast Protectorate.[2] Slaves were 'property', in a sense, and as much money had been invested in them, in a way they represented capital, they were wealth; they formed the basis of labour and production; they could be pawned, and when their owners died they could be passed on as part of the estate. The economic implications of this Act were to have far-reaching consequences. For the people of the Gold Coast, the Act meant finding new means of investment; providing security for debts, and securing a source of labour that the extended family could not fulfil.

The accounts of the prospects of the potential mineral wealth reported by returning British soldiers from the Asante War lured prospectors to the country,[3] with the first European efforts following the Asante to develop gold mining with European capital being undertaken by Pierre Bonnat in 1877. Bonnat had been captured in Ho in 1869 when Asante invaded the Volta region and had been taken with the missionaries Ramseyer and Kuhne to Kumasi. He was released in 1874. On his return to Europe a French mining engineer, Bazin, who had read his adventures in L'Explorateur, approached him with the idea of prospecting gold on the Gold Coast. As a result the Société des Mines d'Or de l'Afrique Occidentale was founded and began prospecting for gold at Awudua in April 1877.[4]

The number of mining companies formed on the Gold Coast after 1877 both by Africans and Europeans exhibited new interests in prospecting for gold in the country. Among the companies were the African Gold Coast Company (1878), the Gold Coast Mining Company (1880), the Wassaw and Ahanta Gold Mines Syndicate (1880), Effuenta Gold Mining Co. (1880), Swanzy Estates and Mining Company (1882), the Wassaw (Gold Coast) Mining Company (1882), the Tarkwa (Tamsu) Gold Mining Company (1882), and the Ginnamon Bippo Gold Mine Ltd (1887).[5]

1 R. A. Freeman, *Travels and Life in Ashanti and Jamon*, London, 1898, p. 477

2 Kimble, *Political History*, pp. 303–4

3 Junner, *Gold on the Gold Coast*, pp. 5–10; Kimble, *Political History*, pp. 15–25; E. D. Morrell, *Affairs of West Africa*, London, 1902, pp. 367–70; Dickson, *Historical Geography*. pp. 179–91; S. D. Neumark, *Foreign Trade and Economic Development in Africa: a Historical Perspective*, Stanford, 1964, pp. 95–96; Dumett, 'Official British Attitudes', pp. 54–71; Francis Hart, *The Gold Coast, Its Wealth and Health*, London, 1904, pp. 24–37

4 Horton, *West African Countries*, p. 265; Kimble, *Political History*, p. 15

5 Dickson, *Historical Geography*, pp. 182–3; Dumett, 'Official British Attitudes', pp. 55–61; C-5620, *Parl. Papers* 1889, liv, Report on Gold Mines, 1889

The Wassaw and Ahanta Gold Mines Syndicate was undertaken by Africanus Horton in conjunction with Ferdinand Fitzgerald of the *African Times*.[1] It has been estimated that 31 of the 109 different concessions registered at Cape Coast between 1878 and 1882 were held by Horton.[2] Other Africans who had mining concessions at this time were Joseph Dawson of Cape Coast at Tarkwa and J. E. Ellis, J. E. Biney and J. P. Brown at Obuasi.[3] In 1882 the Gold Coast Native Concession Purchasing Company was formed by F. C. Grant, J. F. Amissah, John Sarbah, James Brew, G. E. Eminsany and J. W. Sey.[4] Undoubtedly much of this acquisition of mining concessions by Africans was mere speculation. This kind of activity and the role of the new type of middleman who negotiated concessions between mining companies and chiefs must have played an important part in sustaining the waning fortunes of African merchants and the coastal 'middle class'. Obviously, mining concessions (as were the timber and cocoa industries) which were linked with the acquisition of land lay behind some of the political agitation of this period, especially the problem of the land legislation in the 1890s.[5]

Although the mining undertakings of the Africans failed because of the difficulty of raising capital, it is significant that Africans were responding and continuing to give leadership to economic development. It was not only African mining prospectors who lacked the financial resources and the technical and practical skills for carrying on a successful mining operation. As there was no rush to bid for shares in gold mining companies and there was no abundance of knowledgeable mining personnel, a large number of the earlier companies failed.[6] However, because of the advantages European mining companies had in raising capital they were able virtually to exclude Africans from the field.[7]

Most of the pioneering mining companies had failed by 1885 and the surviving companies had not yet installed enough crushing machinery to produce gold on a significant scale. Although there was a rise in gold exports from 1882 to 1888, the bulk of it came from Asante as relations between them and their southern neighbours improved. It was not until 1889 that the mining companies began to export a large amount of the country's gold.[8]

The development of modern gold mining activities on the Gold Coast had a great effect on the country. The mining concession led to an increase in the value of land which consequently brought more wealth to some chiefs. Wealth was

1 Kimble, *Political History*, p. 22   2 Dumett, 'Official British Attitudes', p. 61

3 Dickson, *Historical Geography*, p. 181   4 Kimble, *Political History*, p. 22

5 On the land question, see Kimble, *Political History*, pp. 330–55

6 Dumett, 'Official British Attitudes', p. 62   7 Kimble, *Political History*, p. 22

8 Dumett, 'Official British Attitudes', p. 71. The gold exports for this period were:

Year	Oz	£	Year	Oz	£
1880	9,129	32,865	1888	24,030	86,510
1881	12,567	45,241	1889	28,667	103,200
1882	17,097	61,552	1890	25,460	91,657
1883	14,565	52,435	1891	24,475	88,112
1884	18,385	66,188	1892	27,446	98,099
1885	24,995	89,981	1893	21,972	79,099
1886	20,749	74,829	1894	21,332	76,796
1887	22,549	81,168	1895	25,415	91,497

also accrued to African lawyers who often acted on behalf of the traditional authorities and the concessionaires.[1]

It was not only gold but also rubber that was becoming an export item in the 1880s.[2] Though this trade was short-lived, it formed an important link between the last two decades of the nineteenth century when trade in palm oil was declining and the early years of the twentieth century when the cocoa industry became the mainstay of the Gold Coast economy. Between 1890–1905 the Gold Coast, which ranked fifth in the world production of rubber, was the leading exporter of the product in the British Empire.[3] In the development of the rubber trade African merchants, especially F. C. Grant and John Sarbah, played a key role.[4] Despite its short existence, the rubber trade was an important source of capital for the pioneering Akuapem cocoa farmers to purchase land for cocoa-growing in the 1890s.[5] The trade in rubber was also a source of capital in Asante for investment in cocoa-growing.[6] Polly Hill has observed that before 1900 cocoa had been planted as far north as Akuamdan, south of Takyiman. The cocoa seeds were supposed to have been brought there by Akuapems who engaged in the rubber trade with the Nkoranza area.[7]

The cocoa industry began to assume importance in the economic landscape of the country during the two decades of the nineteenth century and by 1911 the Gold Coast was the world's leading exporter of cocoa.[8] The introduction of cocoa to Ghana dates back to 1857 when the Basel missionaries imported it from Surinam[9] but it was not until a Ga blacksmith, Tetteh Quashie, brought the crop from Fernando Po in 1879 that the crop began to take root.[10] Tetteh Quashie successfully cultivated the plant at Akuapem Mampong and local farmers eagerly bought his first harvest in 1883. Governor William Brandford Griffith also gave the cocoa industry import seeds from Sao Thomé, started a nursery at Aburi and supplied the seedlings to farmers.[11] By 1891 the Basel missionaries were also

---

1 Kimble, *Political History*, p. 21

2 Dumett, 'The Rubber Trade of the Gold Coast and Asante', pp. 79–101; Dickson, *Historical Geography*, pp. 162–5; Hill, *Migrant Cocoa-Farmer*, pp. 164–5

3 Dumett, 'The Rubber Trade of the Gold Coast and Asante', p. 79

4 *Dickson, Historical Georgaphy*, p. 162; Dumett, 'The Rubber Trade of the Gold Coast and Asante', pp. 81–82

5 Hill, *Migrant Cocoa-Farmers*, pp. 164–5. Other sources of capital to buy land for cocoa farming were general trading in: salt, parrots, skins and blankets from the north. Some of the Akuapem migrant farmers were people who had before 1900 travelled to Nigeria and other places in West Africa as traders and craftsmen. *Ibid.*, p. 166.

6 Dumett, 'The Rubber Trade of the Gold Coast and Asante', p. 101

7 See Hill, *Migrant Cocoa-Farmers*, p. 165, n. 4

8 For the study on cocoa, see Polly Hill's classic studies, *Gold Coast Cocoa-Farmer and Migrant Cocoa-Farmers*; see also Dickson, *Historical Geography*, pp. 165–71; Kimble, *Political History*, pp. 33–40.

9 Hill, *Migrant Cocoa-Farmers*, pp. 170–1; Horton, *West African Countries and People*, p. 147

10 Hill, *Migrant Cocoa-Farmers*, pp. 172–3; Dickson, *Historical Geography*, p. 166

11 Hill, *Migrant Cocoa-Farmers*, pp. 173–4; Dickson, *Historical Georgaphy*, p. 166

selling and distributing cocoa seeds to their congregations and African growers.[1] The first recorded export of the crop was 121 lb in 1885 which fetched £6 1s. Thanks to the responsiveness of the African to cocoa farming and the encouragement offered by the government and the Basel Mission, the cocoa industry grew rapidly and by 1895 cocoa culture had spread to all parts of the then Gold Coast Protectorate.[2]

The development of the cocoa industry was based on small-scale production. It is significant that the initial reception to this development came from the Akuapems who had responded early to Christianity and to the social change that it entailed. As Polly Hill observed:

> Many Akwapim men already had highly expansible sets of wants, being aware, through education, travel and contact with others, of conditions in other parts of the world. Apart from the Akwapim traders and craftsmen . . . many of whom had originally (themselves or their forbears) been trained by the Basel Mission, there were labourers and carriers who sought jobs in connexion with the Ashanti wars, on the building from 1898 of the Sekondi railway, or in the expanding coastal towns. Ministers of religion, catechists, teachers, and prominent Christians generally, were among those most sensitive to the possibilities of the new crops and if the 'scholar-farmer' was sometimes derided, though usually only in public, his influence and example were profound.[3]

The leadership and example of those who had already reacted favourably to the trade and economic change that had been taking place in the country were therefore crucial. Another writer commented:

> . . . Clearly the decisive factor was the driving energy of this African class which had the wisdom to see in cocoa-production a new and promising source of wealth and profit. From the very beginning the backbone of the Gold Coast cocoa industry has been, not the simple tribal peasant, but in the real sense a 'middle' class, of traders and entrepreneurs.[4]

The export of timber and kola nuts also assumed some importance during the period after 1874. Overseas export of kola began modestly in 1867 when a small amount of it was sent to Britain and by the 1880s the export was worth about £2,000. Kola was also exported to Lagos in considerable quantity after the 1870s.[5] Timber began to feature in Gold Coast exports around 1887 and by 1894 it had become a major item of export.[6] It was the accelerated development of certain exports during the last quarter of the nineteenth century, especially those of cocoa and gold, that led to the 'economic revolution' beginning in the 1890s.

1 Hill, *Migrant Cocoa-Farmers*, p. 171; Kimble, *Political History*, pp. 33–34

2 Dickson, *Historical Geography*, p. 166

3 Hill, *Migrant Cocoa-Farmers*, pp. 168–9

4 C. K. Meek, W. M. MacMillan, E. J. R. Hussey, *Europe and West Africa*, Oxford, 1940, p. 82

5 Dickson, *Historical Geography*, pp. 151–3   6 *Ibid.*, p. 176

The rapid economic development of the last decades of the nineteenth century was possible because of the earlier economic changes that followed the abolition of the Atlantic slave trade. The prohibition of the slave trade by various European powers during the early decades of the nineteenth century did not bring the slave trade to an end immediately. It continued surreptitiously well into the middle of the 1860s.

The impact of the interdiction of the slave trade upon the Gold Coast was significant. As the slave trade had made inroads into the country's economy its stoppage called for serious adjustments for Africans and Europeans involved in the trade. The end of the slave trade upset the pre-1807 economic arrangements. For the states which furnished the slaves and the brokers for the trade; and those who had provided services pertaining to the trade such as supplying food for the long voyage across the Atlantic, it meant a loss of income. The loss of profits from the diminution of the slave trade also reduced the capacity of the coastal rulers to defend themselves against Asante aggression and led to an increasing dependence on European nations on the coast for protection.

The profits accrued to the Gold Coast rulers, especially the coastal chiefs, and customary presents they had received from European traders had, in part, enabled them to distribute wealth among their people and to fulfil customary and social obligations. With the bulk of the trade that enabled the rulers to fulfil this role removed, the standing of the chiefs began to decline. For Asante, however, the loss of wealth from abolition was by no means disastrous. The demand for Asante kola allowed her to establish alternate markets north in lieu of the abolished trade. Furthermore, Asante gold found a ready market on the coast.

Abolition brought about a strong need to find substitutes for the slave trade, and Europeans endeavoured to encourage the export of old staples like gold and ivory as well as the production of agricultural goods for the overseas trade. Despite efforts to foster the exports of natural produce of the country the disruption caused by local wars, the lack of enthusiastic response from local people, the half-hearted efforts of Europeans to cultivate plantations, and the high duties imposed on African produce made economic change difficult.

By 1830 not much progress had been made on the Gold Coast towards changing the economy from one based primarily on the sale of slaves to one based on natural produce. Often it was alleged that the slow progress of economic change was due to the laziness of the people, but any transformation in the economic lives of the people could only be achieved through some changes in the social and cultural outlook of the people. It seemed to outside observers that much free time was not employed in actual labour, but other obligations in the society like religious and funeral observances took up some of the time when the people were not actually engaged in work.

A new era of trade and economic change began in 1830 under the administration of George Maclean. The peace treaty that the Governor concluded with Asante and the justice he dispensed ushered in an era of peace and tranquillity encouraging to trade. The Maclean epoch marked a key period of economic development and was undoubtedly the most prosperous period of trade up to 1874.

By the time of the presidency of Maclean, palm oil had become a staple export of the Gold Coast; it was the desire to control the eastern region (Akuapem and Krobo) which produced the bulk of the crop which led to a conflict between the English and the Danish authorities on the Gold Coast. Furthermore, the development of the palm oil trade increasingly led to the alienation of land when the people of Krobo began to seek more land outside their home land for the cultivation of palm oil.

It is very possible that there may have been a time in the history of the Gold Coast when the sale or alienation of land was rare, but the trade and economic change of the nineteenth century had a devastating impact on the customary land tenure. Before the commercialisation of agriculture in the nineteenth century, farming had been based on shifting cultivation and land rotation. The cultivation of products like palm and cocoa which continued to yield crops for years initiated permanent cultivation and affected the traditional concept of usufruct. Commercial agriculture thus resulted in an indefinite appropriation of such land planted with commercial trees. Economic development accelerated the process of land alienation which had begun early in the nineteenth century. The sale of land was further intensified during the last decades of the nineteenth century by the mining and cocoa industries.

The period of prosperity and progress in trade under Maclean also saw the rise of an African merchant class which traded on its own account and received credit directly from European firms abroad. In addition to these merchants, a number of Africans coming out of schools established by the Methodist Missionary Society also sought occupations connected with trade. The work done by the Methodist and Basel Mission Societies in education and the economic advancement of the people beginning in the Maclean period was significant for economic progress.

That trade and economic changes could take place during this period was in a large measure due to institutional changes in Gold Coast society. By 1850 the African merchants had begun to eclipse the traditional rulers and chiefs in wealth and influence and had assumed a role in Gold Coast society compatible with their wealth and influence. The fortunes of the African merchants began to decline in the 1860s because of the prevailing system of credit, conflict on the Gold Coast, and partially because of social obligations and the standard of living expected of people of their status. A large number of these African merchants went bankrupt during the 1860s. It is significant that the declining fortunes of the African merchants coincided with the political activities of the Fante Confederation. Although the organisation had the support of most educated people on the Gold Coast, much of the local support came from people who had experienced some difficulty in trade. This is not to deny other legitimate grievances that the greater degree of British potential presence in the country entailed. Although African merchants on the Gold Coast recovered their fortunes after 1874 through the rubber trade and gold mining activities, the trading practices of the 1890s which squeezed them out in favour of large oligopolies among European firms, would force African merchants into further political activities.

Much of the country's economic progress between 1850–1874 was hard-won and during this period some of the problems of economic development were clearly visible. For a rapid economic development to take place, problems like the lack of uniform currency, banks, labour and roads had to be solved. Yet, despite these problems and the often slow progress of development, in 1874 the process of trade and economic change on the Gold Coast reflected important and far-reaching economic advancement. By this time the Gold Coast had made a transition from a trade based on slaves to that based on the natural produce of the country, its resources and labour were increasingly being commercialised;

much of the leadership for commercial development had come from Africans; social and cultural change had followed economic change, and the livelihood of the people was increasingly coming to depend upon the growing external trade as well as the internal one. After 1874 the Gold Coast was indeed entering the era of a truly modern economy.

Appendix 1

TOTAL DECLARED VALUE OF BRITISH AND IRISH PRODUCE AND MANUFACTURES EXPORTED FROM THE UNITED KINGDOM TO THE WEST COAST OF AFRICA

	Senegal and the coast from Morocco to the River Gambia exclusive	Sierra Leone and the coast from the River Gambia inclusive, to the River Mesurada	Windward coast from the River Mesurada to Cape Apollonia	Cape Coast Castle and the Gold Coast, from Cape Apollonia to the Rio Volta	Coast from Rio Volta to the Cape of Good Hope	Total
	£	£	£	£	£	£
1827	718	75,456	9,015	22,414	48,156	155,759
1828	–	62,100	12,009	41,985	75,358	191,452
1829	–	85,700	7,690	46,962	103,901	244,253
1830	–	87,144	9,648	52,889	102,442	252,123
1831	–	85,192	–	59,214	90,362	234,768
1832	650	69,255	12,011	65,291	142,854	290,061
1833	221	58,336	386	86,263	184,004	329,210
1834	795	86,431	3,657	107,627	127,973	326,483
1835	694	75,388	–	87,841	128,617	292,540
1836	7,337	108,978	–	142,063	208,808	467,186
1837	802	109,597	–	89,020	113,519	312,938
1838	2,904	134,470	–	102,685	173,295	413,354
1839	961	123,539	–	131,444	212,426	468,370
1840	1,770	93,640	–	136,877	259,821	492,128
1841	977	96,092	–	133,510	180,219	410,798

Source: *Parl. Papers*, 1842, XII, Appendix

Appendix 2

FOREIGN IMPORTS INTO THE GOLD COAST

	Beads	Salted beef and pork	Coffee	Bugles and glass beads	Cocoa	Cotton manuf. of India	Cowries	Iron bars	Iron and steel manuf.	Rice not in husk	Sugar unrefined	Tea	Silk manuf. of India	Spirits	Tobacco	Wines
	lb	cwt	lb	lb	lb	pieces	cwt	tons	cwt		cwt	lb	pieces	gals	lb	gals
1827	18	–	192	7,433	–	17,325	432	9	99	–	76	128	216	27,281	44,436	2,676
1828	40	13	222	39,624	165	16,686	261	31	209	–	31	160	755	33,485	24,436	928
1829	–	–	222	31,273	–	15,002	878	19	76	–	32	408	319	222,625	35,722	1,076
1830	119	–	443	62,770	530	19,114	648	36	408	–	159	289	383	51,585	54,296	1,954
1831	52	–	509	115,893	512	5,370	1,372	32	462	–	34	570	1,523	64,259	84,216	1,767
1832	93	–	916	100,168	507	3,808	1,465	8	314	225	52	738	1,613	64,928	93,767	774
1833	13	–	160	87,063	–	4,987	338	22	335	–	22	164	367	77,575	69,068	1,937
1834	78	–	376	53,294	866	2,627	1,324	15	348	85	60	317	348	63,625	92,183	4,805
1835	11	1	132	61,631	1,264	1,040	1,860	29	148	40	69	334	377	52,375	109,275	1,075
1836	90	95	160	134,656	1,586	594	3,046	22	521	10	122	859	1,219	106,073	177,751	2,310
1837	28	11	2,856	88,163	549	30	1,476	31	166	141	73	292	1,168	42,051	86,181	746
1838	3	216	126	145,106	2,547	986	2,005	31	227	39	172	1,045	657	56,914	106,585	2,703
1839	125	267	118	104,831	1,276	10	1,289	31	206	240	57	507	594	48,303	86,124	947
1840	–	504	1,664	91,567	1,695	608	2,913	50	250	247	161	777	1,407	45,324	135,510	1,734
1841	–	546	–	100,813	175	1,067	1,195	21	324	204	7	279	1,020	48,902	88,893	1,626

Source: *Parl. Papers*, 1842, XII, Appendix

Appendix 3

QUANTITIES AND DECLARED VALUE OF BRITISH AND IRISH PRODUCE IMPORTED INTO THE GOLD COAST

	Jewellery, plate, plated ware, watches	Salt		Soap and candles		Station-ery	Linen thread, tapes, small wares	Silk manuf.	Sugar refined		Tin, pewter wares, tin plates	Woollen manuf. entered by price	
	£	bushels	£	lb	£	£	£	£	cwt	£	£	pieces	£
1827	130	–	–	4,148	102	19	–	–	34	93	55	492	819
1828	395	–	–	7,005	203	120	–	200	23	60	250	651	1,453
1829	85	–	–	2,322	62	45	–	–	15	41	41	228	416
1830	599	–	–	4,916	190	52	–	–	34	94	83	723	919
1831	283	–	–	1,680	47	47	15	15	31	91	342	1,938	2,456
1832	700	2,400	100	9,643	327	71	–	563	29	83	707	1,178	2,149
1833	68	–	–	9,493	222	89	–	316	36	94	960	793	1,639
1834	206	800	28	11,457	255	109	–	108	72	196	96	829	1,444
1835	40	635	30	9,677	245	117	–	12	50	143	213	567	633
1836	160	600	31	20,385	451	233	11	108	105	299	178	1,062	1,259
1837	24	400	15	13,414	360	47	–	150	64	128	73	1,129	1,113
1838	803	1,400	44	23,546	465	162	30	282	97	243	244	1,450	1,216
1839	40	6,808	253	19,569	435	138	–	40	61	144	242	1,658	1,455
1840	379	2,640	98	15,171	428	89	–	120	93	166	403	945	1,097
1841	132	6,150	155	18,901	395	150	–	365	70	130	202	559	580

Source: *Parl. Papers*, 1842, XII, Appendix

Appendix 4

QUANTITIES AND DECLARED VALUE OF BRITISH AND IRISH PRODUCE IMPORTED INTO THE GOLD COAST

	Earthenware of all sorts		Hardware and cutlery		Iron and steel		Glass of all sorts	Hats of all sorts		Lead and shot		Leather and saddlery	Linen manuf. entered by the yards	
	pieces	£	cwt	£	tons	£	£	doz	£	tons	£	£	yds	£
1827	4,050	49	11	79	63	797	181	5	11	20	431	10	1,402	66
1828	9,500	108	70	402	97	1,020	598	50	125	36	683	191	2,488	157
1829	20,944	226	44	269	151	1,575	294	58	115	35	678	289	3,817	167
1830	44,150	464	55	318	165	1,363	477	70	140	32	470	113	3,831	234
1831	37,540	385	87	543	141	1,383	557	106	122	47	690	204	5,078	276
1832	44,120	484	352	1,754	171	1,563	571	160	188	52	690	334	3,712	252
1833	48,536	478	184	886	245	2,339	336	104	180	46	707	186	1,217	104
1834	81,480	841	673	3,088	293	2,203	426	162	308	63	995	89	4,329	224
1835	51,678	487	129	668	216	2,135	468	93	158	38	833	139	4,602	290
1836	113,458	1,227	422	2,247	277	3,668	986	211	288	68	1,574	327	6,483	332
1837	39,570	465	149	842	112	1,381	422	44	89	41	858	358	4,091	200
1838	85,826	851	298	1,514	205	2,348	576	125	179	58	1,175	267	8,336	497
1839	101,230	1,197	456	2,282	329	4,009	557	101	159	63	1,231	216	7,979	380
1840	61,764	748	698	4,008	301	3,389	749	105	150	56	1,072	182	6,538	265
1841	103,140	1,140	1,085	5,363	256	2,893	572	171	240	56	1,122	104	7,766	330

Source: *Parl. Papers*, 1842, XII, Appendix

Appendix 5

QUANTITIES AND DECLARED VALUE OF BRITISH AND IRISH PRODUCE IMPORTED INTO THE GOLD COAST

	Woollen hosiery and small wares	Empty wooden casks and staves		Woollen by the manufactured yard		All other articles
	£	No.	£	yds	£	£
1827	–	345	235	92	6	871
1828	23	866	755	60	4	1,358
1829	99	1,285	1,079	80	6	1,548
1830	43	1,322	1,152	120	8	1,040
1831	106	1,981	1,441	430	25	1,588
1832	–	1,510	1,049	300	27	1,897
1833	52	4,228	2,814	540	40	1,939
1834	135	1,716	1,138	463	45	2,407
1835	90	1,255	653	1,670	81	1,932
1836	168	1,861	1,032	1,217	76	3,697
1837	129	1,180	721	450	27	3,365
1838	263	1,466	898	284	18	2,500
1839	295	3,878	2,178	–	–	2,413
1840	183	4,446	2,662	230	12	3,319
1841	242	4,984	2,815	4,140	333	2,850

Source: *Parl. Papers*, 1842, XII, Appendix

Appendix 6

QUANTITIES AND DECLARED VALUE OF BRITISH AND IRISH PRODUCE IMPORTED INTO THE GOLD COAST

	Apparel slops and haberdashery	Arms and ammunition in barrels		Beef and pork	Brass and copper manuf.		Cabinet and upholstery wares	Cotton manuf. entered by the yard		Beer and ale in barrels		Butter and cheese		Cotton hosiery and small wares
	£	bls	£	£	cwt	£	£	yds	£	bls	£	cwt	£	£
1827	252	1	5,613	4	21	202	119	311,987	11,905	49	214	39	157	–
1828	742	3	10,426	16	34	273	549	600,127	21,411	86	280	37	164	19
1829	591	90	14,229	338	78	574	80	551,908	23,827	56	204	22	84	–
1830	497	39	15,576	148	84	552	220	746,164	27,446	103	486	33	127	78
1831	765	5	16,508	17	228	1,492	119	765,820	29,195	110	330	37	168	4
1832	990	17	13,922	82	371	2,050	105	922,897	34,049	85	258	41	178	148
1833	841	20	22,655	95	413	2,865	99	1,562,749	45,685	63	217	28	112	145
1834	629	51	21,538	183	564	3,312	168	2,411,053	66,748	109	319	66	253	141
1835	554	23	18,331	85	812	4,809	63	1,558,397	53,774	94	328	40	145	385
1836	796	37	28,572	113	1,331	8,096	527	2,461,547	84,222	170	476	63	288	621
1837	536	26	16,095	120	849	4,857	247	1,783,546	55,660	92	316	41	200	222
1838	919	28	20,683	96	1,380	6,987	368	1,991,487	58,119	165	379	65	308	251
1839	570	4	18,101	15	1,520	8,033	75	2,772,481	85,678	199	491	44	203	614
1840	1,140	35	18,956	155	1,959	10,503	340	2,932,338	84,705	197	565	54	252	752
1841	740	9	24,298	44	2,423	13,343	375	3,004,871	73,606	146	376	36	171	444

Source: *Parl. Papers*, 1842, XII, Appendix

Appendix 7

IMPORTS* 1850–1863: TOTAL VALUE IN £s

	Manchester goods	Spirits and wine	Hardware	Provisions	Beads	Gunpowder	Perfume	Earthen- ware	Wearing apparel	Cigars and tobacco	Sundries	Guns
1850	40,960	7,142	4,733	2,942	5,060	8,256	848	2,061	803	4,599	11,252	no rt.
1851	28,360	15,060	5,085	2,360	5,325	12,895	1,036	1,200	625	5,710	7,296	no rt.
1852	14,000	17,000	3,760	3,610	4,880	12,280	480	240	450	6,440	2,615	5,000
1853	16,000	16,580	6,000	3,320	3,220	3,660	150	300	no rt.	7,100	3,670	no rt.
1854	38,000	21,200	8,500	3,000	6,600	13,400	630	560	490	11,600	3,220	no rt.
1855	68,187	11,383	16,746	1,981	4,084	7,027	961	2,268	1,051	5,445	3,349	no rt.
1856	30,887	36,114	4,918	no rt.	6,179	8,580	no rt.	614	no rt.	9,781	no rt.	no rt.
1857	36,839	24,902	2,345	6,056	2,083	7,531	no rt.	no rt.	no rt.	7,616	no rt.	2,125
1858	42,050	29,175	3,453	no rt.	2,563	8,074	no rt.	no rt.	no rt.	3,828	no rt.	2,471
1859	43,060	29,139	5,839	no rt.	2,910	5,506	no rt.	no rt.	no rt.	7,473	no rt.	1,581
1860	35,089	31,854	5,491	3,235	1,497	6,873	no rt.	no rt.	no rt.	9,326	no rt.	2,129
1861	74,629	39,991	6,924	no rt.	1,005	9,406	no rt.	no rt.	no rt.	6,924	no rt.	2,660
1862	68,000	40,000	11,800	no rt.	no rt.	5,400	no rt.	no rt.	no rt.	7,500	no rt.	3,200
1863	26,000	18,773	14,840	no rt.	no rt.	2,049	no rt.	no rt.	no rt.	6,314	no rt.	2,139

* The table covers only the important imports for the period 1850–1863. Import figures for 1864–1867 are lacking. Figures for 1868–1874 are broken down in headings that do not easily fit into this chart, but the important imports are given in ch. five

Source: Blue Books and C.O.442/10–42

Contemporary sources

1 PRIMARY ARCHIVAL SOURCES

Public Record Office, London

T.70	African Companies: 1799–1820
	Volumes 35, 36, 40, 41, 42, 149, 150, 154 and 1,584–1,606
C.O.96	Gold Coast, Original Correspondence: 1843–1874
	Volumes 2–114
C.O.97	Gold Coast: Acts
	Volumes 1 and 2
C.O.98	Sessional Papers
	Volumes 1A, 1B and 2
C.O.100	Blue Books of Statistics: 1843–1872
	Volumes 2–23
C.O.267	Sierra Leone, Original Correspondence: 1821–1843
	Volumes 55–183
C.O.268	Letters, Instructions, etc.: 1824–1843
	Volumes 21–39
C.O.442	Colonial Statistical Tables: 1834–1868
	Volumes 2–42
Customs 4	Ledgers of Imports: 1809–1869
	Volumes 5–65
Customs 10	Ledgers of Exports: 1809–1874
	Volumes 1–72

Ghana National Archives, Accra

E.C.6/2	Digest of Basel Mission Archives on Ghana, 1828–1851, Manuscripts
E.C.6/3	Digest of Articles on Ghana in the Basel Mission Periodicals, 1828–1851
E.C.6/15	Cocoa Cultivation in Ghana, 1858–1868
S.C.1	Blankson Papers
S.C.2	Bannerman Papers
S.C.3	Cape Coast Historical Society Papers
S.C.4	Freeman Family Papers
S.C.5	Vroom Papers
S.C.6	Sarbah Papers
S.C.7	Ghartey Papers

S.C.8   Schedule of Ocancey Trading Papers
S.C.13   Schedule of J. H. Caesar's Trading Papers

Balme Library, University of Ghana
Furley Collection
Transcript of Dutch material from the State Archives, The Hague, especially
   Archief van het Ministerie van Kolonien 1814–1849

Basel Mission Archives
Correspondence and reports to and from Ghana, 1828–1874
Der Heidenbote, Basel. 1835–1874
Sentimental information for the Swiss and German Missions' friends
Jahresbericht der Basler Mission, Basel. 1835–1874
Compact report and information about the fields and problems – statistics about
   home activity, field workers, native cooperators, institutions and financial
   situation
Evangelisches Missionsmagazin, Basel. 1835–1874
Contains reports and essays on travels, special problems, etc.

Methodist Missionary Archives, London
Gold Coast Correspondence, 1835–1876 (five boxes)

Rigsarkivet, Copenhagen
Guineisk Journal, 1776–1850 (12 volumes)
Sager til Guineisk Journal, 1776–1850
Generaltoldkammer og Kommerce Kontor, 1816–1841
Optegnelser og Akter til Brog for forkelliger Kommissioner til Undersogelse
   af Forhaldene in Guinea, 1816
Akter og Materialier Vedkommde den Guineiske Kommision af 9 January 1833

2 PARLIAMENTARY PAPERS

1816, IV [470]. African settlements and forts Select Committee Report Part I
1816, VII [506]. African settlements and forts Select Committee Report Part II
   with Minutes of Evidence and Appendix
1817, VI [431]. African settlements and forts Select Committee Report with
   Minutes of Evidence and Appendix
1826–7, VII [312]. Sierra Leone and Dependencies Reports of Inquiry Commissioners Part I
1826–7, VII [552]. Sierra Leone and Dependencies Reports of Inquiry Commissioners Part II
1842, XII [551]. Report from the Select Committee on the West Coast together with Minutes of Evidence. Appendix and Index. Parts I and II

190

1844–5, XLVI [187]. An account of the quantity of palm oil annually imported into the United Kingdom from the Western coast of Africa since the year 1790 to 31st day of December 1844

1852, XXXI [46]. Case of Robert Erskine correspondence with the Commander-in-Chief

1854–5, XXXVII [383]. British West African settlements. Copies of legislation defining constitutions

1865, V [412]. Report from Select Committee on the state of the British settlements on the Western African coast of Africa with Proceedings, Minutes of Evidence, Appendix and Index

1882, LXVI [C.3386]. Gold Coast further Correspondence

1883, XLVIII [C.3687]. Gold Coast further Correspondence with a Report by Captain Lonsdale

1884, LVI [C.4052]. Ashanti Kingship/British Policy. Further Gold Coast Correspondence

3 ARTICLES

CAMERON, V. L. 'The Gold Fields of West Africa', *J.S.A.* xxx (1882), 777–85.
'Gold Coast Mining Company Prospectus', pamphlet, London, 1825

PRICE, JOHN EDWARD. 'On Aggri Beads', *J.A.I.* xii (1883), 64–68

SWANZY, A. 'On Trade in Western Africa with and without British Protection', *J.S.A.* xxii (1874), 478–88

—— 'Civilisation and Progress on the Gold Coast of Africa as Affected by European Conduct with the Native Inhabitants', *J.S.A.* xxiii (1875), 415–26

4 NEWSPAPERS

The African Times, London, 1862–1902

5 BOOKS

ADAMS, CAPTAIN JOHN. *Remarks on the Country Extending from Cape Palmas to the River Congo, including Observations on the Manners and Customs of the Inhabitants,* London 1823

ALEXANDER, JAMES EDWARD. *Narrative of a Voyage of Observation among the Colonies of Western Africa,* London 1837

ALLEN, MARCUS. *The Gold Coast, or a Cruise in West Africa,* London 1874

BANDINEL, JAMES B. *Some Accounts of the Trade in Slaves from Africa as Connected with Europe and America,* London 1842

BARBOT, J. *A Description of the Coasts of North and South Guinea,* London 1732

BARTH, H. *Travels and Discoveries in Central Africa,* London 1857

BEECHAM, JOHN. *Ashantee and the Gold Coast,* London 1841

BINGER, L. G. *Du Niger au Golfe de Guinée,* 2 vols, Paris 1892

BOSMAN, WILLIAM. *A New and Accurate Description of the Coast of Guinea,* London 1705

BOWDICH, THOMAS EDWARD. *The British and French Expeditions to Teembo, with Remarks on Civilisation in Africa,* Paris 1821

—— *Mission from Cape Coast Castle to Ashantee,* London 1819

BRIDGE, HORATIO *Journal of an African Cruiser*, London 1845

CANOT, T. *Captain Canot: or, Twenty Years of an African Slaver*, London 1854

CRUICKSHANK, BRODIE *Eighteen Years on the Gold Coast of Africa*, 2 vols., London 1853

DUNCAN, JOHN *Travels in Western Africa in 1845 and 1846*, 2 vols., London 1847

DUPUIS, JOSEPH *Journal of a Residence in Ashantee*, 2 vols., London 1824. 2nd edition, introduction and edited with notes by W. E. F. Ward, London 1966

FORBES, LIEUTENANT, R. N. *African Blockade*, London 1849

FREEMAN, T. B. *Journal of Two Visits to the Kingdom of Ashanti in Western Africa*, London 1843

GORDON, CHARLES ALEXANDER *Life on the Gold Coast*, London 1874

HENTY, GEORGE ALFRED *The March to Coomassie*, London 1874

HOLMAN, JAMES *Travels in Madeira, Sierra Leone, Teneriffee, St. Jago, Cape Coast, Fernando Po, Princess Island*, London 1840

HORTON, J. AFRICANUS *Political Economy of British West Africa*, London 1865

—— *West African Countries and Peoples*, London 1868

—— *Letters on the Political Condition of the Gold Coast*, London 1870

HUNTLEY, H. *Seven Years' Service on the Slave Coast of Western Africa*, 2 vols., London 1850

HUTTON, WILLIAM *A Voyage to Africa*, London 1821

JACKSON, J. G. *An Account of Timbuctoo and Housa*, London 1820

LABARTHE, P. *Voyage à la Côte de Guinée*, Paris 1803

LEE, R. *Stories of Strange Lands*, London 1835

LEONARD, PETER *Records of a Voyage to the Western Coast of Africa*, Edinburgh 1833

MCQUEEN, JAMES *A Geographical Survey of Africa*, London 1840

MATHIESON, W. L. *Great Britain and the Slave Trade 1839–1865*, London 1929

MAURICE, J. F. *The Ashantee War*, London 1874

MEREDITH, HENRY *An Account of the Gold Coast of Africa*, London 1812

MONRAD, HANS C. *Bidrag til en Skildrig af Guinea-Kysten og dens Indbyggere 1805–1809*, Kobenhavn 1822

NAGTGLAS, C. J. M. *What Must the Netherlands Do with Her Settlements on the Coast of Guinea*, translation, London 1864

READE, W. *The African Sketch-Book*, 2 vols., London 1873

—— *The Story of the Ashantee Campaign*, London 1874

RICKETTS, H. I. *Narrative of the Ashantee War*, London 1831

ROMER, LUDVIG F. *Tilforladelig Efterretning om Nogotien paa Kysten Guinea*, Kobenhavn 1750

SMITH, JOSEPH *Trade and Travels in the Gulf of Guinea, Western Africa with an Account of the Manners, Customs and Religion of the Inhabitants*, London 1851

STANLEY, H. M. *Coomassie and Magdala*, London 1874

THOMAS, C. W. *Adventures and Observations on the West Coast of Africa and Its Islands*, London 1864

TILLEMAN, ERIC *En Liden Enfoldig Beretning om det Landskab Guinea*, Kobenhavn 1697

TRAVASSOS VALDEZ, FRANCISCO *Six Years of a Traveller's Life in Western Africa*, I, London 1861

WILSON, J. LEIGHTON (REV.) *Eighteen Years as a Missionary to Africa: Western Africa, Its History, Condition and Prospects*, London 1856

WHITFORD, JOHN *Trading Life in Western and Central Africa*, Liverpool 1877

Later works

1 COLLECTION OF DOCUMENTS

BLAKE, J. W. *Europeans in West Africa, 1450–1560*, 2 vols., London 1942

CARSTENSEN, EDWARD *Guvernor Edward Carstensens Indberetninger fra Guinea 1842–1850*, Kobenhavn 1964

CRONE, C. R. ed. *The Voyages of Cadamosto and Other Documents*, London 1937

CROOKS, J. J. *Records Relating to the Gold Coast Settlements, 1750–1874*, Dublin 1923

DONNAN, E. *Documents Illustrative of the History of the Slave Trade to America*, 4 vols., Washington, D.C., 1930ff

METCALFE, G. E. *Great Britain and Ghana, Documents of Ghana History, 1807–1959*, London 1964

NEWBURY, C. W. *British Policy towards West Africa, Select Documents, 1786–1874*, Oxford 1965

—— *The Western Slave Coast and Its Rulers*, Oxford 1961

WOLFSON, F. *Pageant of Ghana* London 1958

2 BOOKS

ADE AJAYI, J. F. and ESPIE, IAN, eds. *A Thousand Years of West African History*, Ibadan 1965

AGBODEKA, FRANCIS *African Politics and British Policy in the Gold Coast 1868–1900*, London 1971

AKUFFO, BENNETT *Ahemfi Adesua, Akanfo Amamere*, Akropong 1950

ARHIN, KWAME, ed. *Ashanti Northeast*, Legon 1970

BAETA, C. G. *Prophetism in Ghana*, London 1962

—— *Christianity in Tropical Africa*, London 1965

BALMER, W. T. *A History of the Akan Peoples of the Gold Coast*, London 1925

BARTELS, F. L. *The Roots of Ghana Methodism*, Cambridge 1965

BAUER, P. T. and YAMEY, B. S. *The Economics of Under-Developed Countries*, London 1957

BELSHAW, C. S. *Traditional Markets and Modern Exchange*, New York 1965

BENNETT, NORMAN AND BROOKS, GEORGE, E., JR., eds. *New England Merchants in Africa*, Boston University 1968

BERRY, B. J. L. *Geography of Market Centres and Retail Distribution*, New York 1967

BLAKE, JOHN W. *European Beginnings in West Africa, 1450–1560*, London 1937

BOHANNAN, PAUL and DALTON, GEORGE, eds. *Markets in Africa*, Northwestern African Studies, 9, Evanston 1963

BOVILL, E. W. *The Golden Trade of the Moors*, Oxford 1958

BOXER, C. R. *The Portuguese Seaborne Empire: 1415–1825*, New York 1969

BROOKS, GEORGE E., JR. *Yankee Traders, Old Coasters and African Middlemen*: a *History of American Legitimate Trade with West Africa in the Nineteenth Century*, Boston 1970

BROWN, E. J. P. *The Gold Coast and Asianti Reader*, 2 vols., London 1929

BURTON, R. F. and CAMERON, V. L. *To the Gold Coast for Gold*, London 1883

BUSIA, K. A. *The Position of the Chief in the Modern Political Systems of Ashanti*, London 1951

CASELY-HAYFORD, J. E. *Gold Coast Native Institutions*, London 1903

CHALMERS, R. *A History of Currency in the British Colonies*, London 1893

CLARIDGE, WILLIAM W. *A History of the Gold Coast and Ashanti*, 2 vols., London 1918

CLERK, N. T. *A Short Centenary Sketch. The Settlement of the West Indian Immigrants on the Gold Coast 1843–1943*, Accra 1943

CLINE, WALTER *Mining and Metallurgy in Negro Africa*, Mensha 1937

COLLIER, SIR, G. R. *West African Sketches; Comprised from the Reports of Sir G. R. Collier, Sir Charles MacCarthy and other Official Sources 1824*, Legon 1967

COOLHAS, W. P. *A Critical Survey of Studies on Dutch Colonial History*, Gravenhage 1960

COOMBS, DOUGLAS *The Gold Coast, Britain and the Netherlands 1850–1874*, London 1963

CURTIN, PHILIP D. *The Image of Africa*, Madison 1964
—— ed. *Africa Remembered*, Madison 1967
—— *The Atlantic Slave Trade: a Census*, Madison 1969

DAAKU, KWAME YEBOA *Oral Traditions of Assin-Twifo*, Institute of African Studies, Legon 1969
—— *Trade and Politics on the Gold Coast 1600 to 1720*, Oxford 1970

DAENDELS, H. W. *The Correspondence of Daendels*, Legon 1964

DAVIES, K. G. *The Royal African Company*, London 1957

DEANE, P. and COLE, W. A. *British Economic Growth 1688–1959*, Cambridge 1964

DEBRUNNER, H. W. *A Church between Colonial Powers. A Study of the Church in Togo*, London 1965
—— *A History of Christianity in Ghana*, Accra 1967

DICKSON, K. B. *A Historical Geography of Ghana*, Cambridge 1969

DIKE, K. O. *Trade and Politics in the Niger Delta*, Oxford 1956

DOUGLAS, MARY and KABERRY, PHYLLIS M. *Man in Africa*, London 1969

DUBOIS, W. E. B. *The Suppression of the African Slave Trade to the United States of America, 1619–1870*, New York 1965

EINZIG, PAUL *Primitive Money*, London 1949

ELLIS, ALFRED B. *A History of the Gold Coast of West Africa*, London 1893
—— *West African Sketches*, London 1881
—— *The Tshi-Speaking Peoples of the Gold Coast*, London 1887
—— *The Ewe-Speaking Peoples*, London 1890

FAGE, J. D. *Ghana, a Historical Interpretation*, Madison 1961
—— *A History of West Africa*, Cambridge 1969

FIELD, M. J. *Social Organisation of the Ga People*, London 1940

FORDE, C. DARYLL and KABERRY, P. M., eds. *West African Kingdoms in the Nineteenth Century*, London 1967

FOSTER, P. *Education and Social Change in Ghana*, London 1965

FRANKEL, S. H. *Capital Investment in Africa*, London 1938

FREEMAN, R. A. *Travels and Life in Ashanti and Jamon*, London 1898

FULLER, F. *A Vanished Dynasty: Ashanti*, London 1921

GANN, L. H. and DUIGAN, P. *The History of Colonialism 1870–1914*, Cambridge 1969

GARLICK, P. C. *African Traders in Kumasi*, mimeo., University College of Ghana 1959

GOODY, JACK *Technology, Tradition and the State in Africa*, Oxford 1971

GOULD, P. R. *The Development of Transportation Pattern in Ghana*, Evanston 1960

GRAY, J. R. and BIRMINGHAM, DAVID *Pre-Colonial African Trade Essays on Trade in Central and East Africa before 1900*, London 1970

GROS, JULES *Voyages, Aventures et Captivité de J. Bonnat chez les Achantis*, Paris 1884

HANCOCK, W. K. *Survey of British Commonwealth Affairs*, 2 vols., London 1942

HARGREAVES, J. D. *Prelude to the Partition of West Africa*, London 1963

HART, F. *The Gold Coast, Its Wealth and Health*, London 1904

HILL, POLLY *The Gold Coast Cocoa-Farmer: a Preliminary Study*, Cambridge 1956

—— *Migrant Cocoa-Farmers of Southern Ghana*, Cambridge 1963

—— *Rural Capitalism in West Africa*, Cambridge 1970

HODDER, B. W. and UKWU, U. I. *Markets in West Africa*, Ibadan 1969

HOPKINS, A. G. *An Economic History of West Africa*, London, 1973

HOSELITZ, BERT F. *Sociological Aspects of Economic Growth*, Chicago 1960

HUBER, HUGO *The Krobo: the Traditional Social and Religious Life of a West African People*, St. Augustin 1963

IMLAH, ALBERT H. *Economic Elements in the Pax Britannica*, Cambridge, Mass. 1958

JOHNSON, MARION *Salaga Papers*, 2 vols., Institute of African Studies, Legon 1968

JUNNER, N. R. *Gold in the Gold Coast*, Colchester 1935

KIMBLE, DAVID *A Political History of Ghana 1840–1928*, Oxford 1963

KLEMM, HERMAN *Elias Schrenk: der Weg eines Evangelisten*, Wuppertal 1961

KNOWLES, L. C. A. *The Economic Development of the British Overseas Empire*, 2 vols., London 1928

KWAMENA-POH, M. A. *Government and Politics in the Akuapem State, 1730–1850*, London 1973

LAWRENCE, A. W. *Trade Castles and Forts of West Africa*, London 1963

LEWIS, I. M., ed. *Islam in Tropical Africa*, London 1966

LLOYD, C. *The Navy and the Slave Trade*, London 1949

MANOUKIAN, M. *The Ewe-Speaking People of Togoland and the Gold Coast*, London 1952

MARTIN, EVELINE C. *The British West African Settlements 1750–1821*, London 1927

MEEK, C. K., MACMILLAN, W. M. and HUSSEY, E. J. R. *Europe and West Africa*, Oxford 1940

MEILLASSOUX, CLAUDE, ed. *The Development of African Trade and Markets in West Africa*, London, 1971

METCALFE, G. E. *Maclean of the Gold Coast*, London 1962

MEYEROWITZ, EVA L. R. *The Sacred State of the Akan*, London 1951

—— *The Akan of Ghana*, London 1958

—— *Akan Traditions of Origin*, London 1950

MOREL, E. D. *Affairs of West Africa*, London 1902

MACDONALD, GEORGE *The Gold Coast, Past and Present*, London 1898

MCPHEE, ALLAN *The Economic Revolution in British West Africa*, London 1926

NEUMARK, S. D. *Foreign Trade and Economic Development in Africa: a Historical Perspective*, Stanford 1964

NEWBURY, COLIN W. *The Western Slave Coast and Its Rulers*, Oxford 1961

NØRREGARD, GEORG *Danish Settlements in West Africa 1658–1850*, trans. by Sigurd Mammen, Boston 1966

NUKUNYA, G. K. *Kinship and Marriage among the Anlo Ewe*, London 1969

195

OLIVER, ROLAND *The Middle Ages of African History*, Oxford 1967

OLIVER, COL. and MITCHELL, R. E. LT. *Precis of Information Concerning the Gold Coast Colony*, London 1887

OLLENU, N. A. *Principles of Customary Land Law*, London 1962

OWUSU, MAXWELL *Uses and Abuses of Political Power: a Case Study of Continuity and Change in the Politics of Ghana*, Chicago 1970

PADEN, JOHN and SOGA, E. W., eds. *The African Experience*, Evanston 1970

PERHAM, M. *The Native Economies of Nigeria*, London 1946

—— *Mining Commerce and Finance in Nigeria*, London 1948

PETERSON, JOHN *Province of Freedom*, London 1969

PIM, ALAN *Colonial Agricultural Production*, London 1946

POPE-HENNESSY, J. *Verandah*, London 1964

PRIESTLEY, MARGARET *West African Trade and Coast Society*, London 1969

RAMSEYER, F. A. and KUHNE, J. *Four Years in Ashantee*, London 1897

RATTRAY, R. A. *Ashanti*, Oxford 1923

—— *Religion and Art in Ashanti*, Oxford 1927

—— *Ashanti Law and Constitution*, London 1929

REINDORF, REV. CARL CHRISTIAN *History of the Gold Coast and Asante*, 2nd ed. reprint, Accra 1966

RODNEY, WALTER *A History of the Upper Guinea Coast*, Oxford 1970

ROSTOW, WALTER W. *The Stages of Economic Growth*, Cambridge 1960

SAMPSON, M. J. *Gold Coast Men of Affairs*, London 1937

SARBAH, J. M. *Fanti Customary Laws*, London 1904

—— *Fanti National Constitution*, London 1906

SMITH, NOEL *The Presbyterian Church of Ghana*, London 1965

SOUTHON, A. E. *Gold Coast Methodism, the First Hundred Years 1835–1935*, Cape Coast and London 1934

STEVENSON, ROBERT F. *Population and Political Systems in Tropical Africa*, New York 1968

SUNDSTROM, LARS *The Guinea Trade*, Oslo 1966

SZERESZEWSKI, ROBERT *Structural Changes in the Economy of Ghana 1891–1911*, London 1966

THE BASEL EVANGELICAL MISSION ON THE GOLD COAST WESTERN AFRICA FROM 1828–1893, Christiansborg 1894

TORDOFF, W. *Ashanti under the Prempehs, 1888–1935*, Oxford 1965

TURNER, G. W. EATON *A Short History of Ashanti Goldfields Corp., Ltd., 1897–1947*, London, n.d.

UNITED NATIONS *Scope and Structure of Money Economies in Tropical Africa*, New York 1955

—— *Enlargement of the Exchange Economy in Tropical Africa*, New York 1954

WANNER, VON GUSTAF ADOLF *Basler Handelsgesellschaft 1859–1959*, Basel 1959

WARD, WILLIAM E. F. *History of Ghana*, rev. 3rd ed. (6th printing), London 1966

WELMER, C. W. *The Native States of the Gold Coast Ahanta*, London 1930

WILKS, IVOR *The Northern Factor in Ashanti History*, Legon 1961

WILLIAMS, ERIC *Capitalism and Slavery*, Chapel Hill 1944

WILLS, J. B., ed. *Agriculture and Land Use in Ghana*, Oxford 1962

WYNDHAM, H. A. *The Atlantic and Slavery*, Oxford 1935

ZOOK, J. F. *The Company of Royal Adventurers Trading to Africa*, Washington, D.C. 1919

3 *Articles*

ADAMS, C. D. 'Activites of Danish Botanists in Guinea 1783–1850', *T.H.S.G.* iii (1957), 30–46

ADOMAKO, ALBERT 'The History of Currency and Banking in Some West African Countries', *E.B.G.* vii, 4 (1963), 3–17

AGBODEKA, F. 'The Fanti Confederacy, 1865–1869', *T.H.S.G.* vii (1965), 82–123

AMENUMEY, D. E. K. 'Geraldo de Lima: a Reappraisal', *T.H.S.G.* ix (1968), 65–78

—— 'The Extension of British Rule to Anlo (South-East Ghana), 1860–1890', *J.A.H.* ix, 1 (1968), 99–117

ARHIN, KWAME 'The Structure of Greater Ashanti (1700–1824)', *J.A.H.* viii, 1 (1967), 65–85

—— 'Diffuse Authority among the Coastal Fanti', *G.N.Q.* 9 (1966), 66–70

ASANTE, S. K. B. 'Interests in Land in Customary Law of Ghana – a New Appraisal', *Yale Law Journal* lxxiv (1964–1965), 848–85

AUSTEN, R. A. 'The Abolition of the Overseas Slave Trade: a Distorted Theme in West African History', *J.H.S.N.* v, 2 (1970), 257–73

BARTELS, F. L. 'Philip Quaque, 1741–1816', *T.G.C.T.H.S.* i, pt. 5 (1955), 155–77

BENNEH, GEORGE 'The Impact of Cocoa Cultivation on the Traditional Land Tenure of the Akan', *G.J.S.* vi, 1 (1970), 43–61

BEVIN, H. J. 'M. J. Bonnat: Trader and Mining Promoter', *E.B.G.* iv, 7 (1960), 1–12

—— 'The Gold Coast Economy about 1880', *T.G.C.T.H.S.* ii, 2 (1956), 73–86

—— 'Some Notes on Gold Coast Exports 1886–1913', *E.B.G.* iv, 1 (1960), 13–20

BOAHEN, A. ADU 'The Origins of the Akan', *G.N.Q.* 9 (1966), 3–10

BOATEN, K. 'Trade among the Asante of Ghana up to the end of the 18th Century', *I.A.S.E.E.* vii, 1 (1970), 33–46

BOHANNAN, PAUL 'The Impact of Money on an African Subsistence Economy', *J.E.H.* xix, 4 (1959), 491–503

BROOKS, G. E. JR. 'The Letter Book of Captain Edward Harrington', *T.H.S.G.* vi (1963), 71–77

COHEN, A. 'The Social Organisation of Credit in a West African Cattle Market', *Africa* xxxv (1965), 8–20

COHEN, DAVID 'Agenda for African Economic History', *J.E.H.* (1971), 208–221

COLLINS, E. 'The Panic Element in Nineteenth-Century Relations with Ashanti', *T.H.S.G.* v, 2 (1962), 79–144

DAAKU, KWAME YEBOA and DANTZIG, ALBERT VAN 'An Annotated Dutch Map of 1629', *G.N.Q.* 9 (1966), 14–17

DANTZIG, ALBERT VAN 'The Dutch Recruitment in Kumasi', *G.N.Q.* 8 (1966), 21–24

DEBRUNNER, H. 'Notable Danish Chaplains on the Gold Coast', *T.G.C.T.H.S.* ii, 1 (1956), 13–29

DEGRAFT-JOHNSON, J. C. 'Some Historical Observations on Money and the West African Currency Board', *E.B.G.* xi, 2 (1967), 3–19

—— 'Akan Land Tenure', *T.G.C.T.H.S.* i (1955), 99–103

DICKSON, K. B. 'The Development of Road Transportation in Southern Ghana and Ashanti since 1850', *T.H.S.G.* v, 1 (1961), 33–42

DUMETT, R. E. 'The Rubber Trade of the Gold Coast and Asante in the Nineteenth Century: African Innovation and Responsiveness', *J.A.H.* xii, 1 (1971), 79–101

ENGERMAN, STANLEY L. 'Some Considerations Relating to Property Rights in Man', *J.E.H.* xxxiii (March, 1973), 43–65

FAGE, J. D. 'The Administration of George Maclean on the Gold Coast, 1830–1844', *T.G.C.T.H.S.* i, 4 (1955), 104–20

—— 'Slavery and the Slave Trade in the Context of West African History', *J.A.H.* x, 3 (1969), 393–404

—— 'Some Remarks on Beads and Trade in Lower Guinea in the Sixteenth and Seventeenth Centuries', *J.A.H.* iii, 2 (1962), 343–7

FIRTH, RAYMOND 'Leadership and Economic Growth', *I.S.S.J.* xvi, 2 (1964), 186–91

FRASER, A. G. 'The Cult of the Kwahu Hunter on the Question of *Sasa* Animals, especially the Elephant', *G.C.R.* iv, 2 (1928), 155–65

GARLICK, PETER 'The French Trade de Nouveau', *E.B.G.* iii, 2 (1959), 16–25

GROVE, J. M. and JOHANSEN, A. M. 'The Historical Geography of the Volta Delta, Ghana, during the Period of Danish Influence', *I.F.A.N.* xxx, 4 (1968), 1, 374–1,421

HAIR, P. E. H. 'The Enslavement of Koelle's Informants', *J.A.H.* vi, 2 (1965), 193–203

HARROP, SYLVIA 'The Economy of the West African Coast in the Sixteenth Century', *E.B.G.* viii, 3 and 4 (1964), 15–33 and 19–36

HELM, ELIJAH 'The Cultivation of Cotton in West Africa; *J.A.S.* ii (1902–1903)

HILL, POLLY 'Notes on Traditional Market Authority and Market Periodicity in West Africa', *J.A.H.* vii, 2 (1966), 295–311

HOPKINS, A. G. 'Economic Imperialism in West Africa: 1880–1892', *E.H.R.* xxi (1968), 580–606

—— 'Economic Aspects of Political Movements in Nigeria and the Gold Coast, 1918–1939', *J.A.H.* vii, 2 (1966), 133–52

HOSELITZ, BERT, ed. *Annals of the American Academy of Political and Social Science, Agrarian Societies in Transition*, May, 1956

HUTCHINSON, W. F. 'The Gold Trade of the Gold Coast: 1555–1825', *E.D.M.* iii, 11 (1924), 115–18

—— 'The Gold Trade of the Gold Coast 1826 to 1890', *E.D.M.* xii, 3 (1924), 148–50

—— 'The Gold Trade of the Gold Coast 1826 to 1890', *E.D.M.* xiii, 4(1925), 8–10

HYMAN, STEPHEN 'Economic Forms in Pre-colonial Ghana', *J.E.H.* xxx, 1 (1970), 33–50

JEPPESEN, H. 'Danske Plantageanlag po Guldkysten 1788–1850', *Geografisk Tidsskrift*, lxv (1966), 48–88

JOHNSON, MARION 'Migrants' Progress', *B.G.G.A.* ix, 2 (1964), 4–27

—— 'The Cowrie Currencies in West Africa', *J.A.H.* xi, pt. I, No. 1 (1970), 17–49 and pt. II, No. 3, 331–53

—— 'Ashanti East of the Volta', *T.H.S.G.* viii (1965), 33–59

—— 'The Ounce in Eighteenth Century West African Trade', *J.A.H.* vii, 2 (1966), 197–214

KEA, R. A. 'Firearms and Warfare on the Gold and Slave Coasts from the Sixteenth to the Nineteenth Centuries', *J.A.H.* xii, 2 (1971), 185–213

LATHAM, A. J. H. 'Currency, Credit and Capitalism on the Cross River in the Pre-Colonial Era', *J.A.H.* iv (1971), 599–605

LAWSON, ROWENA M. 'The Development of the Lower Volta', *E.B.G.* vii, 4 (1963), 81–90

—— 'The Growth of the Fishing Industry in Ghana', *E.B.G.* xi, 4 (1966), 3–24

—— 'The Traditional Utilisation of Labour in Agriculture on the Lower Volta, Ghana', *E.B.G.* xii, 1 (1968), 54–61

LEVER, J. T. 'Mulatto Influence on the Gold Coast in the Early Nineteenth Century: Jan Nieser of Elmina', *A.H.S.* iii, 2 (1970), 253–61

LIMBERG, LENNART 'The Economy of the Fanti Confederation', *T.H.S.G.* xi (1971), 83–103

MANNING, PATRICK 'Slaves, Palm Oil and Political Power on the West African Coast', *A.H.S.* ii, 2 (1969), 279–88

METCALFE, G. E. 'After Maclean', *T.H.G.C.T.* i, 5 (1955), 178–92

MORRIS, M. D. 'Toward a Reinterpretation of Nineteenth Century Indian Economic History', *J.E.H.* xxiii (1963), 606–18

NATHAN, M. 'The Dutch and the English on the Gold Coast in the Eighteenth Century', *J.A.S.* liv (1904), 33–43

NEWBURY, C. W. 'Credit in Early Nineteenth Century West African Trade', *J.A.H.* xiii, 1 (1972), 81–95

OTOTU BAGYIRE VI, ABIRIWHENE 'The Guans: a Preliminary Note', *G.N.Q.* 7 (1965), 21–24

POLANYI, K. 'Sortings and "Ounce Trade" in the West African Slave Trade', *J.A.H.* v, 3 (1964), 381–93

POSTMA, JOHANNES 'The Dimension of the Dutch Slave Trade from Western Africa', *J.A.H.* xiii, 2 (1972), 237–48

PRIESTLEY, MARGARET 'The Ashanti Question and the British: Eighteenth Century Origins', *J.A.H.* ii, 1 (1961), 35–59

—— 'Richard Brew: an Eighteenth Century Trader at Anomabu', *T.H.S.G.* iv, 1 (1959), 29–46

PRIESTLEY, MARGARET AND WILKS, IVOR 'The Ashanti Kings in the Eighteenth Century: a Revised Chronology', *J.A.H.* i, 1 (1960), 83–96

ROHDIE, SAM 'The Gold Coast Cocoa Hold-Up of 1930–1931', *T.H.S.G.* ix, (1968), 105–18

RODNEY, WALTER 'Gold and Slaves on the Gold Coast', *T.H.S.G.* x (1969), 13–28

ROSS, DAVID A. 'The Career of Domingo Martinez in the Bight of Benin', *J.A.H.* vi, 1 (1965), 79–90

SHERIDAN, R. B. 'The Commercial and Financial Organisation of the British Slave Trade, 1750–1807', *E.H.R.* xi, 2nd Series, 2 (1958), 249–63

SWANZY, H. 'A Trading Family in the Nineteenth Century Gold Coast', *T.G.C.T.H.S.* ii, 2 (1956), 87–120

VANSINA, J. 'Long-Distance Trade-Routes in Central Africa', *J.A.H.* iii, 2 (1971), 375–90

WHITE, GAVIN 'Firearms in Africa, an Introduction', *J.A.H.* xii, 2 (1971), 173–184

WILD, R. P. 'Iron Disc Currency from Ashanti', *Man*, 99 (1936), 78–79

WILLIAMS, J. B. 'The Development of British Trade with West Africa, 1750–1850', *P.S.Q.* L (1935), 194–213
WILKS, IVOR 'The Rise of the Akwamu Empire, 1650–1710', *G.H.S.G.* iii, 2 (1957), 99–136
—— 'A Medieval Trade Route from the Niger to the Gulf of Guinea', *J.A.H.* iii, 2 (1962), 337–41
—— 'Aspects of Bureaucratisation in Ashanti in the Nineteenth Century', *J.A.H.* vii, 2 (1966), 215–32
WOLFSON, FREDA 'A Price Agreement on the Gold Coast – the Krobo Oil Boycott, 1858–1866', *E.H.R.* vi, 2nd Series, 1 (1953–1954), 68–77

4 UNPUBLISHED THESES

AMENUMEY, D. E. K. *The Ewe People and the Coming of European Rule, 1850–1914*, M.A. thesis, University of London, 1964
ARHIN, KWAME *The Development of Atebubu and Kintampo as Market Centres*, Ph.D. thesis, University of London, 1969
DALTON, HEATHER *The Development of the Gold Coast under British Administration 1874–1901*, M.A. thesis, University of London, 1957
DUMETT, R. E. *British Official Attitudes in Relation to Economic Development in the Gold Coast, 1874–1905*, Ph.D. thesis, University of London, 1966
FEINBERG, HARVEY MICHAEL *Elmina, Ghana: a History of Its Development and Relationship with the Dutch in the Eighteenth Century*, Ph.D. thesis, Boston University, 1969
HOPKINS, A. G. *An Economic History of Lagos, 1880–1914*, Ph.D. thesis, University of London, 1964
JAMES, P. G. *British Relations to the Gold Coast 1815–1850*, M.A. thesis, University of London, 1935
POSTMA, JOHANNES *The Dutch Participation in the African Slave Trade; Slaving on the Guinea Coast 1675–1795*, Ph.D. thesis, Michigan State University, 1970
STILLIARD, N. H. *The Rise and Development of Legitimate Trade in Palm Oil with West Africa*, M.A. thesis, University of Birmingham, 1938
TENKORANG, SAMMY *British Slave Trading Activities on the Gold and Slave Coasts in the Eighteenth Century*, M.A. thesis, University of London, 1964
WOLFSON, FREDA *British Relations with the Gold Coast, 1843–1886*, Ph.D. thesis, University of London, 1959

Index

Aboasi, 21
Abokobi, 160, 161
Abomey, 27
Abonce, 17, 25
Abora, 168, 170
Aburi, 157, 160, 177
abusa, 161
Abutia, 27
Accra, 26, 46, 47, 73, 87, 97, 104–6, 112, 126, 129, 174; Confederation, 170–1; fort, 6, 50, 57, 77; James Town, 40, 130, 135, 143, 170; slave trade, 38–42, 89; trade, 15, 20, 25, 54, 60, 61, 62, 71, 74, 88, 89, 90–3, 104–6, 110, 112, 128, 130, 140, 142, 147
Ada and the Adas, 27, 72, 140, 141, 142, 150, 172
Adafo, 89, 142
Adaklu, 27
Adangbe, 20
Adansi traders, 17
Addo, William, 129, 147, 171
Adina, 141
African Aid Society, 142, 172
African Company, 49–50, 156
African Gold Coast Company, 175
African Institution, 66
African merchants, 31, 80, 103–4, 106–14, 118–25, 127, 129–31, 138, 149–50, 151–5, 162–6, 168, 173, 177, 180
African Steamship Company, 119
African Times, 143, 150, 156, 158–9, 161, 162, 163, 167, 172, 176
African traders, 6–7, 54, 55, 81–5, 143, 150, 162
agents, 83, 89, 104, 142, 171
Aggrey, King *see* John Aggrey, *King of Cape Coast and* Joseph Aggrey, *King of Cape Coast*
Aggri beads, 33
Agome, 27
Agotime, 23
agriculture, 20, 24, 28, 45–6, 51, 63–9, 70–1, 93, 161, 169, 179, 180; *see also* plantations *and specific products*
Agwarefo, 30
Ahafo, 9
Ahanta, 16, 26, 55, 75, 175
Ahenkro, 29
Ajguay, 172
Aka, Kweku, 79

Akim and the Akims, 99, 105
Akoas, 18
Akpafu, 23
Akropong, 64, 75, 89, 158, 160
Akuamdan, 177
Akuapem and the Akuapems, 20, 26, 29, 46, 61, 64, 69, 73, 74, 75, 78, 89, 99, 105, 135, 147, 160, 161, 171, 177, 178, 179
Akwamu and the Akwamus, 13, 15, 24, 25, 47, 73, 144, 170, 172
Akwida, 26, 41
Akyem, 13, 17, 20, 24, 25, 26, 27, 62, 73, 74, 78, 135, 147
Akyeremadefo, 30, 31, 32
Akyeres, 19
Amanianpong Temporn, 27
Amankwa, *General*, 39
American, goods, 91; petroleum, 146; plantations, 9, 18; slave trade, 37–8, 39, 41, 51
Amissah, J. F., 168, 176
Ankra, *Chief*, 39, 40
Anfoo Otoo, *King of Aburi*, 168
Anlo, 27, 120, 142–3, 144, 172
Anomabo, 8, 26, 28, 39, 40, 48, 50, 54, 61, 62, 86–8, 99, 108, 109, 111, 112, 168
Ansa, 29, 30
Aowin path, 26
Apam, 41, 44, 108, 109
Apokoo (Gyaasewa treasurer), 32
Apollonia, 23, 26, 28–9, 57, 79, 89
Aquamboes, 105
Arkrah, 108
Asante, David, 160
Asante and the Asanti, crafts, 22–3, 24; fishing, 20; gold, 20, 59, 85, 176, 179; kola, 70, 161, 179; slaves, 12–13, 18, 28, 39–44, 69–70, 82, 142, 159, 172; trade, 15, 17, 28, 30–3, 35, 45, 49, 50, 52, 57–61, 105, 108, 131, 142, 171–2, 177; trade routes, 26, 27, 29, 70, 79, 83, 141, 158–9; treaties, 49, 50, 52, 60, 73–4, 77, 81; wars, 9, 40, 45–7, 57, 60–2, 65, 67, 71–7, 105, 107–10, 113, 114, 116, 120, 130, 134, 139, 144–5, 158, 164, 166–75, 178, 179
Asantehenes, 12, 16, 24, 29, 30, 31–2, 38, 43–4, 46, 52, 60, 73–4, 76, 107, 108, 166
Asiminia, 23
Asoanifo, 30
Asokwafo, 30, 31, 32
Assafa, 108

Assembly of Native Chiefs, 122–4
Assin and the Assins, 15, 20, 23, 26, 29, 30, 55, 74, 78, 134, 159
Asumegya, 30
Atebubu, 27
Atiemo, Obuobi, 64, 74
Atiogbe, Adzoviehlo (De Lima), 141–2
Atoko, 141
Australia, tallow from, 146
Awowas, 18
Awoonah and the Awoonahs, 143, 144
Awudua, 175
Axim, 6, 41, 50, 63, 78, 111
Ayensu, River, 109

Badagry, 154
Baeta, Goncalves, 141
Bana, River, 21
Banda, 21
bankruptcy, 95, 109, 113, 139, 143–4, 150–5, 159, 162, 180
Banner Brothers and Company, 95
Bannerman, James, 39, 73, 80, 82, 99, 107–8, 112, 121, 123, 124, 130, 152, 171
Barnes, George, 77
Barnes, Henry, 80, 105, 112, 113
Barnes, *Mrs* Henry, 113, 163
Barter, Edward, 16, 106
barter trade, 13, 14, 35, 54, 70, 82, 89, 93, 148, 155, 162
Basel Mission Trading Company, 109, 142, 144, 148–50, 163, 171
Basel Missionary Society, 22, 75, 87, 156, 157, 158, 160–1, 177–8, 180
Batafo, 32
Bauer, P. T., 66–7
Bazin, 175
beads, 31, 33, 35, 101, 136, 137, 161, 183, 188
Beecham, J., 22
beer, imported, 187
beeswax, 62, 92, 94
Begho, 17
Begida, 27
Bekwai, 30–1
Belshaw, C. S., 24–5
Benin, 15, 17; Bight of, 10, 11, 12
Beraku, 44
'Beula' plantation, 68
Bevington and Morris, *Messrs.*, 136
Biafra, Bight of, 10, 11
Biney, J. E., 176
Birmingham, firearms from, 59, 91
Bissoo (Mossi slave), 83
Blankson, George (*Jun.*), 168
Blankson, George (*Sen.*), 80, 103, 113, 124, 131
Blekusu, 141
Bond, 1844, 96
Bonduku, 27, 28, 31
Bonnat, Pierre, 175
Bonny, 143
Bono-Manso, 17
Bonwire, 23
Bosman, William, 8
Bosomtwe, Lake, 20, 38
Bowdich, Thomas E., 26, 28, 30, 31, 32, 34, 43–5, 49, 50, 59, 60, 70, 113
brass, coinage, 35; imported, 187

Brazilian slave trade, 38, 41, 89, 141
Bremen missionaries, 136, 144
Brew, James, 176
Brew, *Prince* James Hutton, 109, 168
Brew, Sam Kanto, 8, 44, 80, 108
Brew, Samuel Collins, 108–9, 112, 113, 120, 124, 139
Bridge, H., 113
British, Abolition Acts, 37–8, 42–50, 65, 98, 175; administration, 103–6, 114–17, 120–124, 158–9, 164; anti-slavery ships, 39, 40, 45, 90; Asanti wars and, 72–5, 77, 166–7; Dutch and, 103, 120, 167; forts, 13, 48, 50, 54, 60, 76–8, 84, 95–6, 167; goods, 29, 53, 59, 83, 89–92, 101, 136–7, 182–7; judiciary, 78–80, 96, 105, 152–5, 164–5; merchant houses, 55, 80, 95, 109, 113, 119, 151; merchants, 48, 49, 53–4, 57–8, 60, 73–4, 77, 80, 94–9, 152, 162; Parliamentary grant, 48, 49, 124; plantations, 63, 65, 68; Select Committees on settlements and forts, *Reports, 1816–17* and *1865*, 48, 49, 60, 167, 169; Select Committee on the West Coast, *Report, 1842*, 90, 91, 96; slave trade, 9–11, 37, 40, 89–90, 95–9, 165; trade, 6, 7, 16, 51–62, 73, 89–90, 144; Trade and Navigation Acts, 60
British and African Steam Navigation Company, 119
Broch, *Governor* Niels, 73
brokers, 15–16, 39, 43, 45, 47, 81–2, 148, 179
Brong, 27
Brown, J. P., 176
Brown, Robert, 77
Bruce, E. W., 142
Bruce, W. G., 142
Bruce, William, 135
Buem, 27
Buipe, 27
Burti, 63
butter and cheese, imported, 187
Bwa, Kwamina, 44

canoes, 16, 20, 24, 27, 40, 44, 45, 148
Canot, Theodore, 19, 91
Cape Coast, 104–5; administration, 73–4, 110–12, 116–18, 123, 125, 129, 130, 153, 165, 168, 174, 176; agriculture, 20, 46, 65, 66, 68; Castle, 77; slave trade, 38–9, 42–4, 47, 95; trade, 26, 49–54, 60–2, 83, 86–90, 92, 93, 99, 101, 127, 130, 132, 148, 153, 163, 182
Cape Three Points, 26
capital investment, 161–3
carnelians as currency, 36
carriers, 7, 30, 81–5, 113, 144, 178
Carstensen, Edward, 75, 89
cash sales, 148
casks, imported, 186
cassava, 46
'castle slaves', 13, 18, 84
'castle' trade *see* 'factory' trade
castles *see* forts
charms, 22
chiefs, 30, 47, 120–7; reduction of power of, 79–80, 96, 97, 103, 106–7, 111, 114–18, 120–1, 127, 164–70, 179, 180; slave trade

and, 13, 43–4, 45; tribute to, 9, 15, 21, 22, 29–33, 76, 81, 107, 115–18
Christian VIII, *King of Denmark*, 99
Christiansborg, 40, 54, 72, 73, 108, 117, 126, 130, 149, 157, 160, 161, 170, 171
citrus fruit, 63
Claridge, W. W., 169
Clayton, John, 142
Cleland, Frank, 80, 110, 112, 113
Cleland, George Frank, 110, 171
clients, 113–14
cloth, 20, 22, 23, 24, 28, 31, 35, 70
clothing, imported, 185, 188
cocoa, 69, 161, 176–8, 180, 183
coffee, 62, 64, 65, 68–70, 89, 92, 93, 94, 171, 183
coinage *see* currency
Collier, E. H., 42
Committee of Merchants, 48, 60, 73, 77, 97, 112, 116
commodity currency, 14, 155
Company of Adventurers of London, 9
Company of Merchants Trading with Africa, 13, 38, 42–3, 48, 53–4, 56, 65, 66, 116
Conran, *Lt Col.*, 143, 165
Coomassie *see* Kumasi
copper, coins, 86, 156; imported, 187
corn, 46, 52, 62, 63, 70, 72, 92, 93, 99
cotton, 7, 23, 31, 52, 63–5, 68, 69, 89, 91–2, 136, 142–4, 150, 172, 183, 187
Council of Merchants, 77, 97–8
Court of Mixed Commission, 95, 96
cowries, 28, 33, 34, 74, 85–6, 127–9, 134, 140, 155, 156–7, 183
credit system, 14–15, 80, 83, 84, 95, 109, 112–13, 119, 138, 150–5, 180
Crobo *see* Krobo
Cruickshank, Brodie, 18, 77, 78, 80–3, 88, 89, 101, 104, 108, 121–8, 154
Cuban slave trade, 41, 90, 172
currency, 13–14, 25, 28, 33–6, 85–6, 127–9, 148, 155–7, 180; commodity, 14, 155
Curtin, Philip D., 10, 12, 41–2, 89
customs duties, 29–30, 49, 60, 77, 92, 124, 129, 131–2, 144, 169–70, 179

Daaku, Kwame Yeboa, 16, 115
Daboya, 20, 27, 28
Daendels, H. W., 42, 50, 65
Dagomba, 13, 20, 28, 31, 70
Dahomey, 15, 28, 35
Danes, 10, 37, 39, 47, 50–1, 54, 60, 64–5, 70, 72–5, 78, 87, 99–100, 112, 117, 124–5, 171
Dankua, 109
Dankwa, Ado, 74
Dataise, 23
Datchanso, 23
Davidson, W. E., 168
Dawson, *Governor*, 44, 58
Dawson, Joseph, 168, 176
De Lima, Cesar Cequira Geraldo, 141
debts, 19, 84; *see also* bankruptcy *and* panyarring
defence, 166–7, 168, 179
Denkyera, 15, 17, 20, 26, 55, 74, 79
Denkyina, 78
Dixcove, 26, 50, 60, 61, 62, 80, 111
Dobokrom, 75

Dodi, 141
Domums, 19
Donkos, 12, 82, 105
Dumpasi, 20, 23
Dunkwa, 26
Duos Amigos, 95
Dupuis, Joseph, 21, 26, 29, 43–4, 45, 49–50, 60
Dutch, 6, 7, 9, 10, 16, 37, 39, 42, 47, 49–51, 54, 60, 63, 65, 68–9, 75–6, 78, 87, 103, 115, 120, 124, 167

earthenware *see* pottery
'educated' Africans, 103–4, 106, 120, 125, 150, 151–2, 165, 168–9, 170
education *see* schools
Edwards, W., 129
Effuenta Gold Mining Company, 175
Egyah, 108
Ejura, 27
Ekumfi, 111
Ekwea, 23
elephants, 22, 94
Ellis, J. E., 176
Elmina, 5, 6, 15, 26, 41, 50, 57, 60, 63, 68, 75, 76, 78, 99, 111
Eminsany, G. E., 176
Engmann, Jeremia, 171
exports, 56, 61–2, 69, 71, 88–95, 100–102, 131–8, 139, 144–7, 176–7

factories, 6, 7, 49, 108, 109, 149, 172; *see also* slave factories
'factory' trade, 53–4, 93, 95
Fage, J. D., 17
Fante and the Fantes, 9, 12, 15, 26, 40, 45–7, 50, 55, 57, 60, 77, 82, 83, 105, 118; Confederation, 109, 111–12, 120, 163, 167–71, 180
Ferguson, S., 168
firearms and gunpowder, 22, 28, 30, 31, 44, 45, 50, 53, 57, 59–60, 91, 92, 101, 114, 142, 145, 171, 172, 185, 187, 188
Firth, Raymond, 119–20
fishing, 16, 28, 38, 109, 141
Fitzgerald, Ferdinand, 163, 176
Fleischer, Paul, 171
'floating' trade, 53–4, 93, 95
Fomena, 83
Forster, Matthew, 53–4, 55, 77, 151, 153
Forster and Smith, *Messrs*, 55, 80, 90, 95, 108, 109, 112, 113, 119, 121, 122, 126, 127, 129, 140, 148, 153–4, 158, 163
forts, 6, 8, 12, 13, 15, 27, 39, 46, 48–51, 53, 54, 57, 60, 76–8, 84, 95–100, 115, 124–5, 127, 156, 167
Fosu, 25, 45
Fotuosanfo, 32
free traders, 53–6, 107
Freeman, Thomas B., 83, 108, 120–1, 165, 174
French, 10, 11, 37, 38, 91
Fry, R. F., 73
furniture, imported, 138, 187
Fynn, W. C., 168

Ga, 160, 177
Gaman, 27
Gato, 7

German goods, 91, 150
Ghana Presbyterian Church, 75
Ghartey, Robert Johnson, 80, 109, 112, 113, 120, 168
ginger, 63, 92, 93, 94
Ginnamon Bippo Gold Mine Ltd, 175
glass, imported, 185
gold, adulteration of, 14, 57; currency, 8–10, 33, 34, 76, 81–2, 85, 86, 127–8, 155–7, 161; mining, 9, 20, 21, 75–6, 109, 161, 175, 176, 180; prospecting, 5, 9, 175; trade, 5, 7–9, 17, 28, 30, 35, 48, 49, 52–3, 56–9, 61, 62, 64, 70, 83, 92–3, 100, 101, 106, 109, 132–4, 139, 145, 157, 176, 178, 179; washing, 20, 21, 76
Gold Coast Aborigines' Rights Protection Society, 173
Gold Coast Corps, 120
Gold Coast Legislative Council, 108, 110, 111, 121–2, 123, 125
Gold Coast Mining and Trading Company, 55
Gold Coast Mining Company, 175
Gold Coast Native Concession Purchasing Company, 111, 176
Gold Coast Rifle Volunteer Corps, 110
goldsmiths, 24
Gomes, Fernão, 5
Gonja, 27, 70
Goody, Jack, 35
Grand Bassam, 26, 55
Grant, Francis Chapman, 80, 105, 110–11, 170, 176, 177
Grey, Henry George, *3rd Earl Grey*, 103, 122, 124, 125
Griffith, William Brandford, 177
ground nuts, 99, 133, 136, 147
guinea grains, 58, 62, 92–4, 133, 136, 147
gum, 58, 62, 92, 93, 94, 133, 135, 147
Gunnell, W. P., 142
gunpowder *see* firearms and gunpowder
Gyaasewa, 32
Gyaasewahene, 32
Gyaman, 9, 22
Gyateh Kumah III, *Chief of Winneba*, 109

haberdashery, 136, 187
Hansen, J. C., 80, 112
hardware, 101, 136, 138, 185, 188
Hatton, W. B. and Sons, 80
Hausa traders, 70
Hein, *Governor* L. V., 73
Henry Acquah I, *Chief of Winneba*, 109
Henty, George Alfred, 106, 113
Hesse, L., 80, 112
hides, 7, 92–4, 133, 135–6, 147; *see also* leather
Hill, H. W., 89, 96–9, 123–6, 130
Hill, Polly, 177, 178
Ho, 27, 175
Holm, Samuel, 171
Hope, L., 171
Horton, Africanus, 118, 136, 139, 166, 176
hotels, 105–6
Housch, 75
Hughes, Thomas, 80, 105, 111–12
hunting, 20, 22
Huntley, *Sir* Henry, 82

Hutchinson, Robert, 80, 105, 110, 111, 129, 130–1
Hutchinson, W. F., 91, 148
Hutton, T. and Company, 55, 95
Hutton, William, 77
Huydercooper, W., 45, 49, 76

imports, 62, 88–95, 100–104, 131–8, 182–8
Indian goods, 91–2, 146, 183
indigo, 52, 63, 64
Insiadoo, J. M., 168
Inta, 28, 31, 70
interior, trade with the, 15–17, 28, 30–3, 49, 52–3, 70, 81, 83–5, 100, 105, 141, 143, 148–50, 152, 153, 157–9
Irish goods, 182–7
iron, 22–3, 53, 70, 92, 183, 185; currency, 33
Isert, Paul, 64, 74
Isuta, 27
ivory, 5, 9, 14, 22, 25, 35, 48, 49, 52–3, 56–62, 70, 83, 92–3, 100, 101, 107, 109, 132–134, 139, 146, 157, 179

Jackson, John, 77
James Town *see* Accra, James Town
Jellee Coffee, 144
Jeremie, *Sir* John, 98
jewellery, 184
John Aggrey, *King of Cape Coast*, 164–5
Johnson, Marion, 128
Josenhaus, Joseph, 160
Joseph Aggrey, *King of Cape Coast*, 111, 116, 118
Juaben, 20, 31, 33

Kabes, John, 16, 106
Kaneshi, 40
Katamansu, Battle of, 40, 47, 72
Kennedy, *Sir* Arthur Edward, 155, 170
Keta, 6, 27, 41, 89, 141, 142, 144, 172
King, R. and W. *Messrs*, 95, 127
Kintampo, 27
Koelle, S. W., 13
Kofi Akrashie, *Manche of James Town*, 110
Kofi Amissah, *King of Cape Coast*, 110
Kokofu, 31
kola, 13, 17, 28, 30, 70, 161, 174, 178–9
Komenda, 16, 21, 26, 46, 49
Konny, John, 16, 106
Kormantin, 44, 97
Kpando, 27
Kpene, 27
Kpong, 28, 139, 140, 142, 150
Krakje, 27
Krepi and the Krepis, 13, 27, 105, 142–4, 150, 170
Krobo and the Krobos, 23, 61–2, 69, 74, 78, 99, 110, 112, 120, 129–30, 134–5, 139–42, 144, 160, 161, 179–80
Kuhne, J., 175
Kumasi (Coomassie), 23, 26–9, 31, 43–5, 49, 50, 76, 83, 174, 175
Kumawu, 31
Kuntu, *Chief of Egyah*, 108
Kwahu, 13, 22, 25, 27, 141, 157
Kwasi, Obodum, *Asantehene*, 12
Kwesi, Edoo, *King of Mankessim*, 168
Kwisa, 83
kyenkyen, 23

La Fama Africana, 44
Labadi, 89, 126, 130
labour, 25, 64, 66–9, 75, 85, 106, 175, 178, 179, 180; *see also* carriers *and* slave *labour*
land tenure, 64, 68, 69, 159–61, 176–80
Last, *Colonel*, 76
lead, 53
leather, 24, 28, 58, 185; *see also* hides
Lincoln, Abraham, 38
Lind, *Governor* H. G., 141
linen, imported, 184, 185
liquor *see* wines and spirits
Liverpool, lead from, 91
livestock, 28, 30, 99
Locher, C. W., 160
Lome, 27
Lutterodt, William, 54, 73, 80, 112, 171

MacCarthy, *Sir* Charles, 60
Maclean, George, 73–80, 84, 95–8, 104, 108, 112, 116–18, 130, 153, 159, 179, 180
Madden, Richard, 96, 98
Mafi, 142
Malfi, 64
Mamfe, 29
Mampong, 27, 177
Mamprusi, 28
Manchester goods, 89, 91, 101, 136–7, 188
Mande, culture, 23; traders, 5
Mankessim, 112, 118, 168, 170
Mankwadi, 108
Mansu, 25, 45
manumission, 84, 159, 160, 161
markets, 17, 23–5, 28, 106, 141
meat, imported, 183, 187
merchant houses, 55, 80, 95, 109, 113, 119, 151, 153, 180
Meredith, Henry, 34, 46, 48, 52, 57, 105, 115
metal, 30; work, 20, 22–3, 24
Metcalfe, G. E., 73, 78–9
Methodist missionaries, 68, 180; *see also* Wesleyan Mission
middlemen, 15, 44, 142
mining, 55, 111, 169, 173, 175–7; *see also* gold mining, iron *and* quartz mining
missionaries, 63, 68, 75, 86–7, 98–9, 103–4, 108, 136, 144, 148–50, 158, 160, 175, 177–8
Moisy, 23
monetary system *see* currency
monkey hides, 133, 135–6, 147
monopolies, 5–6, 30, 53, 95, 99, 119, 130
Monrad, H. C., 65
Moravian Brethren, 63
Morch, Frederick S., 74–5
Mossi, 83
Mouree, 6, 26
mulatto slave traders, 39, 44, 108
Muslim traders, 29, 35, 70

'Napoleon' plantation, 68
'native capitalists', 162–3
'native' trade *see* 'floating' trade
Newbury, C. W., 36, 92
Nicholls, John George, 55, 77
Nieser, Jan, 65
Nkonya, 27
Nkoranza, 27, 177

Nkwansrafo, 32
Nkwanta, 27
nnaabo, 33
nsitiri, 30
Nyankumasi, 29
Nzima, 79

Obuasi, 176
Obuokrom, 23
Odente, 27
Odonkos, 19
Odumase, 33, 158, 160, 161
Oforika, Wilhelm, 160
Omanhenes, 30, 33
Osei Bonsu, *Asantehene*, 29
Osei Kwadwo, *Asantehene*, 12, 32
Osei Kwame, *Asantehene*, 12, 46
Osino, 23
ounce trade *see* commodity currency

Palime, 27
Palm, Frederick, 171
palm nut kernel, 109, 135, 146, 150
palm oil, 7, 21, 52, 58, 60–2, 69–72, 74, 75, 85–6, 89, 93, 94, 99–101, 107, 112, 129–130, 133–5, 139–46, 150, 154, 156–7, 172, 177, 179–80
palm trees, 63, 99, 180
palm wine, 138
Pankrono, 23
panyarring, 13, 17, 19, 42, 73, 79, 154
pawns and pawning, 18–19, 81, 84, 98–9, 159, 161, 165, 175
Peki, 27
pepper, 58, 63, 92, 94
perfume, imported, 188
Pine, Benjamin, 105, 126–7, 165
Pine, Richard, 139
Pine, William, 166
plantains, 46
plantations, 9, 18, 51, 63–9, 70, 171, 179
police, 79, 97, 113, 122
Poll Tax Ordinance, 111, 120, 124–31
Pong *see* Kpong
Pope-Hennessy, *Sir* John, 111, 168
Popo, 89, 172
Portuguese, 5–9, 17, 37–9, 41, 51, 89
pottery, 20, 23–4, 136, 138, 185, 188
Pra, River, 63, 159
Prampram, 49, 110, 140, 142
Principe, 51, 89
protection, 79, 81, 97, 143
provisions, imported, 188

Quaqua cloth, 7
Quaque, Philip, 112
quartz mining, 21
Quashie, Tetteh, 177
Quissah *see* Kwisa
Quist, Karl, 171
Quittah *see* Keta

Ramseyer, F., 175
Rattray, R. A., 30
Reid, Joseph, 77
Reindorf, Carl Christian, 39, 46, 47, 171
rice, 52, 92, 94, 183
Richter, H., 54, 73, 74, 112, 129
Richter, J. E., 80, 112, 130, 171

Riis, Andreas, 75
roads *see* trade routes
Rottman, H. L. and Company, 142, 149
Royal African Company, 8, 9, 10
Royal African Corps, 78
rubber, 111, 136, 147, 161, 173, 177, 180
Russia, tallow from, 134, 146

Sadame, 27
Salaga, 13, 23, 25–8, 31, 70
salt, 7, 16, 20, 27–31, 35, 70, 72, 141, 172, 184
Saltpond, 109, 111, 135, 157
Sampson, M. J., 108, 109
Sanahene, 32
Sao Tomé, 9–10, 51, 89, 177
Sarasu, 20
Sarbah, John, 80, 111, 176, 177
Sarbah, John Mensah, 111, 115
Saresso, 23
sasammoa, 22
schools, 86–8, 103–4, 110, 112, 156, 169, 171, 180
Schrenk, Elias, 22, 156, 158
scrivelloes, 22
seahorse teeth, 58
Sekondi, 49, 63, 71
Sewell Ross and Company, 95
Sey, J. W., 176
Shai, 23
Shama, 6, 26, 63
shea butter, 28, 30, 31
Sierra Leone, 11, 12, 50, 60, 63, 76, 77, 91, 92, 95, 101, 103, 143, 167, 182
silk, 28, 70, 183, 184
silver, 61; coins, 62, 86, 155–6, 157
Simbo, 68
Simpson, W. H., 170
slave factories, 90–1, 96, 141
slave labour, 18, 21, 46, 64, 65, 68, 83, 98–9, 152, 160, 175
slave trade, 5, 8–13, 25, 28, 30, 31, 35, 36, 40–2, 159; abolition, 17, 37–8, 42–50, 64, 65, 89, 98, 100–101, 104, 151, 175, 179; firearms trade and, 44, 45, 50, 59–60, 114, 142, 172; *Madden Report*, 96, 98–9; revival, 38–45, 50, 58, 82, 89–91, 95–6, 141–2, 172, 179
slaves, as capital, 19, 33–5, 83–5, 159, 161, 165, 175; as carriers, 7, 81–4; conscription of, 76, 120–1; domestic, 13, 17–19, 28, 38, 82–3, 99, 108, 113, 120–1, 151–3, 159–61; payment for, 8, 9; raiding for, 12–13, 17, 24; *see also*, manumission, panyarring *and* pawns and pawning
Small Cormantine, 180
Smith, H., 123
Smith, John Hope, 38–9, 42–4, 48, 57, 58
Smith, Joseph, 80, 105, 110, 112, 113, 153–4, 159
soap and candles, imported, 184
Société des Mines d'Or de l'Afrique Occidentale, 175
sorting *see* commodity currency
Spanish slave trade, 37–9, 41, 42, 44, 89
spirits *see* wines and spirits
Starrenbury, *Colonel*, 141
stationery, 184
steamships, 119, 151

Steffens, P. S., 39
Stooves Brother, 109
sugar, 64, 183, 184
sumans, 22
Svaniker, Thomas, 171
Swanzy, Andrew, 68, 78, 80, 113, 131, 132, 134–8, 151, 152, 153, 163
Swanzy, F. and A., *Messrs.*, 55, 90, 95, 109, 110, 113, 119, 121, 125, 127, 129, 140, 148, 158, 163
Swanzy, Frank, 122, 123, 125–6
Swanzy, James, 68
Swanzy, *Mrs.* Kate, 113
Swanzy Estates and Mining Company, 175

Tafo, 23
Takoradi, 27
tallow, 134, 137, 146
tamarides, 63
Tandoe, J., 105
tanning, 24
Tantumquerry, 46, 48, 49
Tarkwa, 176
Tarkwa (Tamsu) Gold Mining Company, 175
tea, 183
Tema, 40
Teshi, 89, 126, 130
Tete, Benjamin, 160
Thompson, James Robert, 80, 105, 110, 148
timber, 52, 58, 62, 72, 92–4, 109, 176, 178
tin, imported, 184
tobacco, 63, 64, 68–9, 89, 91, 101, 136, 183, 188
tolls, 28–30, 32, 169–70
Torrane, George, 47, 52
tortoiseshell, 62
trade routes, 15, 26–30, 50, 69, 70, 73, 79, 108, 157–9, 169, 172, 174–5, 180
'trust' *see* credit system
Tsibu, Kojo, 79
Twifu, 78

Ussher, H. T., 168
Uthman Dan Fodio, 70

Vay, 89
Verver, *General*, 76
Victor, M. and Sons, 142
Vierra, La Rocha, 68
Vodza, 141
Volta, River, 27, 28, 38, 64, 67, 72, 99–100, 139, 141, 142, 144, 157, 172, 182
Wassaw, 20, 26, 55, 57, 62, 78, 83, 111, 147
Wassaw and Ahanta Gold Mines Syndicate, 175, 176
Wassaw (Gold Coast) Mining Company, 175
Waya, 27
weaving *see* cloth
Wesleyan Mission, 87, 98–9, 108, 110, 112, 113
West Indies, 68, 71, 72, 75, 76, 97
White, *Governor*, E. W., 46, 52
'whitewashing', 155
Whydah, 9–10, 49, 89, 143
Widermann, George, 160
Windward Coast, 10, 11, 46, 55, 89, 182

wines and spirits, 28, 30, 70, 89, 91, 101, 107, 124, 136–8, 142, 183, 188
Winneba, 15, 48, 49, 52, 97, 108, 109, 111, 135
Winniett, *Sir* William, 108, 121, 124, 141, 156
Wolseley, *Major-General Sir* Garnet, 159
wood-workers, 20, 24
woollen goods, imported, 184, 186

Wrisberg, Christian, 171
Wrisberg, J. P., 64

Yamey, B. S., 66–7
yams, 46
Yeji, 27
Yendi, 27, 174–5
Yomoho, 20

Zimmermann, J., 160